BUDDHISM BEYOND BORDERS

SUNY series in Buddhism and American Culture
John Whalen-Bridge, editor

BUDDHISM BEYOND BORDERS

New Perspectives on Buddhism in the United States

EDITED BY
SCOTT A. MITCHELL
AND
NATALIE E. F. QULI

SUNY
PRESS

Cover art © Bigstockphoto/daboost

Published by State University of New York Press, Albany

Printed in the United States of America

For information, contact State University of New York Press, Albany, NY
www.sunypress.edu

Production, Diane Ganeles
Marketing, Anne M. Valentine

Library of Congress Cataloging-in-Publication Data

Buddhism beyond borders : new perspectives on Buddhism in the United States /
Edited by Scott A. Mitchell and Natalie E.F. Quli.
pages cm. — (SUNY series in Buddhism and American culture)
Includes bibliographical references and index.
ISBN 978-1-4384-5637-9 (hc : alk. paper)—978-1-4384-5636-2 (pb : alk paper)
eISBN 978-1-4384-5638-6 1. Buddhism—United States.
I. Mitchell, Scott A. II. Quli, Natalie E. F.
BQ736.B83 2015
294.30973—dc23

2014026036

10 9 8 7 6 5 4 3 2 1

CONTENTS

PREFACE

Buddhism beyond Borders

SCOTT A. MITCHELL AND NATALIE E. F. QULI

In the fall of 1994, with the generous support of the Numata Foundation, the Institute of Buddhist Studies at the Graduate Theological Union in Berkeley, California, hosted a twelve-week lecture series titled Buddhism in America: An Expanding Frontier. The series brought together some of the leading scholars in an emerging subfield of Buddhist studies dedicated to the study of Buddhism in Western contexts. One of the fruits of this conference was the volume *The Faces of Buddhism in America*, edited by Charles Prebish and Kenneth Tanaka (1998). Together with Prebish's later volume, *Luminous Passage: The Practice and Study of Buddhism in America* (1999), the conversations begun at this lecture series and subsequent publications have been the foundation of this subfield for more than a decade. Scholars continue to wrestle with questions of ethnicity and identity, adaptation and authority, engagement and activism, and the scholar's role as academic, practitioner, or both.

Reflecting on this seminal lecture series, we noted how much the subfield has grown, deepened, and matured—and the new paths it has taken. Some of the original questions remain important. What roles do ethnicity and race play in the adaptation of Buddhism to US culture? How has the democratization of *sangha* leadership and practice altered Buddhist institutions? Has increased social, political, and environmental leadership affected Buddhist philosophy or ethics? Other research vistas were not even possible in the early 1990s. The Internet was barely visible on the horizon, and in the intervening years it has fundamentally changed the way the world communicates. In what way has this change impacted US Buddhism? Since the turn of the century, Buddhist ideas and practices are increasingly appearing in non-Buddhist contexts, whether in advertising and popular culture or in psychotherapeutic contexts such as Mindfulness-Based Stress Reduction programs. Regardless of the total number of Buddhist practitioners in the United States, it is clear that Buddhism is having an impact on the broader culture. What are the consequences to US culture of this Buddhist influence, and what are the consequences to Buddhism?

It is something of a cliché to say that we live in a globally interconnected world. Yet Buddhist studies as a discipline has, until rather recently, seemingly resisted this idea, having been dominated by area studies and its focus on the bounded category of nation or a broadly defined cultural area. Recognizing that certain Buddhist ideas, persons, and whole communities now freely and easily cross geopolitical borders, scholars are increasingly focused on the imaginary or global culture. More recent scholarship, for example, has been concerned with the transient nature of culture, what Arjun Appadurai (1996)—building on the idea of Benedict Anderson's "imagined communities" (1983)—calls "imagined worlds," cultural landscapes that transcend national boundaries. These imagined worlds, defined by the movement of ideas, persons, artifacts, technologies, and commodities, in many ways define how we interact with persons the world over. Scholars such as Manuel Vásquez and Marie Friedmann Marquardt (2003) and Thomas Tweed (1997b, 2006) have argued convincingly that we cannot understand the locality of US religious culture without looking beyond our borders for the influences and sources of cultural flows leading into and out of the United States proper. Transnational currents such as immigration, refugees and diaspora communities, international trade, and the Internet have a profound impact on how religious communities come into being, where they settle, and how they understand themselves in relation to their current locality. How then do these border crossings impact and affect local US Buddhist communities?

Arguably, US Buddhism is the direct result of such transnational forces. US Buddhism is defined by movement, be it late-nineteenth-century Chinese and Japanese immigrants, the importation of Buddhist artifacts and texts, post-1965 Asian immigration and refugee communities, or the more contemporary spread of Buddhist ideas and practices via the Internet. It is difficult to discuss Buddhism in the United States without being attentive to these historical and contemporary global cultural flows. Given this connectivity, one might ask whether the category of "US Buddhism" is even still relevant. The short answer, of course, is yes. As Roland Robertson has argued, globalization is the universalization of the particular and the particularization of the universal (Robertson 1992, esp. chap. 6). While we cannot study US Buddhism without being attentive to transnational cultural flows, we must also be aware of how such transnational flows express themselves uniquely within the particular local context of the United States, *within* borders.

It was with these methodological questions in mind that we decided that a continuation of that original conversation, begun in Berkeley in 1994, was long overdue. The result was a four-day conference, titled Buddhism without Borders, held in March 2010 at the Institute of Buddhist Studies—a conference that brought together some of the original voices, scholars who had been there at the beginning and set the terms of the debate, as well as younger voices, newer scholars who represent the future of the field. We recognized that whereas our field began with the bounded category of "America" or "the United States," increased global connectivity has changed the face of Buddhism in both Western and Asian contexts. How have global communication networks spread the Buddha's teachings to unexpected areas? What are the effects of immigration, migration, diaspora? How are younger generations of American Buddhists transcending ethnic divisions that seemed so rigid a generation ago? How have Buddhist practices moved beyond the confines of Buddhist communities and influenced US culture, art, and even other religious traditions?

The present volume, based on lectures given at the 2010 conference, is the result of such questions. Aware of the global interconnectivity of Buddhism as a modern world religion, as well as the seemingly endless varieties of its local iterations, we collected a handful of papers from the conference that best spoke to these concerns, with special attention to not only the local and translocative nature of Buddhism in the United States but to boundary maintenance and boundary crossings more generally.

In section 1, "Boundaries, Borders, and Categories," authors grapple with theoretical issues of borders and categories. Thomas Tweed, in his "Theory and Method in the Study of Buddhism: Toward 'Translocative' Analysis," applies his recently published theory of religion to the specific case of Buddhism. With references to various essays in this volume, his chapter draws connections between the chapters and lays the groundwork for theorizing Buddhist developments in the contemporary United States, with special attention to the border-transgressing flows of people and ideas across national and cultural boundaries. Jeff Wilson, by contrast, argues for increased attention to the small-scale boundaries within the United States in "Regionalism within American Buddhism," suggesting that different Buddhist cultures mirror their American geographical surroundings. Wilson argues that too often the translocative nature of Buddhism in the United States has been emphasized without attending to more specific regional adaptations. In the last chapter in this section, Wakoh Shannon Hickey attends to a different kind of boundary. "Two Buddhisms, Three Buddhisms, and Racism" addresses the issue of scholastic categories, as Hickey unpacks the racial dynamics implicit in the two and three Buddhisms typologies and argues against rigid and static typologies of US Buddhism that do not account for hybridity or change over time.

Section 2, "Crossing Borders: Transcultural and Translocative Flows," focuses on several case studies that demonstrate cultural flows across both physical and social "place." Michihiro Ama's "'First White Buddhist Priestess': A Case Study of Sunya Gladys Pratt at the Tacoma Buddhist Temple" unpacks how individual Buddhists have transgressed both racial and gender boundaries in US Buddhism, looking specifically at the case of a female Caucasian convert to the Japanese American community of the Buddhist Churches of America before the Second World War. The mechanics of Buddhist cultural flows are at issue in Jeannine Chandler's piece, "Invoking the Dharma Protector: Western Involvement in the Dorje Shugden Controversy." This controversy has continued life in part because of the ability of devotees of Dorje Shugden to connect via the Internet. Moreover, because of this interconnectivity, new actors have become involved in what was once an exclusively Tibetan issue, thus crossing the divide between "Westerners" and ethnic Tibetans, modernists, and traditionalists. In the final contribution to the section, Helen J. Baroni considers the "distant membership" correspondence of American Zen teacher Robert Aitken. Based on her extensive study of the Robert Aitken archive in Hawaii, Baroni's piece details the ways in which US Zen practitioners interacted with this pioneering Zen Buddhist teacher. She notes how Aitken developed relationships with students at a distance, demonstrating how

Zen Buddhism spread across the local boundaries of the United States and exploring why such a service was so popular.

Section 3, "Free-Floating Dharma Discourses," considers how Buddhist ideas flow across Buddhist groups, and at times across the boundary of "Buddhism" itself. In chapter 7, "Dharma Images and Identity in American Buddhism," Richard Hughes Seager explores what he calls a "free-floating Dharma discourse" in US Buddhist culture wherein Buddhist ideas flow into non-Buddhist contexts. Focusing his attention on contemporary art, he examines several artists who have been influenced by Buddhist teachings but may or may not self-identify as Buddhists, and as such the Buddhist ideas they use in their work have become decontextualized and freed from their Buddhist moorings. Kimberly Beek similarly explores how Buddhist ideas are flowing beyond the category of "Buddhism" into the world of American literature. In "Telling Tales Out of School: The Fiction of Buddhism," she details the emergence of a new genre of literature, which she identifies as explicitly Buddhist fiction. Finally, Mira Niculescu considers the secularization of Buddhism in her "Mind Full of God: 'Jewish Mindfulness' as an Offspring of Western Buddhism in America," arguing that as Buddhist ideas flow beyond the category of "Buddhism" into secularized contexts, those ideas can be more readily imported into new religious contexts. In an important contribution to this subfield, Niculescu looks specifically at the interplay of Buddhist Jewish mindfulness practices, noting the manner in which Buddhism has become reduced to secularized mindfulness. Because the specifically Buddhist context of mindfulness has been removed, the practice can be safely appropriated into Judaism without theological conflict.

Section 4, "Modernity and Modernities," returns to more theoretical issues involved in the globalization of Buddhism. The division of Buddhism into "modern" and "traditional" varieties is complicated by Erik Braun's chapter, "The United States of *Jhāna*: Varieties of Modern Buddhism in America," wherein he discusses how *jhāna* meditation practices are deployed within different types of Buddhist discourses, blurring the boundaries between what is traditional and what is modern. In "Buddhism and Multiple Modernities," David L. McMahan argues for a more nuanced understanding of modernity, one that takes into account different regional varieties. Comparing Chinese examples of Buddhist modernity to American ones, McMahan argues for the idea of multiple Buddhist modernities that differ based on local contexts. In the section's last chapter, the editors' "Buddhist Modernism as Narrative: A Comparative Study of Jodo Shinshu and Zen," Natalie Quli and Scott Mitchell argue against a monolithic, acultural model of modernity and instead focus on how modernities are constructed in different cultural environments. Specifically, we explore how the Zen and Shin Buddhist traditions are understood as variously modern or traditional in the United States, while those same traditions are defined in an opposite manner in Japan. This draws our attention to the manner in which "modernity" is not a real, definable force but rather a set of contested narratives about the contemporary world and Buddhism's place in it.

The Buddhism without Borders conference from which these essays were drawn would not have been possible without the generous support of the Institute of Buddhist Studies and the Jodo Shinshu Center in Berkeley, which hosted the event. We would like to thank IBS faculty, staff, and students who assisted with the event, from helping set up conference rooms to refilling coffee. Kumi Hadler, Reverend David Matsumoto, Daijaku Judith Kinst, Lisa Grumbrach, Yufuko Kurioka, Diana Thompson, Sayaka Inaishii, and Takashi Miyaji made this conference possible. We thank the respondents, who read and replied to the papers while also moderating their respective panels. Our gratitude to Todd Lewis, Martin Verhoeven, and Lisa Grumbach for their work in this regard.

The editors are also grateful to those whose insightful and interesting papers, due to limited space, time constraints, or publication in other venues, were not included as essays in this volume. Daniel Veidlinger raised tantalizing questions on the role and influence of the Internet on contemporary understandings of Buddhism. Ruth Fitzpatrick explored women's experiences of a female Tibetan deity among contemporary Australians. Charles Prebish, truly a pioneer and founder of the subdiscipline, contributed to our understanding of Buddhism as it is practiced in the local context of Mormon-dominated Utah. Duncan Ryuken Williams relayed the story of Japanese Americans who served in the military during World War II. Chapla Verma looked at the practice of Zen in two different national contexts, the United States and Japan. Transnationalism and networks between Thai Buddhists in Thailand and the United States was the focus of Todd Perreira's presentation. Christine Walters proposed a new way of categorizing American Buddhists based on Buddhist denominations.

Mindy McAdams contributed new research on the role of blogs in the American Buddhist world. Jitka Cirklová focused on the development and role of Buddhism among Czechs. Eve Mullen discussed two Buddhist institutions in the United States that care for the dying and their families. Zach Zimmerman focused on children's programs offered by several Buddhist groups. Richard Payne discussed the construction of sacred biographies through a study of the little-known twentieth-century Chinese Buddhist master Yogi Chen. Franz Aubrey Metcalf drew our attention to issues of authenticity and ethics in his discussion of Hakuyu Taizan Maezumi Roshi's legacy in the White Plum Asanga. Galen Amstutz presented on the marginalization of Shin Buddhism in the West. While their papers are not part of this volume, these scholars raised fascinating and important issues that helped shape the lively discussions at the conference.

Finally, the editors would like to thank IBS dean Richard Payne for his continued support and guidance. We were both fortunate enough to be under his attentive tutelage as graduate students, and his faith in our abilities, coupled with his tendency to push us—sometimes gently, sometimes with significant force—to be better scholars is characteristic of both his generous spirit and his dedication to high-quality scholarship. With deep bows and much thanks.

ACKNOWLEDGMENTS

An earlier version of chapter 2, "Regionalism within North American Buddhism," by Jeff Wilson, was published in chapter 1 of Jeff Wilson's *Dixie Dharma: Regionalism and Identity at a Buddhist Temple in the American South*. Copyright 2012 University of North Carolina Press. Used by permission of the publisher, www.uncpress.unc.edu. We thank the University of North Carolina Press for permission to publish it here.

An earlier version of chapter 3, "Two Buddhisms, Three Buddhisms, and Racism," by Wakoh Shannon Hickey, was published in thc *Journal of Global Buddhism* 11 (2010).

SECTION I

BOUNDARIES, BORDERS, AND CATEGORIES

The selection of essays in this section calls our attention to boundaries. Each of the authors questions previous modes of scholarly analysis, challenging us to review theoretical models and develop new, more nuanced means of studying Buddhism as a living religion.

Since serious academic study of US Buddhism began in the 1970s, scholars have generally approached the subject as a bounded category: "American Buddhism." Such a boundary makes sense to the extent that studies of US Buddhism grew out of Buddhist studies proper, a field that is dependent upon an area studies model with scholars focused on South Asian Buddhism, for example, or specialists in Japanese Buddhism. In his opening essay, Thomas Tweed challenges us to "follow the flows" and in so doing disrupts the area studies emphasis on stable, physical locations. Drawing on his theory of religion as "confluences of organic-cultural flows" (2006, 54), here he proposes five axioms for the study of Buddhism in global contexts: follow the flows; notice all the figures crossing; attend to all the senses; consider varying scales; and notice how flows start, stop, and shift. These axioms allow the researcher the flexibility to notice how religious cultures and persons are neither bound nor solely defined by the default categories of nation-state and cultural area. Such an orientation challenges the seeming naturalness of scholarly constructions of physical and cultural boundaries and points us toward a more process-oriented approach that brings needed attention to exchange, movement, and dynamism.

With his fourth axiom—consider varying scales—Tweed explicitly reconsiders the nation-state as default category and urges us to "move agilely across varying scales of analysis, from neural pathways to global trade routes." Seemingly inspired by this axiom, in his contribution Jeff Wilson proposes regions, hyper-local areas, as an appropriate scale of analysis, suggesting that where Buddhist communities are located is a determining factor in how Buddhists practice their religion and engage the broader culture. While an attentiveness to movement across borders may be an important corrective to more reifying tendencies, Wilson warns us that location and specific cultural environments still play important roles in the shaping of religious communities.

Wakoh Shannon Hickey is concerned with a different type of boundary. She draws our attention not only to how rhetorical boundaries of ethnicity and race have been employed as categories of scholarly analysis but how scholars' own social locations may color their perceptions of the Buddhists whom they study. Deconstructing the long-held binary typology of "two Buddhisms" in America, she pointedly notes how the assumptions of white privilege have shaped scholarship. Indeed, this is a critical mechanism by which cultural flows stop and shift, and such racial discourses have played an immense role in the development of both the study and practice of US Buddhism.

ONE

THEORY AND METHOD IN THE STUDY OF BUDDHISM

Toward "Translocative" Analysis

THOMAS A. TWEED

This volume's title—*Buddhism beyond Borders*—announces an influential theme in scholarship on US Buddhism and the study of religion more generally. It calls attention to scholars' interest in "globalization" or "transnationalism." This academic interest surged during the 1990s just as intensified transnational migration and emerging new media prompted scholars to seek new language to name the "time-space compression" experienced by those who had access to new communication and transportation technology (Harvey 1990, 241). The world grew smaller, many observers said, and the pace of life accelerated, just as it had with the introduction of earlier innovations in communication and transportation. As with scholarship during the earlier phases of the academic study of Western Buddhism, especially in the United States, this chapter and the others in this volume are a product of their time. Most importantly, they appear after this so-called transnational turn.[1] It's not that earlier generations did not notice connections across the globe. They did. They used different categories, however, and their interpretive terms—and the assumptions those terms embedded and the values they encoded—led scholars to particular conclusions about what they should study and how they should study it.

During the 1950s and 1960s, a few scholars trained in history, literature, or sociology began to write about US Buddhism, though without any sense they were participating in a common subfield. With historians tracing the "history of ideas" (Ahlstrom 1962; Chisolm 1963; Hay 1956; Jackson 1968; Wright 1957) and sociologists analyzing "Americanization" (Rust 1951), these scholars noticed "international" influences but tended to interpret them as their guiding term implied and their theoretical framework dictated: as episodic connections between two static, bounded, and autonomous national units.

By the next phase, which began in the 1970s, the scholarship shifted from a concern for the history of ideas to an interest in the history of meaning, as the symbolic anthropology of Clifford Geertz and others prompted a "cultural turn." This period saw the first classic studies of US Buddhism, including those that focused on a single geographical region (Hunter 1971) and those with wider ambitions (Layman 1976; Prebish 1979).[2] Although in the 1970s and 1980s influential scholars continued the earlier emphasis on the history of elites' ideas (Ellwood 1979; Jackson 1981), a new focus on Buddhist institutions also emerged simultaneously, as some sociologists (Horinouchi 1973; Kashima 1977) and some organizations (Buddhist Churches of America 1974) produced volumes that focused on ethnicity and race and the ways that the descendants of Asian migrants resisted or accepted acculturation. For all of its erudition and impact, like other research in the human sciences at the time, most scholarship on US Buddhism still assumed that "culture"—and "religion" as a cultural system of symbols—was fixed and consensual.

Things changed during the 1990s, when scholars in the humanities and social sciences began to decouple "place" and "culture" and attend more fully to diasporic groups that had been displaced, just as interpreters began to emphasize that cultures were contested (not shared) and changing (not static). Several intellectual movements that had begun in the 1960s and 1970s transformed the study of US Buddhism during the 1990s, when a multidisciplinary specialization aligned with the broader study of "Asian religions" in the West or "Western Buddhism" began to form (Tweed 1997a, 190; Tweed and Prothero 1999; Tweed 2000, xv–xvi), and the subfield boasted comprehensive bibliographies and literature reviews (e.g., Baumann 1997; Gregory 2001). Postructuralism, feminism, and postcolonial theory combined with other intellectual movements to increase scholars' attention to the role of race, class, gender, and nationalism and shift the focus from the making of meaning to the negotiations for power (e.g., Clarke 1997). The swelling number of transnational migrants after 1965—and not only in North America—also changed the social context in which scholars worked. Some who already had been doing research on US Buddhism attended to the demographic changes and embraced the intellectual shifts, and some Buddhist studies specialists began to focus on migrants in the United States (e.g., Numrich 1996). For the first time, scholars trained in US religious history also began to turn their attention to Buddhism (Tweed 1992; Prothero 1996; Seager 1999). Their work reflected their training in cultural history, which predominated during the earlier phase, but traces of the newer concerns for transnational exchange and social power also shaped their scholarship, including Stephen Prothero's *The White Buddhist*, which attended to colonialism and "creolization," and my own "Nightstand Buddhists and Other Creatures" (1999), which complicated identity and emphasized "hybridity." Buddhist studies scholars edited several collections that also pushed the subfield in new directions, including by attending more fully to racialized identities, ethnic institutions, and transnational migrants (Prebish and Tanaka 1998; Williams and Queen 1999). Transnational collaborations shaped those volumes and others, and scholars writing from and about various places expanded and enriched the conversation. Scholars of US Buddhism increasingly were in conversation with those who analyzed historical or contemporary expressions around the world, including in Canada (Van Esterik 1992; McLellan 1999), Britain (Almond 1988), Australia (Spuler 1999), France (Raphael and Etienne 1997), and Germany (Baumann 1993). In this third phase, impassioned debates ensued about how to classify US Buddhists (Hickey 2010; Nattier 1998; Prebish 1993; Tweed 1999), but those disputes obscured some emerging agreement: even if interpreters did not use the term, some in the subfield had begun to presume that their focus should be "transculturation" (Ortiz 1995, 97–103), two-way cultural transformations, rather than the earlier concern to understand ethnic minorities' "acculturation" to the dominant society or to trace ideas' unidirectional "international" influence.

Although it's difficult to discern shifts as they are happening, I think another phase in the subfield's history began around 2000, the year the *Journal of Global Buddhism* published its initial issue, with its title reaffirming the global focus of scholarship about Buddhism "in industrialized non-Asian countries."[3] After 2000, edited volumes expanded what we knew about some understudied Buddhist groups, including Koreans, Thais, and Cambodians, and added new research topics, including environmental activism, stress reduction, and prison ministry (Iwamura and Spickard 2003; Perreira 2004; Queen 2000). One of those volumes, *Engaged Buddhism in the West*, continued and extended the global emphasis by including chapters not only on North America, Europe, and Australia but also Africa (Queen 2000), just as other scholars writing about the so-called "Global South"—Africa (Clasquin and Krüger 2000) and Latin America (Rocha 2006)—also have widened the subfield's scope. In a similar way, recent research on Japanese Buddhism in the Americas has helpfully framed the narrative in terms of the Western Hemisphere (Williams and Moriya 2010). Specialists in Japanese Buddhism who studied "occidentalism" as well as "orientalism" built on earlier research (Ketelaar 1990) and became increasingly interested in contacts with the West, including the United States (Snodgrass 2003). Some Japanese scholars have not only analyzed Western exchanges in Japan but also have made important contributions to the history of US Buddhism (Ama 2012; Moriya 2000; Yoshinaga 2005). Some specialists in US religion, in turn, have traced the transnational flow of practices back and forth across the Pacific (e.g., Wilson 2009). Interpreters trained in religion and sociology also have devoted more attention to transnational migrants in the United States (e.g., Cadge 2005; Chandler 2004; Chen 2008). Wanting to acknowledge both the importance of global connections and the persistence of local variations, hoping to attend to negotiations for power while not erasing individual agency or overlooking quests for meaning, these scholars' concerns—including attention to geographical variations, two-way exchanges, gendered practices, racialized representations, and new media—have been transforming the subfield since 2000.

This emerging scholarship also has its unstated assumptions, however, and as far as I can tell no fully adequate theoretical or methodological framework has emerged. I do not mean to suggest that a single theory or method is necessary, or even helpful: A subfield thrives by its differences and debates as much as by its shared views about what to study and how to study it. May many flowers bloom in the field! My point is just this: most prevailing interpretive models, which are borrowed from scholars not trained in religious studies, remain indifferent or hostile to religious practice—as with many poststructuralist and postcolonial frameworks—or specialists draw on models from religious studies that commit the interpreter to a static and bounded notion of culture that offer little aid to those who want to study the dynamics of religious practice in the era of global flows. Further, whether the guiding models are derived from religious studies or not, the models' moral implications are not always examined. The emergent concerns of the subfield, in other words, are not well served by the available theories of religion and the usual methodological prescriptions. To address that problem, in this chapter I propose one possible framework for the "translocative"—not international, transnational, or global—study of Buddhism. I identify some advantages of my theory of religion, which emphasizes movement, position, and relation, and note how it harmonizes with Buddhist commitments and provides tools for the study of that tradition. Next, systematizing the theory's methodological principles, I propose five axioms for the translocative analysis of Buddhism in the contemporary world and in global history. Finally, I conclude by considering the theory's moral implications, since theoretical models and interpretive categories always enact particular values.

RELIGION AS CROSSING AND DWELLING

Although I continued my research on transnational Asian migrants and the circulation of Buddhist practices as I was writing my theory of religion, that theory emerged most directly from my study of a Cuban Catholic shrine. The Cuban exiles I met in Miami during five years of fieldwork at the Shrine of Our Lady of Charity, which honors the national patron of Cuba, seemed preoccupied with where they were and where they used to be. They wept as they told me about their former lives on the island, and they grinned as they imagined their return from exile. As I argued in the ethnography I wrote about the shrine, for them religion was *translocative*, a term I coined to make sense of what I found during fieldwork: religious rituals, stories, metaphors, institutions, and artifacts propelled them back and forth between the homeland and the new land (Tweed 1997b).

Standing at the Shrine of Our Lady of Charity—and at the annual feast day rosary and mass in a downtown Miami stadium—I began to formulate my theory of religion (Tweed 2006). It emerged as I tried to articulate what I found lacking in other theories. To make sense of the practices of those transnational migrants—as well as the circulation of Buddhist migrants, ideas, artifacts, and institutions—I needed a different theory, a self-consciously positioned sighting that highlighted movement and relation. I cannot lay out that theory here, but let me give my definition of religion and explain a few of its most important commitments.

As I understand them, "*Religions are confluences of organic-cultural flows that intensify joy and confront suffering by drawing on human and suprahuman forces to make homes and cross boundaries*" (Tweed 2006, 54). This definition draws on aquatic metaphors in order to emphasize movement, avoid essentialism, and acknowledge contact. Each religion, then, is a flowing together of currents—some institutionally enforced as "orthodox"—traversing channels, where other religions, other transverse confluences, also cross, thereby creating new spiritual streams. Religions cannot be reduced to economic forces, social relations, or political interests, but they always emerge from the swirl of transfluvial currents, as both religious and nonreligious streams propel religious flows. These flows are also "organic-cultural," in my view, so I invoke the hyphen to suggest that both natural forces and cultural processes are at work in religion: we can talk about constraining organic channels and shifting cultural currents. So religions are processes in which social institutions (the temple or the family) bridge biological constraints and cultural mediations to produce reference frames that yield a variety of representations (rituals, artifacts, and narratives) that draw on suprahuman agents (gods, buddhas, or bodhisattvas) and imagine an ultimate horizon of human life (Amida Buddha's Pure Land or the Kingdom of God). It is this appeal to suprahuman forces and an ultimate horizon that distinguishes religion from nonreligion, in my view, though it can be useful to classify practices and artifacts on a continuum that allows us to acknowledge that some cases—for example, Mindfulness-Based Stress Reduction programs in medical centers and Buddhist-influenced paintings in art museums—might fall between the imagined poles of the fully secular and the fully religious.

All this helps us understand what religion *is*—and even how we might identify quasi-religious practices—but how does religion *function*? I suggest, first, that religion "intensifies joy and confronts suffering." Religions involve emotion as well as cognition. They not only interpret and ease suffering—disease, disaster, dislocation, and death—but also provide ways for humans to imagine and enhance the joys derived from encounters with the natural world, including comets and rainbows, and transitions in the lifespan, including childbirth and marriage. Religions provide that idiom and transmit those practices.

Religions, in other words, are about enhancing the wonder as much as wondering about evil (Tweed 2006, 69–73).

Second, shifting to spatial metaphors, I suggest that religions "make homes and cross boundaries" (Tweed 2006, 73–77). Religions are about finding one's place (dwelling) and moving across space (crossing). As dwelling, religions are spatial practices that orient humans in time and space, situating devotees in four *chronotopes*, or time-spaces: the body, the home, the homeland, and the cosmos. They function, I suggest, as watch and compass. But religions make sense of the nomadic as well as the sedentary in human life and involve another spatial practice—crossing. Religions enable and constrain corporeal, terrestrial, and cosmic crossings. They mark and traverse the boundaries of not only the natural terrain, as in pilgrimages and missions, and the limits of embodied life, including illness and death, but they also chart and cross the ultimate horizon, whether that final crossing is imagined as transport or transformation, as ascending to heaven or attaining enlightenment.

THE THEORY'S BUDDHIST PARALLELS AND METHODOLOGICAL IMPLICATIONS

Some readers have interpreted *Crossing and Dwelling* as providing a *Catholic* theory of religion or as primarily reflecting on *modernity*. It's true that I hoped to make sense of the most prominent conditions of late modernity—including migration, pluralism, and the time-space compression produced by advances in technology, like computers and jet planes. So I noted that religion is always mediated by communication and transportation technology, and I emphasized both the movement of peoples and the confluence of traditions. Readers celebrating the theory's Catholic parallels also have a point. They have welcomed my deemphasis of the creedal as they simultaneously criticize the ways that Protestant assumptions—including assumptions about the centrality of beliefs—have shaped most modern Western thinking about religion. Those readers are right that the theory did arise most directly from my immersion at a Catholic site, and that my account's acknowledgment that artifacts, institutions, and rituals play an important role might provide tools for making sense of devotional life in late modernity.

Yet even if I was in conversation with those thinking about both Catholicism and modernity, I also think it might help to note the theory's Buddhist parallels. Those who have understood themselves as "Buddhists" have varied widely from period to period and from place to place. The more you attend to differences in practice, the more you sense that it's not easy to identify what, if anything, they've shared. We can have some sympathy, then, with the early Western interpreters who, until the middle of the nineteenth century, could not imagine that the Buddhist traditions in, for example, Burma, Japan, and Tibet claimed the same founder and a common history. I recall a recent conversation with a Buddhist studies scholar on that topic, and we concluded that the most we could say was that "Buddhists" are those who have taken refuge in the Buddha, the Dharma, and the *sangha*—however they understood that classic formulation. You might have your own sense of the nature and extent of Buddhist commonality. In any case, I think it's fair to say, most Buddhist philosophical schools also have accepted the claim that there are three characteristics of the phenomenal world, the world we all live in: suffering (*duḥka*), no-self (*anātman*), and impermanence (*anitya*) (Anderson 2004).[4] And all three themes find a place in my theory, either explicitly or implicitly. The most obvious trace of Buddhist influence is my definition's emphasis on the first of these characteristics: religions, I proposed, "confront suffering." However, the other two doctrines—no-self and impermanence—are as important. Impermanence means that all things, including the self and the world, change. They change over time and are affected by—even brought into existence by—other things. The Buddhist idea of *anātman* or no-self also affirms the processive and relational character of beings and objects. There is no substantial and enduring stuff. Humans are no more—or less—than constitutive elements flowing together: body, sensation, perception, habit, and consciousness. All persons and things are in a state of flux, and all are interdependent, conditioned by other things. In the book, I noted the intellectual resources for reimagining religion in motion and in relation, by employing metaphors from natural sciences (like physics and hydrodynamics) and by incorporating the insights of Western thinkers (like Heraclitus and Alfred North Whitehead). But I also acknowledged the usefulness of Buddhist ideas of impermanence, no-self, and dependent co-origination (Tweed 2006, 56–60). I even self-consciously used Buddhist terminology when trying to address some vexing problems facing any theory of religion. For example, how do we understand the relation between religion, politics, society, and economy? My solution was to emphasize the "mutual intercausality" of these cultural forces, while also acknowledging the ways that the cultural, in turn, emerges in relation to the biological (Tweed 2006, 60).

So I am happy to acknowledge the Buddhist influences, but what are the theory's *methodological* implications? What might it tell us about how to study the historical and contemporary expressions of Buddhism? All theories, I proposed, have blind spots (Tweed 2006, 14–15 and 171–177). All schemes illumine some things while they obscure others. This theory, with its Buddhist-like emphasis on flux and interrelation, proposes a different understanding of a religious "tradition" and, more specifically, offers a different perspective on the history and geography of Buddhism. In 1951, Edward Conze, the British-born translator of Buddhist texts, published a popular interpretation entitled *Buddhism: Its Essence and Development*, and that volume had many strengths. But in terms of the role-specific obligation of scholars, it is not helpful to talk about Buddhism—or any tradition—as having an "essence," an unchanging core of teachings or practices. As I noted, turning to aquatic metaphors, every tradition, including Buddhism, is a flowing together of currents (Tweed 2006, 60). There is no pure substratum, no static and independent core called "Buddhism"—in the founder's day or in later generations. What we have come to call "Buddhism" was always becoming, being made and remade over and over again in contact and exchange, as it was carried along in the flow of things. Buddhist leaders have the right—even the role-specific obligation—to determine what constitutes "authentic" Buddhism, but scholars—and practitioners as they contribute to academic conversations—have another duty, I suggest: to follow the flows wherever they lead. To study the historical or contemporary expressions of Buddhism is to trace the flow of people, rituals, artifacts, beliefs, and institutions across spatial and temporal boundaries.

We should not overlook the ways that Buddhism orients devotees in time and space, situates them in the body, the home, the homeland, and the cosmos. In short, we should remember that religion is also about *dwelling* (Tweed 2006, 80–121). But this emphasis on *crossing*—this effort to reimagine the Buddhist "tradition" as a confluence of streams—illumines some things, including many of the topics addressed by the contributors to this volume.[5] It helps to interpret the interactions of Buddhist temples' "Distant Correspondents" (Baroni, chap. 6 in this volume) and the two-way flows of Buddhists' "conspicuous compassion" (Chandler, chap. 5 in this volume). The mixing of religious traditions—for example, the emergence of Jewish Buddhists—makes more sense if we take a theoretical perspective that highlights movement and relation; so does the contact and exchange evident in regional expressions of Buddhism in the Protestant South (Wilson, chap. 2 in this volume). And if we keep in mind the ways that communication and transportation technology mediates religion in modernity, Buddhist blogs and social networking sites in virtual space seem to be yet further compelling examples of crossing. Perhaps we'll find that my theory of religion obscures some things we want to study—again, blind spots always remain—but to give you a better sense of what I am suggesting, let me summarize two of my recent attempts to apply this approach and then systematize my methodological proposals by offering five axioms or guidelines for the study of Buddhism.

TWO CASE STUDIES: FLOWS IN THE ATLANTIC WORLD AND THE PACIFIC WORLD

In an article-length study (Tweed 2005), I began with a simple question (the approach I advocate starts small and gets big). I asked: How did D. T. Suzuki (1870–1966), the twentieth-century Japanese popularizer of Buddhism, come to be influenced by the thought of Immanuel Swedenborg (1688–1772), the eighteenth-century Swedish mystic? I won't repeat my findings here—or those of the Japanese scholar Shin'ichi Yoshinaga (2005), with whom I've collaborated—since my article, "American Occultism and Japanese Buddhism," is available, but I just want to note that the process of research, which I called "translocative analysis," led me to trace the flow of ideas, people, and objects across Asia, North America, and Europe.

In the same way, a journal article asks a question that begins on the other side of the Pacific but opens out to global flows (Tweed 2011): How has Buddhism influenced the post-1945 United States, especially but not only American visual artists? How, I wondered, did American artists, especially painters like Jasper Johns and video artists like Bill Viola, come to make art the way they did? That essay makes a larger point about the tradition's influence and then focuses on the visual arts. In a process of *transcultural collage*, I proposed some American artists between the 1940s and the 1960s assembled other kinds of found objects—Dadaism, Japanese aesthetics, and "Suzuki Zen"—to create new art forms that valued spontaneity and irreverence; experimented with line, color, and space; and emphasized the vernacular glance and the meditative gaze.

These are just two examples of what I have in mind. In both studies, I tried to follow the flows and begin to work out the methodological implications of my theory of religion. But what I have in mind still might not be clear, so let me try to say more about the *translocative analysis* I propose by suggesting a few specific methodological guidelines, five axioms for the study of Buddhism in the contemporary world and in global history.

AXIOMS FOR THE TRANSLOCATIVE STUDY OF BUDDHISM

(1) *Follow the flows.* Religions are spatial processes that involve settling in and moving across, and in the study of Buddhism we should attend to the kinetics of both itinerancy and homemaking. This means noticing, on the one hand, that even things that seem static, like landscapes and temples, are always changing. It means, in other words, putting landscape in motion. We do this by excavating the layers of human migration and settlement—and noticing all the traces left on the terrain, from the so-called natural world to the built environment. It also means, this axiom suggests, that we follow the flows of people, artifacts, institutions, and practices that have transformed indifferent space into familiar place.

(2) *Notice all the figures crossing.* To follow the flows and provide the richest representation of a practice or a site, we need to creatively use a variety of sources to try to recover all those who have had a presence, ordinary devotees as well as religious leaders, women as well as men, and (we need much more research on this) children as well as adults. Notice all those who are present—while also noticing those who, for one reason or another, are absent. Ask: Who's there? Who's not there? And, as with Buddhists' critics, who's present only as an incorporeal presence, as the other who haunts the landscape?

(3) *Attend to all the senses and all religion's components*. The humans crossing the water or the landscape are embodied beings, and religions are multisensorial spatial practices. Humans mark boundaries and cross them by appealing to all the senses—sight, smell, taste, touch, and hearing—and by using all religion's components—stories, moral codes, artifacts, architecture, and rituals. For example, we might focus on an ordinary artifact, a single stick of incense (tracing its production, circulation, and use), and then inquire about a sense that scholars of Buddhism have underemphasized: smell.

(4) *Consider varying scales*. If we follow the flows wherever they lead—and that's easier said than done—we often will find that we need to extend our study's temporal span and expand its geographical scope. The traces might be very recent or quite ancient, and we should expand and contract the historical frame of our study accordingly. In turn, if we follow the flows, the geographical scale of our analysis will sometimes be larger and sometimes smaller than the nation-state. We should not assume the nation as the default level of analysis but instead move agilely across varying scales of analysis, from neural pathways to global trade routes, from the local to the transregional, or wherever the movements we're tracing take us. So we might reframe the study of Buddhism and not only think about Buddhism in North America, Latin America, Europe, Africa, Australia, or "the West." New angles of vision might open up if we situate what we study, the Buddhist flows we're following, in the Atlantic world, the Indo-Pacific world, the Western Hemisphere, or the Global South.

(5) *Notice how flows start, stop, and shift*. Religions, as I understand them, negotiate power as well as make meaning, and the kinetics of dwelling and crossing are always mediated not only by transportation and communication technology but also by institutional structures. All space is striated, marked by the traces of social power wielded by institutions and their legal and moral codes. In the same way, there are no unimpeded flows. The flows—of people, things, and practices—are propelled, compelled, and blocked, directed this way and that, by institutions. Extending the aquatic metaphor to explain how institutional power—as well as individual agency—is at work, we might say that institutions channel and regulate religious flows, functioning like a dam.[6] In those sorts of hydrodynamic engineering systems, walled structures divert the water's direction and "control valves" modulate its rate of flow. A large organization—a legal system or a corporation—usually

constructs and maintains the dam, yet that collectivity also authorizes a particular person, who is subject to transmitted codes intended to constrain individual choice, to turn the valve and control the flow. Similar processes are at work, I suggest, as social institutions, including nation-states, divert and modulate religions' organic-cultural flows. It's important for scholars of Buddhism to notice this—and, so, to attend to the ways that power is enacted and not only the ways that meaning is made. For example, we know something—but not enough—about the reception of the racist US immigration act of 1924 in Japan (Stalker 2006), and some scholars have studied the impact of President Roosevelt's 1942 executive order mandating internment camps for Americans of Japanese descent (Williams 2002). But in which *other* ways have legal codes and institutional structures—within US boundaries or beyond them—compelled and constrained Buddhists' crossings?

MORAL IMPLICATIONS: TOWARD A KINETIC AND RELATIONAL ETHIC

The fifth axiom, which concerns power, raises other issues about right and wrong—about scholarly obligations, individual morality, and public policy. And I want to conclude by briefly pondering the moral implications of my theory of religion and the methodological approach that emerges from it. As one philosopher put it, fact and value are "entangled" (Putnam 2002, 28–45). To restate the point using my aquatic metaphors, we might talk about the "transfluence of fact and value." All of us who study Buddhism enact epistemic values (like coherence and clarity) and moral values (like fairness and inclusiveness) when we prefer one interpretation to another. In one piece (Tweed 2009), I started to think about the moral implications of my theory, noting how it highlights the virtue of humility and how another virtue, reciprocal generosity, might provide a basis for civic engagement.

I now want to identify other moral values that emerge from the perspective I've proposed. Before I do that I feel compelled to acknowledge that, as I consider scholarship's moral implications, I'm recalling an unpayable debt to a Jodo Shinshu practitioner and member of the Buddhist Churches of America, Masatoshi Nagatomi (1926–2000), a professor of Buddhist studies at Harvard. While I was researching my dissertation during the 1980s, I consulted with Professor Nagatomi, and, although I never told him this, it was a story he'd recounted in 1980 that originally set me on my career path—and that has haunted me ever since. I've never mentioned this publicly before. It was Professor Nagatomi's story to tell, and I've forgotten some of the details, so I won't dishonor him or his memories by attempting to report it in full. Let me relay only its outlines and its impact. While his parents were interned at Manzanar and he was in Japan studying during World War II, the nineteen-year-old Nagatomi was riding on a train. In the distance, suddenly he and his fellow passengers eyed a mushroom cloud on the horizon, the billowing traces of the atomic bomb. A white Christian missionary nearby, the Harvard professor recalled decades later, announced to the Japanese passengers that the bomb was God's just condemnation of the "heathen." I was stunned by that heartbreaking story, my eyes filling with tears. That was the moment I decided to go on for a PhD in religion. Even though I have no idea what Professor Nagatomi thought about my subsequent Buddhist research—or what he might have thought about my theorizing—I am grateful to have a chance to consider the ways that research has its moral sources and effects.

So what are the moral and political implications of my theoretical perspective? To put it negatively, my understanding of theory and method challenges alternatives that privilege stasis, homogeneity, and purity. To put it more positively, my kinetic and relational account values movement, manyness, and mixing.[7] That, in turn, has implications not only for imagining scholarly obligations and personal morality but also for assessing public policy. Those who've thought about Buddhists, including about Asian Buddhist migrants in the nineteenth and twentieth centuries, often have presupposed that stasis is the norm. People, they've presumed, are supposed to be stationary. But both the peopling of the hemisphere, which began with migrants crossing from Asia fifteen thousand years ago, and the theory of religion I favor, suggest instead that movement is the norm. In turn, we need to revalue the migrant and challenge any immigration policy that obscures our shared history of crossing.

In a similar way, it seems wrong to assume that homogeneity, or uniformity, has been the norm in human history or in Buddhist life. In many times and places, leaders of villages, cities, nations, and empires have imagined the dominant tradition as the only tradition. But the more we follow the flows, the more we recover the full complexity of ways of being Buddhist—as well as the many ways of being American or Brazilian, Japanese or South African. We have historical grounds and theoretical resources for challenging any nationalist public policy or intolerant institutional mandate that coerces or condemns, or does violence to those who dissent.

Sometimes those who've advocated violence—or prescribed coercive legal and religious codes—have defended their actions by celebrating the "purity" of their lineage and condemning the impurity of others. But in both heritage and religion mixing has been the norm. There was no pure spiritual origin, in my theory, and there is no pure race. There is only ceaseless contact and exchange. Creolization in language, culture, and religion is the *usual* way of things. Any personal stance or public policy that rests on an imagined "purity" is both morally dangerous and historically unfounded. Because all things are interdependent and in flux, my Buddhist-inflected theory and method suggests, we should value movement, manyness, and mixing.

And if you are not ready to celebrate "translocative analysis" and adopt my theoretical framework and its guiding categories, I hope we still can agree that all of us who study Buddhism after the heightened attention to asymmetrical power relations and circulating transregional flows can't find a stable place on shore, a vantage beyond the flows we study. We can only aim to be as self-conscious as possible, scrutinizing our framework's methodological guidelines and moral implications. So recognizing the transfluence of fact and value and the mutual intercausality of all things—including our own scholarship—perhaps we should just lay back, point our toes, look skyward, and let the swirl of the cultural currents we study toss us this way and that. Let the fullness of the Buddhist tradition, in all its meanderings, wash over us, as we examine methodological assumptions and moral commitments, as we follow the flows that carry all of us along.

NOTES

1. My own specialization is US Buddhism and this chapter focuses on that, even if it includes a wider geographical area. I offer a tentative periodization of the history of the study of Western Buddhism or Buddhism outside Asia, especially but not only in the United States. This periodization traces primarily two changes:

varying notions of connections across regions and varying notions of culture. In this scheme, I propose, there are four phases of the subfield: (1) *national studies*, which focused on the nation-state: 1950s to 1960s; (2) *international studies*, which focused on interactions between two or more nation-states: 1970s and 1980s; (3) *transnational studies*, which trace movements across national borders: 1990s to 2000; (4) *global studies*, which emphasize circulations back and forth across regions: since 2000. One scholar of Atlantic history has distinguished two major approaches to "global history": (1) "*inter*-national histories," "a history of competitive but mutually recognizing territorial nation states," and (2) "*trans*-national histories," "a narrative of globalization predicated, like oceanic history, on borderlessness, fluidity, and . . . a lack of territorial fixity" (Armitage 2007, 9). That is something like I have in mind here. I want to emphasize the shifting terms and their varying implications.

2. Some important texts in this period were not produced by scholars of religion, not only as is the case with Layman, who was a psychologist, but by journalists (Fields 1986) and specialists in American studies and cultural history (Lears 1981, 225–240).
3. "About the Journal," *Journal of Global Buddhism* (retrieved from http://www.globalbuddhism.org/dig.html). The *Journal of Global Buddhism* also has published useful bibliographies that focus on different nations and regions, and those have been crucial for the emerging subfield and its increasing geographical scope.
4. There is an enormous scholarly literature about these three concepts, of course. I cite Anderson's entry on *anitya* (impermanence) because she mentions the "three characteristics of the phenomenal world," and that entry might be a place to start for those (including specialists in US religion) who are unfamiliar with the scholarship. Entries in that reference work on *anātman* (no-self) and *pratītyasamutpāda* (dependent origination) also might be helpful.
5. Other scholars of global Buddhism already have used my theory to study the relocation of Lao migrants to Canada (e.g., White 2010) and the transmission of a ritual from Japan to the United States (Wilson 2009), but I think it might have even wider uses in the subfield, as I hint here and later.
6. For this clarification and expansion of my theory, I am indebted to many readers and audiences in the United States, Canada, and

Europe. A number of commentators in conference sessions and university symposia suggested that I reconsider institutional power (especially Bruce Lawrence, Kim Knott, and Manuel Vásquez) as well as faculty members and graduate students I met during lectures or conferences in London, Turku, and Tromsø. It was during another conference session in Atlanta dedicated to the theory's implications for scholars of the history of Christianity that Marie Marquardt (2010, 13) suggested that "the religious institutions that shape religious flows look more to me like retaining walls, levies, and dams that divert flows, and that create great pools of stagnant water." A scholar in the audience, Michael Ostling, then added a related suggestion: that I should consider "the analogy of valves or filters." He followed up with a helpful note (Michael Ostling, November 15, 2010, email to the author). I learned more in an online discussion with graduate students enrolled in a seminar taught by Michel Desjardins at Wilfrid Laurier University in Waterloo. With these helpful suggestions in hand, I then went to research how dams and valves actually work, and I draw on that information in my analysis here.

7. I take the word "manyness" from Catherine L. Albanese, who has used it as a synonym for diversity.

TWO

Regionalism within North American Buddhism

JEFF WILSON

INTRODUCTION

American religious history as an object of study was constituted at its inception with an interest in regional motifs, when Cotton Mather, in 1702, published his weighty *Magnalia Christi Americana, or, The Ecclesiastical History of New-England*. Regionalism as an interpretive motif was still going strong in 1844, just before the initial arrival of Buddhism, when Robert Baird published his *Religion in America*. Baird's examination paid attention to the major geographic areas of America, to the ethnic and religious origins of the settlers of various places, and noted distribution patterns for an already diverse set of denominations. And when American religious history began to coalesce as an academic field in the early twentieth century, regionalism was a major analytical key, whether it was the contrasts between North and South or East and West, or the influence of Frederick Turner's frontier thesis (Turner 1921). A perusal of current introductory textbooks on American religious history will quickly reveal that regionalism remains an ongoing strategy for discussing the historical interaction between various religious groups and the wider culture (see, for example, Lippy 2009).

Likewise, the regional nature of Canadian religion has been an essential trope for its historiography. Scholars have long noted the French or English domination of particular areas, inter-ethnic and interreligious strife on the Pacific Coast, and regional factors in the decisions of individual Presbyterian churches as to whether or not to join the United Church of Canada, among many other possible examples.

Despite this prevalence of regional awareness in American and Canadian religious history, studies of North American Buddhist regionalism have lagged far behind those on Christianity and other traditions. Among the various important studies that have appeared in the past fifteen years, nearly all have been based on work in a few restricted areas that are nonetheless held up as representative of American, Canadian, or even North American Buddhism as a whole. In American Buddhist studies, California, the urban Midwest, and the Northeast are somehow transformed into the entirety of the United States. Consider our book-length ethnographies: Wendy Cadge's work was done in Boston and Philadelphia, Eve Mullen's was done in New York City, Paul Numrich's research was done in Chicago and California, and Carolyn Chen, Sharon Suh, and Joseph Cheah's work was done in California (Cadge 2005; Cheah 2011; Chen 2008; Mullen 2001; Numrich 1996; Suh 2004). Or think about more general interpretive works, such as James William Coleman's *The New Buddhism*, whose argument about an emergent convert-based, pan-sectarian neo-Buddhism home-grown in America has been widely influential (Coleman 2001). The seven sites for his fieldwork were four California centers (three of which were in the Bay Area alone), one in Boston, one in New York, and one in Boulder, Colorado. We see similar patterns in the various book chapters of the collected anthologies in the field, and in the stand-alone articles in relevant journals: time and again, the lion's share of work on American Buddhism is done in a few specific places but is then extrapolated to somehow represent phenomena at the national or even international level. Meanwhile, relatively little attention is paid to how the specifics of the local environment impact the particular sites under study, or how these Buddhist temples themselves affect the differing regions in which they find themselves.

Buddhism in Canada doesn't fare much better. All of our published book-length ethnographies have focused on the Greater Toronto Area (such as Van Esterik 1992; McLellan 1999; and Campbell 2009), which isn't even representative of Ontario as a whole. Bruce Matthews's (2005) edited volume on Buddhism in Canada does have a regional view but only in terms of description, not comprehensive analysis. Full-length ethnographies of Mexican or Caribbean Buddhism—regional or otherwise—simply don't exist.

Descriptions of Buddhism in America do not usually involve a sophisticated understanding of Buddhism's differing manifestations in various parts of the country. Most often, American Buddhism is taken as a monolithic geographic/cultural movement, diverse in terms of groups but with little indication that there might be more Vipassana in Boston than in Phoenix, or more Chan in Houston than in Chicago. Ironically, the partial exception to this is found among historians of general American religion who do not focus on Buddhism specifically. Well familiar with the regionalism trope, they sometimes make a small-scale attempt to indicate that Buddhism is in some ways a regional religion—for example, Laurie Maffly-Kipp in "Eastward Ho!" (her contribution to Thomas Tweed's revisionist anthology, Tweed 1997c), Edwin Gaustad in his fabulous county-by-county atlas of American religion (and its 2001 update with Philip Barlow), and Bret Carroll in his more classroom-oriented atlas all demonstrate the largely Western nature of the Buddhist Churches of America (BCA) (Carroll 2000; Gaustad 1962; Gaustad and Barlow 2001; Maffly-Kipp 1997). The BCA is singled out for attention because it is organized into congregations, saddled with the comfortable "church" label, and has a central authority that is easily queried for statistics. That this particular organization is the one that is almost invariably gestured toward by nonspecialists perhaps illustrates the scant level of penetration of research on American Buddhism into the field of American religious studies more generally. And this inclusion of a single Buddhist group into surveys of American religious regionalism almost hurts as much as it helps. While it opens the important question of American Buddhist regionalism, it starts to shut it as well by allowing one established institution to stand in for the hundreds of Buddhist lineages operating in the United States. Worse yet, it merely confirms an unvoiced suspicion: Buddhism is a California phenomenon, obscuring the possibility of Southern, Midwestern, or other significant Buddhist regional phenomena.

The time has come to recover regionalism and apply it in a more systematic and sophisticated way to the various Buddhist phenomena of North America. Regionalism can serve both creative and critical functions in our studies. For example, it can generate new avenues of research that expand our understanding of the issues we have already identified within the subfield. One of these common topics is how

Americans seek to explicitly Americanize Buddhism so that it loses or changes aspects of its Asian heritage (often described negatively as trappings or baggage) and is adapted in new forms to a specifically American cultural environment. Attention to regionalism might lead us to inquire whether this process takes different forms in different regions of the United States. After all, no one really lives in "America" as a whole—we live in Oakland, California; Salt Lake City, Utah; Denver, Colorado; San Antonio, Texas; Kansas City, Missouri; Rockford, Illinois; Waynesville, North Carolina; or New Britain, Connecticut. America looks different to the people who live in these separate places, and while they share much, they have particular regional understandings of what America is and what it means to be American. Surely this will have an impact on how they pursue the holy grail of Americanized Buddhism.

Likewise, regionalism can help us to rein in some of our enthusiastic narratives about Buddhism in the United States. It has become common to trumpet the amazing diversity of Buddhism in America, where allegedly every form of Buddhism is present and has the unique opportunity to interact with every other form, leading to previously unimaginable inter-Buddhist exchanges that could give rise to syncretistic Buddhisms undreamed of in Asia. For the pluralists among us this is an appealing vision, but when we begin to look more systematically at American Buddhism from a regional perspective, we must introduce a note of caution about such imagined developments. In fact, most Buddhists in America live in places where they have limited opportunities for substantive inter-Buddhist contact and exchange. Los Angeles may house a staggering diversity of Buddhist groups, but most people interested in Buddhism don't live in LA. And even in Southern California there is a clear tendency for what inter-Buddhist contact that does exist to happen mainly among co-ethnics, which puts a brake on the great American Buddhist mash-up we are supposedly all rushing toward. The vast majority of Americans only have at best one or two local forms of Buddhism to interact with, and even most Buddhist practitioners have very constricted options within their immediate communities. In the few truly pluralistic sites (mainly certain big cities), Buddhist groups are almost invariably more interested in the growth and expansion of their own traditions than they are in actively learning about other forms of Dharma. A regional lens helps us to correct possible distortions that creep into our view when we look at American Buddhism merely on a national scale.

FIVE FORMS OF REGIONAL ANALYSIS

If we are now going to carry out our studies with expanded attention to region, what are the approaches that we should take to the subject? I suggest five specific modes of investigation that will help us produce a more nuanced understanding of the Buddhist regions of North America. First is distribution. We need to know what groups are located in which areas, and why. This mode can be broken down in an almost infinite number of ways, but several immediately suggest themselves. First, we can pay greater attention to the distribution patterns of particular Buddhist ethnic groups. For example, Kalmykian American Buddhists have mainly been found in the narrow corridor between New York City and Washington, D.C. Taiwanese American Buddhists, by contrast, are far more widely distributed throughout the United States, but their single greatest concentration is in the San Gabriel Valley outside Los Angeles. Are nightstand Buddhists uniformly distributed throughout the country, and does their ratio to local "card-carrying Buddhists" differ in separate regions (Tweed 1999)? In what areas do retreat centers tend to cluster? Where do Americans build *stūpas*? And, of course, beyond the simple numbers and concentration ratios, the important question behind each of these projects will always be: Why do we see these regional differences? What are the factors driving them?

A second approach to use in regional studies of North American Buddhism is to examine how different American cultural regions affect the Buddhisms within them. Buddhism not only differs in concentration and diversity of sectarian affiliation between the West Coast and the South, but the experience of Buddhists across the board is different in these separate regions. We may object that regional subcultures are not as strong as they once were. True enough, but that also suggests that our historical studies of North American Buddhism should pay attention to different regions. And I argue that while modern transportation, communication, and economic realities have somewhat eroded the regional subcultures that existed in earlier periods, there is still considerable variation that persists between separate parts of the country.

We can look to a number of factors in our analyses. One is climate and terrain. Theravada monks in Quebec, Alaska, and Minnesota cannot go about with bare feet and head, one shoulder uncovered, and just the traditional thin robes. They must develop new costumes that enact creative new interpretations of the Vinaya in order to survive in these areas, a process that monks in Florida do not have to undergo (Prebish 2003). We can also look to economics among different areas: West Coast housing prices and cost of living put a high burden on newer religious groups, affecting their choices of what to build, how, and where. And of course regional culture cannot be ignored. The simple fact is that Southern culture and religion make it harder to be a minority, decrease the chances of attracting resident teachers to new meditation groups, and put significantly more pressure on locals enmeshed in conservative family and social networks not to convert to Buddhism compared to newcomers from other areas of America. Thus, we can combine these factors to describe general regional differences between different parts of the country. Buddhists today in San Francisco have access to large numbers of other Buddhists, a wide range of choices of Buddhist traditions, a moderate climate, a relatively liberal and tolerant surrounding atmosphere, a long history of absorption of Asian culture, a high cost of property values, and other particular local forces with which to contend. Buddhists in Charlotte, meanwhile, practice in a region with far fewer Buddhist adherents, more constricted sectarian choices, a relatively more conservative and exclusively Christian dominant public culture, sweltering temperatures, lower historic Asian immigration, lower cost of living, and other circumstances. These regional differences will make specific impacts on the Buddhist groups and individuals who seek to dwell in these separate regions, and they will need to resort to different types of adapting practices as they navigate their local cultural terrain. And surely there are yet finer, more detailed subregional distinctions within these sorts of regional North American Buddhisms that can be profitably mined.

Beyond distribution patterns and regional environmental influences, a third area for study is how Buddhists themselves are affecting the different regions in which they are found. *The Trap* depicts the relationship between Francophone Cape Breton lobstermen and the Tibetan Buddhists in their midst (Verchery 2007). The Buddhists buy lobsters and release them back into the sea in a ritual designed to show compassion to these beings and generate merit for their benefactors.

In the process, the fishing industry must come to an understanding of their neighbors and the religious framework in which they operate. In Hawaii widespread devotion to the bodhisattva Jizo has altered the landscape itself, with many statues and markers erected in public spaces to protect and warn fishermen, swimmers, and surfers about the presence of dangerous currents and wave-prone beaches (Clark 2007). Thus, it is not simply that different regions affect their Buddhisms in diverse ways; the various Buddhisms within particular regions reciprocate in different ways as they in turn change what it means to live in Nova Scotia or Hawaii. The South is not the same South as it used to be once Buddhists arrived, nor is the West Coast, nor the Midwest. These encounters and changes were not and are not nationally uniform.

The fourth aspect of regionalism that I invite us to study is differences within denominations or lineages themselves. I think this is one of the most potentially interesting avenues for research. Currently, we act like Shambhala Buddhism is the same in Halifax as it is in Kitchener. Is Suzuki Zen the same in San Francisco as it is in Richmond, Virginia? I doubt it. In the San Francisco Bay Area there are many practitioners and centers in this line, and people interested in pursuing a formal meditation practice can easily locate instructors. In the Southeast, on the other hand, this lineage is far less represented, and indeed Zen on the whole does not have a strong hold on the South. Due to lack of local resources, Southern practitioners who identify with the Suzuki lineage are less likely to stress the need for close study with a trained meditation master, emphasizing instead more of a private, individualistic approach to Zen. They are also more likely to display eclecticism in their understanding of Zen, as they often have to rely on whatever books from various lineages they can obtain rather than working directly with and mirroring the approach of sanctioned teachers of this San Francisco Zen Center–based movement. And those teachers from this lineage who do live in the far-flung region of the Southeast may tend to exhibit relatively more diverse personal styles, since they are geographically distanced from the critical surveillance of their co-lineage holders.[1] People in San Francisco and in Virginia may be part of the same network, but we deceive ourselves if we imagine networks merely as Indra's nets, with every jewel equally reflecting every other jewel. Where you are specifically placed in a real-world network matters. It is one thing to practice at the central headquarters and another thing to practice at the end of a far-flung network.

Let us take the Buddhist Churches of America as an example, since it is one of the few groups that receives some acknowledgment as having a regional identity. Geographically, the BCA can be largely divided into those temples west of the Rockies and those to the east. Jodo Shinshu temples in California have a large pool of Japanese Americans (and new Japanese immigrants, workers, and students) upon which to draw. Demographically they are most often dominated by people of Japanese descent, and many temples harbor a relatively traditional approach to Buddhist practice. This contrasts with Jodo Shinshu temples east of the Rocky Mountains, which draw from a much smaller pool of Japanese Americans and Japanese immigrants. These temples are often much more racially and ethnically mixed, and they display significantly more eclecticism in terms of practice and organization. It is from temples east of the Rockies that many new innovations arise—such as quiet meditation in a Shinshu context and lay teachers (now called minister's assistants)—and the BCA's first Caucasian president was produced, perhaps in part because being so far from the centers of power, he was a nonthreatening neutral party who was seen as not beholden to any particular faction. Indeed, so marked are regional variations within American Jodo Shinshu that they can become a source of tension, with geographically based factions competing among themselves; even on the West Coast the BCA's Southern District is sometimes seen as a self-sufficient, at times self-satisfied, enclave that doesn't need the Bay Area District and could leave the BCA should certain conditions arise. This is a much richer, more interesting narrative to tell than "The Buddhist Churches of America are a Japanese American Pure Land church, mostly found in California, end of story."

A fifth and final major area for regional analysis moves away from looking at separate swaths of the country and considers instead differences as ingrained within varying types of built environments. On the other hand, even though Buddhism in America can be found in many environments, it is especially an urban phenomenon. It is large cities that attract the majority of Asian Buddhist immigrants: Cities offer better job prospects, opportunities for air travel back to their countries of origin, a critical mass of others from their home countries, and the diverse and relatively liberal atmosphere that allows minority ethnic and religious groups to find a niche. Furthermore, cities function as important engines for exposure of new demographics to Buddhism—the presence of Asian immigrants, established transnational transportation routes, libraries and museums with Buddhist artifacts and texts, and the urban atmosphere of exploration and tolerance all contribute to the growth of Buddhism among more established American racial and ethnic groups. And there is the common phenomenon of younger persons moving to "the big city" specifically to explore new and allegedly exotic ways of living. Perhaps it is no surprise then that North American Buddhist ethnographies almost invariably take place within large cities.

We need to be careful, however, about allowing a handful of the largest metropolitan areas in North America to stand in for the totality of the Buddhist experience. There are different forces operating on Buddhists in small cities as opposed to large ones. We need projects that examine urban Buddhism versus suburban Buddhism, and rural Buddhism needs far greater attention.[2] It may be that Buddhism in Atlanta, Georgia, shares more in common in certain ways with Buddhism in Honolulu, Hawaii, than it does with Buddhism in small-town Videlia, Georgia. We also need to pay attention to the built environment of Buddhist groups in Asian cultural contexts compared to the types of places they inhabit in North America. If a Buddhist demographic or lineage was primarily rural in Asia and now exists mainly in urban spaces in the United States or Canada, what specific tensions or adaptations emerge? This applies to missionary figures as well: Is it significant that Shunryu Suzuki, who ended up teaching Buddhism to urban Westerners, came from a small village outside Yokohama? Would he have been as insistent on establishing Tassajara Zen Center in the Los Padres National Forest if he had spent his childhood in bustling central Tokyo? Regionalism as an interpretative trope should be applied not only to current North American phenomena but also to their Asian antecedents as we seek to understand the transnational element of local North American Buddhisms.

FACTORS IN NORTH AMERICAN BUDDHIST REGIONALISM

Together, I think these five areas offer useful ways to begin theorizing and researching North American Buddhist regionalism. Of course, beyond the identification of different types of regionalism, there is the necessity to account for the production of these regions. I have hinted at some specific factors, but let me take a moment to look at this more systematically. Arguably the single greatest influence is differing immigration patterns. Asian Buddhist immigration has not been uniform in its spread within the United States. There are more Vietnamese along the Caribbean coast than in the landlocked Western states; more Japanese on the Pacific Coast than on the Atlantic; more Thai in the South than the North. Thus, the Buddhisms that these immigrant groups bring show definite regional patterns of distribution. We can further analyze the reasons behind these various immigration patterns. One is basic chance: A family from Cambodia moves to an area, and soon many others follow simply because they know there are Cambodians there. Or perhaps a church or other organization sponsors refugees from an Asian Buddhist nation, resulting in the accumulation of immigrants from that area. A second reason is proximity to the Old World: The Chinese played a major role in nineteenth-century Western American life because they arrived via trans-Pacific ships, disembarking on the Pacific Coast and finding eastward dissemination slow due to difficult travel conditions and dangerous racism. And a third reason results from actually choosing certain regions because of their specific characteristics. In the Vietnamese case, the Gulf Coast provides the subtropical environmental conditions familiar to immigrants from Vietnam, as well as substantial fishing opportunities for arrivals from a coastal country with a significant fishing industry. This is one reason why Vietnamese Buddhists have settled more densely in coastal Texas, Louisiana, and Florida than in Idaho or Montana.

A second factor to pay attention to is missionary patterns. Buddhism follows in the wake of missionary efforts by both Asian missionaries and Americans who have either encountered Buddhism in Asia or discovered it through reading and seek to propagate it to others. In either case, the presence of a dedicated missionary in a region can substantially influence the amount and type of Buddhism that one encounters in that location. When Leslie Dawson—now Ananda Bodhi Bhikkhu—returned to his home city of Toronto in 1965 after years spent studying and teaching Buddhism in Asia and Europe, he became one of the first teachers to spread Buddhism outside the city's Asian immigrant communities (Namgyal Rinpoche 2004). Soon thereafter he was recognized as an incarnate lama and renamed Namgyal Rinpoche. His eclectic blend of reformist Theravada and Tibetan

Buddhism has been locally impactful through the influence of his Dharma Centre of Canada and groups founded by his disciples. In many other parts of Canada, however, few Buddhists know the history of this Canadian *tulku*.

And of course a third factor has already been alluded to: North American cultural regionalism. The existence of subcultures within the United States and Canada is itself a productive element within the creation of Buddhist regionalism. California isn't just the shore closest to Buddhist Asia, it is also a state famous in recent decades for relative tolerance of new and nonmainstream groups. Likewise, Buddhism's relative success in places like New York and Boston comes not only from their characteristics as large cities with significant trade with Asia but is also due in part to their reputation as centers of learning, acceptance, and diversity. On the other hand, the perception of the South as overwhelmingly Christian and relatively intolerant is a factor in the decision of whether to attempt missionization there at all. The Richmond Zen Center, for example, has had no luck in wooing a permanent teacher from the Bay Area, despite courting many prospective resident priests. They simply are unable to attract a Zen teacher from liberal, highly Buddhist San Francisco to conservative, sparsely Buddhist Richmond. Another impact from American cultural regionalism may be apparent in distinctive traits that groups display. Because many Buddhist centers in the South tend to draw heavily on converts who are rejecting Christian backgrounds they perceive as punitive and superstitious, groups that especially stress Buddhism's tolerant and rational nature are particularly successful. Furthermore, once these former Southern Baptists and evangelical Methodists join such groups, they help to produce a Buddhism that avoids formal missions and rejects prayer. These new Buddhists become an embattled liberal religious bastion, which helps to create group solidarity but also limits the ability to adapt in ways that would allow for growth beyond particular narrow demographics and retards the further penetration of Zen into the South. Meanwhile, their Southern location prompts other responses to the local environment, such as a recent event where Richmond Zen Center members performed walking meditation along the city's old slave trail and then gathered at the slavery memorial to meditate before using the statue of two enslaved Africans about to be sold in the slave market across the street as the group's object of worship during *pūjā* (Wilson 2012). This is a practice that simply does not happen in California.

CONCLUSIONS

We should be aware that the regions we "discover" are in fact partially a product of the observer's particular interests. We can find different Buddhist regions if our concerns are political or cultural or meteorological or geographical, and so on. Furthermore, these general regions may apply for some types of Buddhism, while being nearly useless for the interpretation of certain other denominations or groups that require attention to what unique regions manifest in their particular networks. And, of course, the regions we identify are not static. Regionalism may appear at different times and disappear at others. For example, regionalism, religion, and assimilation issues sometimes made for a volatile mix in Japanese American World War II military units. Hawaiian and mainland Buddhists in the military sometimes clashed because of cultural styles that developed in these different regions. The mainlanders called the Hawaiians "Buddha-heads," while the Hawaiians called the mainlanders "Katonks," neither of which was meant affectionately. Yet that very contact during the 1940s led to greater cooperation and understanding in the postwar period. Nor does regional Buddhism remain the same over time. To be a Southern Buddhist meant one thing in the 1950s, when Jack Kerouac meditated behind his mother's house in Rocky Mount, North Carolina; it means something else today.

I also want to suggest the importance of looking at not just regionalism but microregionalism as well. For example, the Bay Area has been one of the most heavily studied areas of Buddhism in America, and yet without attention to its unique properties, even within California, it may be one of the worst sites for research on American Buddhism. Why do I make such an outrageous claim? Simply because the Bay Area in its wonderful diversity is so completely unrepresentative of Buddhist America. This is the only place outside Japan where Shugendo (a syncretic form of tantric Japanese Buddhism) has been practiced (Layman 1976, 111–114). If we make the Bay Area stand in for America as a whole, we distort the picture of Buddhism in the United States. But, on the other hand, if we recognize it as a unique microregion, we can explore it fruitfully. For example, there is a particular clustering of Zen groups and teachers that have been produced by the San Francisco Zen Center and, in many cases, have been reluctant to leave the Bay Area for thankless missionary work in the hinterlands. This leads to the possibility of Zen overcrowding, which may itself be productive of new developments in American Buddhism that then subsequently get exported to other regions.

In conclusion, bringing regionalism to our awareness can benefit our studies in many ways. In particular, it can serve first to prevent us from mistaking local phenomena as representative of North American Buddhism generally. Second, it can stimulate new studies that look at regionalism specifically as an interpretive lens. And finally, it can add depth to projects that are not about regionalism specifically. Just as we have learned the value of paying attention to gender, race, and class even when they are not the primary subjects of our research, so too we may find that keeping regional specificity in view as we conduct our projects will make them richer, more accurate portraits of whatever group or topic we are studying.

NOTES

This essay is an updated version of my talk, "Regionalism in American Buddhism," delivered at the Buddhism without Borders conference in March 2010. An earlier version of this work was published as chap. 1 of Jeff Wilson, *Dixie Dharma: Regionalism and Identity at a Buddhist Temple in the American South* (Chapel Hill: University of North Carolina Press, 2012). Used by permission of the publisher; www.uncpress.unc.edu. Readers are referred to that book for additional information about Buddhist regionalism in the United States. I thank University of North Carolina Press for their permission to reprint selections from that book here.

1. These comments come from my observations at San Francisco Zen Center and the Richmond Zen Group, as well as thoughts provoked by observations at Chapel Hill Zen Center and other local groups in the Suzuki lineage visited in various parts of the country.
2. I thank Janet McLellan for first bringing the lack of rural research to my attention.

THREE

Two Buddhisms, Three Buddhisms, and Racism

WAKOH SHANNON HICKEY

For several summers I taught a class in the San Francisco Bay Area on Buddhism in the United States. Visits to a variety of Buddhist communities enabled students to experience for themselves the incredible diversity of traditions. In just the three cities of Berkeley, Oakland, and Emeryville, we had easy access to two Jodo Shinshu temples, a Soto-shu temple, at least three different lineages of American Zen, two kinds of Korean Zen, and Thai Theravada, Vipassana, Nyingma, Shambhala, Soka Gakkai, and Chan communities. For decades, scholars have tried to make sense of this dizzying variety.

A number of scholars have tried to provide clarity by proposing sets of broad categories of Buddhist groups for purposes of comparison. Elsewhere, I examined eleven different taxonomies.[1] Typically, these divide Buddhist groups and practitioners into two or three major types. The criteria vary. Some focus on styles of religious practice; others on the religious identity of members, or the mode by which a tradition was transmitted from Asia to the United States. Several distinguish between so-called "ethnic" Buddhists and "convert" Buddhists. The former refers to immigrants and refugees from Asian Buddhist cultures and their descendants; the latter refers to those whose ancestry is not Asian and whose religious heritage is not Buddhist. The majority of converts have European ancestry.

This "ethnic-convert" bifurcation may seem to make sense at first glance. One can indeed observe significant differences between groups that cater primarily to Buddhist converts and those that cater primarily to people whose cultural heritage is Buddhist. Communities in each category tend to practice differently and to serve different purposes for their members. Yet this conceptual division is also problematic in a number of ways. The category "ethnic Buddhism" is especially problematic.

Among the scholars who argue for a typology distinguishing between converts and "ethnic" or "heritage" Buddhists, Paul David Numrich has been a strong and particularly thoughtful advocate. His support for this approach is based on research he conducted in Thai and Sinhalese Theravada communities in Chicago and Los Angeles during the late 1980s and early 1990s (Numrich 1996). He found what he called "parallel congregations" operating side-by-side: one composed of immigrants and their descendants who engaged in cultural and merit-making activities, and one composed of converts who were mostly white and who were interested primarily in meditation and Buddhist philosophy. These congregations interacted relatively little.

I will say more in a moment about Numrich's "two Buddhisms" and other writers' "three Buddhisms." I intend to offer several critiques of this model, but I will begin by acknowledging its value. It accounts for the fact that Buddhist temples frequently perform different functions for immigrants and refugees than they do for converts. It also points to the realities of race dynamics in the United States, where Asian and white Buddhists may not interact very much, and where whites have more power and access to resources than recent Asian immigrants (Numrich 2000). These differing needs and race-based disparities of power and access are real and important, and Numrich is right to stress them. He also suggested a number of ways that scholars might advance the field. Among these were to study "inter-generational dynamics, denominational and ecumenical issues, and the effects of racism and minority social status" (Numrich 2006, 224).

Here, I have three goals. One is to offer some observations about how racism has affected American Buddhisms "on the ground." More than that, however, I want to reflect upon ways white observers have *described* how American Buddhisms are practiced on the ground. Specifically, I want to examine several taxonomies that for many years seemed to dominate the academic discourse, and I want to explain how I think unconscious white privilege manifests in that discourse. My third goal is to propose some alternative ways to think about the varieties of Buddhism in the United States. My proposal is based in part upon observations about intergenerational dynamics. My analysis is also informed by recent theoretical work on postcolonialism, globalization, transnationalism, and racialization, and on research by scholars in several disciplines, including American religious history, the sociology of religion, and Buddhist studies.

SOME DEFINITIONS: RACE, RACISM, AND PRIVILEGE

Because the terms "racism" and "white privilege" can be so loaded, I'd like to begin with some definitions. According to Michael Omi and Howard Winant, "Race is a concept which signifies and symbolizes social conflicts and interests by referring to different types of human bodies" (Omi and Winant 2004, 116). It is a social construct, it varies by time and place, and it draws upon arbitrary criteria for categorizing people. Differences in skin color, hair, and facial features may be invoked as criteria distinguishing "white" from "black" from "Asian," for example, but this need not be the case. In the nineteenth century, many Anglo-Saxons did not regard my Irish ancestors as "white" when they immigrated to North America during the Potato Famine. Likewise, immigrant Jews, Muslims, and Christians from Southern or Eastern Europe were not considered white when they arrived by the millions during the late nineteenth and early twentieth centuries. Ideas about whiteness, blackness, and Asianness have changed over time. Filipinos have sometimes been defined as Asian, and sometimes not. Not so long ago in the United States, if one had *any* ancestor with African heritage, one's blood was considered black and one was legally categorized as black.

Racism "creates or reproduces structures of domination based on essentialist categories of race" (Omi and Winant 2004, 113). A key feature of racism is *essentialism*: a belief that most or all members of a racially defined group have fundamental and immutable characteristics. Again, the specific features that are essentialized may differ by time and place. One need not be white to have attitudes that could be called "racist," that is, to assume that some racially defined group is essentially different from one's own group and to feel prejudice toward that "other." But the definition cited here emphasizes what certain forms of racial essentialism *do*: they create and reinforce *dominance*, that is, systems of unequal access to power and resources. That is the manner in which I'm using the term "racism" here.

Privilege is a set of "unearned assets conferred systematically. . . . If we want to determine whether a particular advantage qualifies as a privilege, we need to look at that advantage macroscopically in order to observe whether it plays a role in keeping complex systems of dominance in place" (Bailey 2004, 305). If one belongs to a dominant group, one benefits from its privileges *regardless* of whether one wants or intends to do so and regardless of whether one is personally prejudiced toward nondominant groups. Privilege is a characteristic of *systems* of dominance into which we are born and which condition us all our lives. It is usually exercised unconsciously and unintentionally.

It is possible to have privilege in some areas—for example, as an educated, middle-class white person in the United States—and simultaneously to lack it in other ways: as a woman; as a gay, lesbian, transsexual, or transgendered person; as someone with a disability; as a non-Christian. I enjoy white privilege based on my culture's current understanding of whiteness. I can arrange to be around other white people most of the time. I can talk about racism without being regarded as self-serving or having a chip on my shoulder. I am more likely to get favorable interest rates on loans and less likely to be stopped by police or incarcerated if I commit a crime. I am not presumed to represent all white people, and I have seldom felt rejected or threatened because of my race. I have, on the other hand, been bullied, harassed, legally discriminated against, and rendered invisible because I am lesbian, and I have been threatened with rape and other forms of violence, taken less seriously, and paid less money than male colleagues because I'm female.

After compiling forty-six examples of white privilege, Peggy McIntosh observed,

> Some privileges make me feel at home in the world. Others allow me to escape penalties or dangers that others suffer. Through some, I escape fear, anxiety, insult, injury, or a sense of not being welcome, not being real. Some keep me from having to hide, to be in disguise, to feel sick or crazy, to negotiate each transaction from the position of being an outsider or, within my group, a person who is suspected of having

> too close links with the dominant culture. Most keep me from having to be angry. (McIntosh 2004, 323)

A key feature of privilege is that when we have it, we are largely oblivious to it: we take it for granted as normal, natural, or deserved. We may deny or fail to notice that we receive advantages, access to resources, and more positive attention simply because we belong to a dominant group, and that our advantages depend directly upon other people's disadvantages. *Privilege means not having to notice that we have it.*[2] The advantages of privilege are cumulative. Better housing, higher net worth, better health, better schooling, better mentoring, better access to professional networks, better job prospects, better pay, and more affirmation from mainstream society: all lead to more confidence, more access to resources, and greater likelihood of success.

Having defined these key terms, I want to make some of my own assumptions clear. First, I believe that ethnic identities are real and not necessarily bad. I am proud of my own ethnic heritages. Ethnic identity is simply a sense of shared language, culture, and/or national origin. It can help to locate and orient us in the world and can be a source of pride. Pushed to extremes, however, ethnic pride can fuel xenophobia, nativism, and genocide. Second, I believe that a long American history of white racism and minority groups' concomitant distrust have contributed to the development of racially segregated Buddhist communities in the United States. I am not suggesting, however, that any of the authors whose work I discuss are racist. I repeat: *I am not calling anybody racist.* Most of these scholars have dedicated their lives to sympathetically understanding Asian histories, cultures, and religions. Rather, I believe that some of the *assumptions* underlying *taxonomies of American Buddhism* reflect unconscious white privilege. That is why I distinguish between racism and privilege. I want to shine some light on ways that privilege can manifest unconsciously in one area of discourse. I do this reflexively as a white scholar specializing in this field. Because privilege is a consequence of systems of domination, a necessary step in shifting such systems is for those who have privilege within them to notice how their privilege works. That is my primary aim: to notice and describe it, in order to help work against systemic inequality. Having laid this groundwork, I turn to examining several taxonomies.

TWO AND THREE BUDDHISMS IN THE STUDY OF AMERICAN BUDDHISM

The first such taxonomy was developed by psychologist Emma McCloy Layman (1976). She profiled about twenty communities[3] and saw them as falling into three broad categories based on their styles of practice: "church-like" (e.g., the Buddhist Churches of America, Jodo-shu, Nichiren-shu, and Buddha's Universal Church); "evangelical" (Nichiren Shoshu-Soka Gakkai); and "meditational" (e.g., convert-oriented Zen, Tibetan Tantra, Theravada, Chan, and Tiantai organizations). The range of groups was ethnically diverse, but Layman focused on the American-born members of the meditation groups. They were typically white, middle-class, well-educated, single people between the ages of twenty-one and thirty-five.

Most of the groups Layman categorized as "church-like" catered to people of Japanese, Chinese, or Southeast Asian ancestry. Their members' age range was much broader. Children typically grew up in these communities, departed during their teens, and returned after marriage and childbirth. These groups tended to focus on sutra study and/or cultivating virtue. The "evangelical" group, Soka Gakkai (SGI), was then 35 percent Caucasian; the rest were a mix of Asian, Asian American, African American, and Latino/a members. This group continues to be the most ethnically diverse Buddhist group in the United States, by far. (British scholar Sharon Smith [2003] observed that SGI promotes an ideal of "global citizenship" in a way that decenters whiteness, it actively addresses the needs and concerns of ethnic minority members in a variety of ways, and it promotes their leadership.)

Shortly after Layman's study, Charles Prebish mused on "two Buddhisms" he saw in America. Many new religious movements were popping up, and the distinction he drew between categories was based on the degree to which a group seemed institutionally stable. While some forms placed "emphasis on sound, basic doctrines [and] solid religious practice" and were thus stable, other groups based "their attraction on the promise of something new, frequently centered in the personal charisma of a flamboyant leader" (Prebish 1978, 171). Prebish hinted at an ethnic divide, as Layman had, and likewise focused on the convert Buddhists rather than those with Buddhist heritage. He remarked that converts included "a veritable 'mixed bag' of serious, mature, understanding students and practitioners, and a group of no less serious, but seriously limited students who understand little, perceive less, but are wildly vocal" (Prebish 1978, 155). His general observations about that era seem apt, but it is not clear which organizations he saw as "stable" or "flashy." San Francisco Zen Center, for example, attracted hippies and generated considerable press in the late 1960s and early 1970s as it sought to raise funds for the first Buddhist monastery outside Asia and launched various business ventures. It could have been considered "flashy," but like other high-profile groups, it became more institutionalized over time and more concerned with stable, "painstaking practice."

Two decades later, Paul Numrich described "two Buddhisms" explicitly divided along racial lines. He examined only immigrant-oriented Theravada communities, however, so his findings do not apply to multi-ethnic or multiracial congregations, some of which have developed since his study. Nor does his "two Buddhisms" model account for people with Asian heritages who become interested in Buddhism *after* they arrive in the United States and therefore could be considered converts. Numrich addressed this critique in 2006, saying,

> For ethnic Asians in the West, it is really not a matter of "conversion" to Buddhism even if one's family or ethnic group was not Buddhist in Asia in recent times. It is rather a matter of reversion, or of revisioning their Buddhist heritage, even if that heritage has suffered hiatus for some time, or has to be created in response to the social pressures involved in minority group identity formation. (Numrich 2006, 223)

I disagree with him about that. It seems to me comparable to assuming that a person whose ancestry is American or British, and who immigrates to Thailand, is tacitly Christian. If she decides in Thailand to practice Christianity, she is simply "reverting" to her "heritage faith." But what if her ancestors were Jewish? Similarly, Malaysians or Indonesians who immigrate to the United States probably would be considered Asian, but their ancestral countries are predominantly Muslim, not Buddhist. A Korean American's family religion may very well be Presbyterian. Because we cannot link nationality or ethnicity to religion so tidily, we cannot assume that any ethnically Asian person who begins to practice Buddhism in the United States is reverting to a heritage faith. Of course, it is also very problematic to speak of "Asians" and "Asian Americans" as if they were homogeneous. "Asian" is a broad, racialized category, just as "white" is, and both contain great ethnic, cultural, and religious diversity, with associated tensions.

A more important problem with the ethnic-convert divide is that it tends to break down over time because of generational change, exogamous marriage, and cultural exchanges with the dominant culture. Numrich found, for example, that some immigrants he met became more interested in meditation, and some converts took on more Theravada ritual behaviors. Converts in one temple were enlisted to promote Buddhism as compatible with modern science among second-generation youth and to help those youth affirm their Thai or Sinhalese cultural heritages (Numrich 1996, 77).

Some communities outside the scope of Numrich's study blur the lines even further. Sociologist Wendy Cadge, who studied American Theravada groups a few years after Numrich, noted that the "divide between Asians and non-Asians is often described as one of the main characteristics of Buddhism in America. While this has often been the case, the current picture is considerably more complex" (Cadge 2001, n.p.). While the "parallel congregations" that Numrich observed are "not uncommon," Cadge has observed that many American Theravada temples demonstrate considerably more mixing than the "Two Buddhisms" bifurcation suggests.

Numrich's "parallel congregations" concept could apply, however, to convert groups that began practicing meditation with Japanese Zen missionaries who initially served immigrant-oriented Zen temples but who eventually split off to form separate communities. It could also apply, in a limited way, to more recent cases in which members of minority groups, such as people of color or LGBT practitioners, form communities or conduct special retreats within majority-culture institutions, as has occurred at San Francisco Zen Center and Spirit Rock Meditation Center in California. These specialized groups or events do not necessarily involve different forms of practice; they simply provide a supportive environment for meditators frustrated by insensitivities they encounter within the dominant group.[4]

"AMERICAN BUDDHISM" VERSUS "BUDDHISM IN AMERICA"

A far more problematic "two Buddhisms" typology than Numrich's or Prebish's was proposed by Helen Tworkov in a 1991 editorial for the Buddhist magazine *Tricycle*. She observed:

> There is no one way to be a Buddhist. . . . The many sects that now exist in the United States reflect the compelling and flexible dimensions inherent in any body of ideas that has been tested by time and has crossed continents. There are a growing number of voices here concerned with the shape of American Buddhism, concerned with arbitrating which interpretations seem appropriate for this society and which may be better left behind in Asia. But whose America? Whose Buddhism? . . . The spokespeople for Buddhism in America have been, almost exclusively, educated members of the white middle class. . . . Asian American Buddhists . . . so far . . . have not figured prominently in the development of something called American Buddhism. (Tworkov 1991, 4)

Although Tworkov was actually lauding pluralism, this remark sparked an understandably irritated response from members of the Buddhist Churches of America, both Japanese and Euro-American, who pointed out that the BCA had been developing an American Buddhism for more than a century. Tworkov seemed to be equating "American" with "white," they said. Reverend Ryo Imamura, an eighteenth-generation Jodo Shinshu priest, remarked:

> It was my American-born parents and their generation who courageously and diligently fostered the growth of American Buddhism despite having to practice discreetly in hidden ethnic temples and in concentration camps because of the same white bigotry. It was us [*sic*] Asian Buddhists who welcomed countless white Americans into our temples, introduced them to the Dharma, and often assisted them to initiate their own Sanghas when they felt uncomfortable practicing with us.[5] (Ames 1994)

Tworkov did not deescalate the debate when she insisted on her distinction between "American Buddhism," represented by middle-class, mostly white converts, and "Buddhism in America," which serves the needs of predominantly Asian communities. "White Buddhism evolved essentially independent of Asian communities," she said. This unleashed a storm of ink, and stereotypes flew in both directions: White Buddhists were called arrogant, overly focused on enlightenment, self-absorbed. Asian Buddhists were called too devotional, too hierarchical, overly focused on social and cultural activities.

HOW RACISM AND PRIVILEGE OPERATE IN THIS DEBATE

Regardless of whether anyone involved in this debate is or isn't personally racist, this conflict certainly reveals the systemic racism that affects all of us. As noted earlier, racism "creates or reproduces structures of domination based on essentialist categories of race" (Omi and Winant 2004, 113). Both Tworkov and her critics made essentializing statements about the members of racially defined groups, that is, whites are one way and Asians are another. These statements both express and reinforce a long history of conflict, in which people with European ancestry have dominated people with Asian ancestry.

From 1878 to 1952, a series of court decisions and laws barred immigrant Chinese, Japanese, Filipinos, and Asian Indians from becoming citizens of the United States. Immigration itself was barred in various ways from 1858 to 1965. Women citizens were stripped of their citizenship if they married Asian immigrant men. Noncitizens were barred from owning land. And, of course, there were countless acts of terrorism and violence against Asian immigrants, from the ghettoization and lynching of Chinese to the WWII internment of Japanese and Japanese Americans, many of whom were citizens by birth.[6] Such events create distrust. As Reverend Imamura noted, Asian immigrants and their descendants developed ethnically focused communities partly in *response* to the white racism promoted by law, propaganda, and force (Numrich 2006, 219).

Partly in response to internment, the Buddhist Churches of America adopted many of its so-called "Protestant" reforms—church buildings with pews; hymns; Sunday services and Sunday schools, among others—to appear less "foreign" to xenophobes and thus to reduce racist persecution (Horinouchi 1973; Tanaka 1999, 8). So although cultural and linguistic continuity is an important need *internal* to an immigrant group, we should not overlook *external* forces that create both a need for places of refuge and ambivalence about practicing alongside white converts. Similar dynamics affect historically black Christian churches.

Tworkov's remarks about "American Buddhism" reflected white privilege in at least three ways. First was the presumed authority to define what "American Buddhism" is for everyone. In 1994, Rick Fields noted in the pages of *Tricycle* that "a powerful aspect of racism [I would say white privilege] . . . is the power to define. . . . [I]n the ongoing discussion about the meaning of an emergent 'American Buddhism,' it is mainly white Buddhists who are busy doing the defining. Nor is it surprising that they're defining it in their own image" (Fields 1994, 55; cf. Fields 1998, 200). In the same issue of the magazine, bell hooks critiqued the sense of entitlement "that allows white comrades to feel so comfortable with their 'control' and 'ownership' of Buddhist thought and practice in the United States" (hooks 1994, 44; cf. Hori 1994). A sense of entitlement is often an aspect of privilege, and it is one of the reasons that white people (including me) sometimes feel defensive when our privilege is pointed out to us.

Second was the assumption that "white Buddhism" is authentic American Buddhism, and that "Asian Buddhism" is an essentially foreign thing that happens to reside on American soil. This idea is not confined to white people. Because the dominant culture does often equate "American" with "white," some members of minority groups internalize this assumption, which serves to reinforce white dominance. Numrich noted, for example, "many if not most of the Asians in our temples are American citizens, and yet they commonly refer to the non-Asian members of the temples as 'Americans'" (Numrich 2006, 219). Internalized racism can be more pernicious than overt hostility.

Third, as the white editor of a glossy popular magazine, Tworkov could command a larger audience than Reverend Imamura could in a BCA newsletter. In general, white Buddhists have gained disproportionate public attention from white scholars and journalists, who have focused on people like themselves in terms of race, class, and education. The advantages of privilege are cumulative, and cumulative advantage reinforces the system of privilege by determining whose voices are heard most easily.

A more recent example was a 2008 Pew Forum study of religion in the continental United States. Of the 35,101 survey respondents, 405 (or 1.15 percent) identified themselves as Buddhist. Forty-five percent of them lived in the western United States, 23 percent in the South, 17 percent in the Northeast, and 15 percent in the Midwest.

Fifty-three percent of the Buddhists were white, and 32 percent were non-Hispanic Asians.[7] However, the survey was conducted in English and Spanish, and therefore these results probably exclude Buddhists (and others) who speak Asian languages. Residents of Hawaii, whose population is 39 percent Asian,[8] were also excluded from the survey. Yet a demographic map indicated that 11 to 20 percent of Hawaiians identify with Buddhism, compared to less than 2 percent in every other state.[9] Thus, the linguistic and geographic parameters of the study revealed affluent white Buddhists and obscured Asian and Asian American Buddhists.

ELITE, ETHNIC, AND EVANGELICAL BUDDHISMS

Like Emma Layman, several scholars have proposed taxonomies with three categories: one for Asians and Asian Americans whose heritage is Buddhist, one for converts, and one for a group that does not fit well into either of the other two.[10] Jan Nattier (1995) argued for a three-part taxonomy similar to one proposed earlier by Prebish (1993), based on the mode by which a given form of Buddhism is transmitted to the United States. "Elite Buddhism," Nattier said, is *imported* by people with money and leisure enough for books and meditation retreats. It is characterized by the middle-class income and college education of (most of) its adherents, rather than by their ethnicity, although a majority is Caucasian. Elite Buddhists tend to emphasize meditation but generally eschew monasticism and devotional practices, deemphasize ethical precepts except in the wake of scandals, and look down their noses at Buddhists who are concerned with worldly benefits and social activities. Thus, while claiming to represent authentic Buddhism, elite Buddhism actually bears "the least resemblance to Buddhism as practiced in any Asian country" (Nattier 1995, 45).

"Ethnic Buddhism" is brought to the United States as "cultural baggage" by Asian immigrants and provides social support and cultural continuity. "Evangelical Buddhism," represented by the multi-ethnic Soka Gakkai, draws members from a range of economic and educational backgrounds. Nattier remarked that members of all three groups are "unwittingly engaged in the practice of defining large groups of our fellow Buddhists out of existence" by not recognizing them as "real" Buddhists (Nattier 1997, 76).[11]

While instructive, Nattier's categories apply less well to the Buddhist Churches of America, to groups that have multi-ethnic constituencies, or to groups that have a monastic core of converts but serve Asian immigrants and their descendants, such as some Chan communities, or some of the Theravada communities described by Cadge (2005). Nattier would place BCA temples among "ethnic" congregations, and it is true that the BCA remains overwhelmingly Japanese and Japanese American. After four or five generations in the United States, however, it is neither an immigrant community nor composed primarily of converts. Its members' income and education levels are probably similar to those classified as "elite," but I do not have the data.

To say that "elite" forms of Buddhism are *imported* is also to assume that affluent white Americans are the primary agents, which obscures the agency of Asian missionaries who had their own agendas for bringing Buddhism to the United States. Sōen Shaku, for example, had religious, political, and economic motives for attending the World's Parliament of Religions in 1893, touring the United States, and sending D. T. Suzuki to work with writer and editor Paul Carus. These motives included opposition to unequal treaties with the United States and support for the Japanese government's nationalist and imperialist agendas at the time (Heisig and Maraldo 1995; Ketelaar 1990, 1991; Sharf 1995c; Snodgrass 2003; Victoria 1997). Although neither Sōen nor Suzuki established temples in the West, both were extremely influential in shaping Western perceptions of Zen.[12] Shunryu Suzuki and Taizan Maezumi, founders of San Francisco Zen Center and Zen Center of Los Angeles, respectively, were not imported by white elites. They were sent as missionaries to Japanese communities and later chose to devote their energies to converts. Immigrant Theravada communities also invite Asian-born monks to run temples they have established, and those teachers sometimes reach out to converts. So, as postcolonial theorists have noted, between dominant and nondominant groups, agency flows in both directions.

All taxonomies shed light on certain dimensions of Buddhism in the United States and obscure others. Their categories are based upon different criteria, so they are difficult to compare, and they do not always account for hybrids that cannot fit neatly into one category. As Max Weber observed long ago, this is true of all ideal types. Fixed categories can be useful even when they apply imperfectly, by bringing exceptions and hybrids into clearer view. A more significant limitation is that communities change over time. Each generation must wrestle with adapting to mainstream American culture, which is predominantly Protestant and individualistic, and with preserving traditions and values that may run counter to that culture.[13]

PROBLEMS WITH THE CATEGORY "ETHNIC BUDDHISTS"

Although ethnic identity is important to many people, academic typologies of American Buddhism based on racial or ethnic categories must be viewed with caution. First, such categories can reify qualities that may be multiple and fluid and that become more complex when describing successive generations and the children of mixed parentage. The longer an initially insular (and/or persecuted) ethnic group is present in a country, the more likely is exogamous marriage and mixed ethnic identities. It is also problematic to lump together diverse Asian ethnic and cultural groups as if they were homogeneous. To do so risks racial essentializing.

When historians of religion discuss American Catholic history in the nineteenth century, we talk about ethnic churches: those that served predominantly German immigrants versus those that served Irish or Italian immigrants, for example. There were debates about how much to preserve particular languages and cultural traditions and how much to assimilate. But all of the Buddhism taxonomies discussed here were proposed by white scholars,[14] and those that include an "ethnic Buddhism" category apply the term "ethnic" *only* to people who are not white. To presume that whiteness is the norm against which "ethnic" is measured is another example of unconscious white privilege. A white-Asian dichotomy also obscures the presence of Buddhists who are neither, such as Latino/as, African Americans, Pacific Islanders, or people of mixed heritage (Foye 1994, 57).

Although Euro-American converts have diverse heritages, we are "ethnic Buddhists." Ryo Imamura (1998), Sharon Smith (2003), and others have pointed out that Euro-American Buddhists often approach Buddhism in a very individualistic manner, which does not always meet the needs of people whose cultural heritage regards the individual as embedded in a web of social relations. A resource guide called *Making the Invisible Visible: Healing Racism in Our Buddhist Communities* makes it clear that majority-white American Buddhist groups have cultural characteristics to which members of minority groups must adapt if they wish to participate (Adams et al. 2000). White people may not notice these characteristics—either because it is easy for us to associate mostly with people who are like us, which leaves our cultural assumptions unchallenged, or because we may be reluctant to face the full, painful implications of white privilege.

Both scholars and practitioners of Buddhism in the United States must attend carefully to these issues, and we can do so without defining practitioners in simplistic, racialized terms. Even the terms "cultural" or "heritage" or "diaspora" Buddhists are less racializing than "ethnic" Buddhist, as that phrase is typically used.

DEVELOPMENTAL MODELS

Methods of describing Buddhism in the United States must account for change over time. Models that take into account developmental processes, fluidity, and intergenerational dynamics may be more useful in understanding the ways Buddhism has taken root, produced offshoots, and given rise to hybrids and new forms in the United States.

Martin Baumann, drawing on a theoretical framework developed by Michael Pye, described the process by which Buddhism has been transplanted to Europe (Baumann 1994; cf. Pye 1969). The first stage is *contact*: A foreign religious tradition is transferred into a new culture by individuals, groups, buildings, texts, styles of activity, and so on. Over time, "missionaries" and first converts begin to appear in the public sphere, important texts are translated, and missionary activities begin. Next is a stage of *confrontation and contact*: The transplanted tradition begins to confront the host culture, challenging its cultural assumptions. The extent to which this challenge is tolerated depends on a variety of political, legal, and social factors. Eventually, however, *ambiguities* arise: To what extent should the tradition adapt to its new environment, in order to make itself more comprehensible, and how much should it resist accommodation? The host culture may also adopt elements of the transplanted tradition. Questions of orthodoxy will begin to arise. A period of *recoupment* will follow, in which a supposedly "pure" or original version of the tradition is reasserted. In addition, new forms and interpretations will emerge in a process of *innovative self-development*. In each of these stages, groups will use a variety of strategies: translating key ideas; simplifying or deemphasizing elements unacceptable to the host culture; tolerating previously unacceptable customs in the host culture; reinterpreting teachings or practices; absorbing elements of the host culture into rituals or systems of meaning; and assimilating converts into foreign practices.

Prebish suggested another process-oriented way to look at American Buddhist groups, as "established religion and emergent religion," categories developed by Robert Ellwood (Prebish 1993; cf. Ellwood and Partin 1988). "Established" groups are marked by constancy, rejection of what is radical, and duration. "Emergent" groups can become established within a few generations. Such a typology can encompass virtually all varieties of Buddhism in America, without valuing any one as more or less "legitimate" than the others.

For example, the BCA is an "established" religion, but it *emerged* as distinct from Japanese Jodo Shinshu, particularly during the internment of Japanese Americans during World War II. Second-generation, American-born members consciously adapted themselves to American Protestant norms, developing English-language services, Buddhist hymns, Sunday school classes, youth groups, basketball leagues, Christian-style wedding ceremonies, and so forth.[15] More recently, the Order of Buddhist Contemplatives (OBC) *emerged* as a result of Reverend Master Jiyu-Kennett's work modeling her community on both the Japanese "Soto Zen Church" and the Church of England. Today, the OBC is run by the first and second generations of her students and has a decidedly churchy ethos.[16] San Francisco Zen Center (SFZC) and Zen Center of Los Angeles (ZCLA) likewise *emerged* from the established Japanese communities Sokoji and Zenshuji. Now, after forty years in the United States, both SFZC and ZCLA are well established. They, like other convert groups, are continuing the process of acculturation and looking for ways to make their practices accessible to working families with children, to prisoners, and to homeless and dying people.

A more nuanced way of thinking about "established" and "emergent" groups might be to add a few more categories. I would define an *established* group as one that has endured for at least four generations, simply because that is about as long as any Buddhist group has been present in the United States. The BCA, Soto-shu, Nichiren-shu, and some Chinese Buddhist groups would qualify. An *offshoot* group emerges from an established group, sometimes by schism and sometimes by a more gentle process. The Theravada temples that

Paul Numrich studied gave rise to such offshoots. The San Francisco Zen Center and Zen Center of Los Angeles are offshoots of Soto-shu temples.

A *transplant* is an established group that moves into a new environment. Soka Gakkai; most Theravada and Soto-shu temples; many Tibetan groups; Shingon, Jodo, and most Nichiren groups; and the BCA in its early stage of missionary activity are all transplants.

A *new movement* is developed by someone who is not ordained or authorized by an established group but who develops and promotes a form of religion that may draw upon elements of an established tradition. Richard Payne has suggested referring to these as "entrepreneurial groups" and cautions that we must be careful not to privilege older groups as somehow more "pure" or "authentic" than newer ones (Payne 2010).

These categories are neither mutually exclusive nor static. Soka Gakkai, for example, was a new movement in the 1920s, then affiliated with an established group (Nichiren Shoshu), then transplanted itself to various locations, and later was excommunicated from its parent. The Vipassana movement is an offshoot of established Thai and Burmese Theravada groups, though it also has features of a new movement. I propose these categories tentatively, knowing they need testing and critique to determine their applicability and usefulness. Eva Neumaier-Dargay (1995) offered some important caveats about horticultural metaphors such as "transplants," "offshoots," and "hybrids." In "Is Buddhism Like a Tomato?" she notes that unlike tomato plants, neither cultures nor religious traditions are discrete objects with clearly identifiable boundaries. The forms of Buddhism that were transplanted to Western countries already had been altered before they arrived, through complex interactions among Asian and Western actors, particularly during the late nineteenth and early twentieth centuries.[17] The virtue of a developmental model, however, is that it presumes change, which more static terms such as "immigrant" and "convert" do not.

We could also use Buddhist categories. Scholars certainly are not obliged to use insider terms, but we do categorize Christian groups broadly as Catholic, Protestant, or Orthodox; Jewish groups as Orthodox, Conservative, Reform, Reconstructionist, or Renewal; Muslim groups as Sunni, Shi'a, or Sufi (in the United States we would add Nation of Islam and Moorish Science). Likewise, Buddhist groups can be described as belonging to the broad "streams" of Theravada,

Mahayana, Vajrayana, or unaffiliated/eclectic. Tweed has pointed out that individual Buddhists might not identify strongly with one of these categories: they might, for example, see themselves first as Thai, then as Buddhist, but not necessarily as Theravadin.[18] Nevertheless, a Thai lay Buddhist probably would find "Theravada" less reductionist or offensive than "ethnic Buddhist"; she probably could recognize her religious tradition as Theravada within the broader context of global Buddhism. A Mahayanist is also likely to recognize her tradition as distinct from Theravada. To borrow an aquatic metaphor from Thomas Tweed (2006), who defines religions as "confluences of organic-cultural flows," within the three broad "streams" (i.e., "vehicles") of Buddhism, one can identify different "currents" that converge and diverge: Zen, Pure Land, Shingon, Vipassana, among others.

If we want to consider questions of religious identity, categories suggested by Tweed are useful. *Cradle Buddhists* are people born into Buddhist families, regardless of their race or national origin, so this group includes both immigrants and the children of converts. (Some have objected to this term, however, calling it infantilizing, so "heritage" Buddhists may be preferable.) *Converts* include both immigrants and people born in the United States who were not raised Buddhist but who later identify themselves with Buddhism and formally affiliate with it in some way. *Sympathizers* are people who identify primarily with other religions, or with no religion, but are influenced by Buddhist thought and may engage in Buddhist practices (Tweed 2002). In more recent scholarly literature, categories of "dual belongers" have also emerged: for example, Christian-Buddhists and Jew-Bu's.[19]

My point is that we can examine the development of American Buddhist groups without defining them by simplistic or static categories based on race. I am not suggesting we should overlook ethnicity or race—quite the contrary. I am saying that to typecast people in those terms obscures more than it reveals. It is probably more helpful to consider racial dynamics when analyzing particular communities or the culture at large.

CONCLUSION

Any attempt to describe or categorize the myriad forms of Buddhism now present in the United States must use a more layered approach rather than static typologies. We can identify a particular organization or group of organizations as falling within the broad streams of Theravada, Mahayana, or Vajrayana, or as unaffiliated and eclectic. And we could think of them in denominational terms, as we do other religious groups in the United States: Buddhist Churches of America, Soka Gakkai, Soto-shu, Shunryu Suzuki lineage, White Plum Asangha, Shambhala, Vipassana, Community of Mindful Living, Kwan Um school, Won Buddhism, among others. Some groups, however, cross sectarian lines. Scholars are not obliged to use insider categories, but we should at least take seriously how members of groups we study describe themselves, even as we question those self-descriptions. We might then explore how a given group formed and its stage of development. Next we could consider participants' religious identities and degrees of affiliation, as well as broader constituencies of sympathizers. We can consider its racial, gender, class, and generational dynamics; its practices; and the sociological needs it fulfills for members.

Our descriptions must account for exceptions, parallels, blends, and developmental processes, and they must pay attention to the history and ongoing effects of racism and white privilege. As a white scholar, I have tried to use the privilege I have to draw attention to some of those effects, in support of efforts to dismantle them. If we cannot do this, then as Jan Nattier once warned, "there will always be 'two Buddhisms' in America: Us and Them, however we define each other" (Nattier 1995, 49).

NOTES

1. This chapter is an adaptation of a shorter conference paper and a longer article, Hickey (2010).
2. For an excellent discussion of privilege, see Johnson (2006). The process of learning to see it is ongoing.
3. Layman studied the Buddhist Churches of America (True Pure Land/Jodo Shinshu), Vajrayana (tantric) groups founded by the Tibetan masters Chögyam Trungpa (now called Shambhala International) and Tarthang Tulku (the Nyingma Institute and Dharma Publishing Co.), Japanese Shingon and Shugendo organizations, Zen groups serving Western converts, Nichiren Shoshu of America-Soka Gakkai, various Chinese temples and monasteries, and a

handful of Theravada communities. She did not include the older Soto Zen temples that were founded on the mainland United States by Japanese missionaries, who came to serve Japanese immigrants and their children: Zenshuji of Los Angeles, founded in 1921, and Sokoji of San Francisco, founded in 1933. This is interesting, because she spoke Japanese (see Layman 1976, n. 35).

4. See http://www.spiritrock.org for information about Spirit Rock's diversity programs. For San Francisco Zen Center programs, see http://www.sfzc.org. It offers meditation instruction in Spanish and retreats and scholarships for people of color. A website devoted specifically to practitioners of color is http://www.rainbowdharma.com.
5. In a study of Asian American Christian churches that tried to create multicultural congregations, Jeung observed that new African American and Latino members had a much easier time adapting to environments in which they were a minority, because they had long experienced doing so. White congregants had a much harder time adapting to marginal status and tended to leave (Jeung 2005).
6. See Takaki (2008, chaps. 8, 10, and 14). See also "Race, Racism, and the Law: The Racial Classification Cases," http://academic.udayton.edu/race/01race/White05.htm; and the Center for Educational Telecommunications, "Ancestors in the Americas: Asian American History Timeline," http://www.cetel.org/timeline.html.
7. Fifty-three percent were also male; 70 percent were between the ages of thirty and sixty-four. http://religions.pewforum.org/portraits, subcategory "Buddhists."
8. http://quickfacts.census.gov/qfd/states/15000.html.
9. http://religions.pewforum.org/portraits, subcategory "Buddhists." Thanks to Michael Jerryson of UC Santa Barbara and Al Bloom, formerly of the Institute of Buddhist Studies, for pointing out these language issues in posts to the Buddhism forum of Humanities Net on March 3, 2008.
10. In the interest of space, I'm only going to note a few examples, but please see the full version of this essay (Hickey 2010) as well as Numrich (2006) for summaries of all of the two- and three-Buddhisms typologies.
11. About the tendency for members of each group to define others as not "real" Buddhists, Nattier said: "Allowing others who are unlike ourselves to want what we want is 'small inclusiveness.' Large

inclusiveness is to view what others want—even if it is radically different from our own needs and preferences—as deserving of equal respect." Nattier finds this tolerance most common among elite Buddhists (Nattier 1995, 49).

12. A similar argument could be made about a number of Tibetan teachers, including the Fourteenth Dalai Lama, who have promoted Buddhism in the West, both for religious reasons and to raise awareness of the plight of Tibetans under Chinese control.
13. In a study of the Jodo Shinshu organization Buddhist Churches of Canada (BCC), Mark Mullins observed that Canadian-born Jodo Shinshu Buddhist Temples of Canada (formerly BCC) members had different expectations of clergy than their immigrant parents because of their exposure to Protestant clergy. *Issei* members were more likely to expect clergy to perform ritual services, for which they made appropriate donations. *Nisei* and subsequent generations were more likely to expect pastoral visits. Exacerbating the problem was the fact that most clergy were sent from Japan for relatively short terms of service before they took over hereditary temples in Japan. These Japanese clergy had relatively low pay and few benefits and chafed at the loss of status and power they experienced in lay-controlled communities, where they were regarded as employees. The Japanese clergy's difficulty in relating to Canadian-born members led to declining membership and decreased financial support, which in turn discouraged Canadian parents from nudging their children to pursue ministerial vocations. The frequency of exogamous marriage also seemed to diminish active involvement in an ethnically identified church (Mullins 1988).
14. I am personally acquainted with all of the scholars named here except Emma McCloy Layman (1910–2002). I could not locate a photograph of her, but I did locate the following information. She earned a PhD from the University of Iowa in 1937, and that university library's "Resource Guide to University Firsts" notes that the first African American woman to receive a PhD from it or any other Iowa institution was Lulu Merle Johnson in 1944 (http://www.lib.uiowa.edu/speccoll/Archives/faq/faqfirsts.htm). According to two articles about Layman in a newsletter published by the University of Colorado at Boulder Library's US Navy Japanese/Oriental Language School Archival Project, Layman grew up in China, studied Japanese at the US Navy Japanese Language School, and served as

a Japanese language officer for the Navy during World War II. She was chair of the Psychology Department at Iowa Wesleyan College from 1955–1975, and at her death, belonged to Christ Episcopal Church of Oberlin, Ohio. *The Interpreter* 23 (June 1, 2001): 1, and 51 (August 15, 2002): 1. Both issues are available at http://ucblibraries.colorado.edu/archives/collections/jlsp/#interpreters, accessed January 4, 2010. In the only photographs from her church that are available online, all the clergy and acolytes appear to be white. http://www.christchurchoberlin.org/clergy and http://www.christchurchoberlin.org/grove, accessed January 5, 2010. An article in the faculty newsletter at Oberlin College noted that Layman was class president at Oberlin in 1930. *The Observer* 16, 18 (May 25, 1995). These details, particularly her educational credentials, lead me to infer Layman probably was white.

15. Jaffe notes that some of these changes also had begun to take place in Japan in the late nineteenth century, particularly in the Nishi Honganji, the parent of the BCA (Richard Jaffe, pers. comm.). The BCA is now rethinking some of these adaptations (Boyce 2006, 53).
16. By "churchy" I mean its system of lay-oriented parish temples, its licensure of lay ministers, and the detailed regulations that govern its celibate clergy in the wake of Jiyu-Kennett's death, not necessarily the OBC's use of organ music and Gregorian chanting for sutra recitations.
17. See Heisig (2002), Jaffe (2004), and Sharf (1995a). Some of the early Buddhist missionaries were also people marginal to the mainstream forms of Buddhism in their home countries, Neumaier-Dargay (1995) noted. One example is the Harada-Yasutani lineage of Zen, or Sanbōkyōdan, which has been enormously influential in the United States and Europe and in Buddhist-Christian dialogue but is not prominent in Japan (see Sharf 1995b). Another example is Shunryu Suzuki, founder of San Francisco Zen Center, a large and highly influential convert organization. In Japan, Suzuki was a minor figure (see Chadwick 1999). On the other hand, some missionaries, such as Shaku Sōen, were prominent Buddhist leaders.
18. Thomas Tweed (pers. comm.).
19. I am a Soto-shu priest with long experience in Buddhist-Christian dialogue and have occasionally referred to myself as "Buddhapalian."

SECTION II

CROSSING BORDERS

Transcultural and Translocative Flows

Tweed's theory of religion and the axioms he proposes in this volume focus on the confluence of flowing cultural streams, but they also highlight *crossing*. Crossing involves specific persons, ideas, icons, or practices moving not only from one spatial location to or another but from one cultural location to another or even from one religious tradition to another. Such crossings often rely on preexisting networks of communication and cultural movement, and they call into question the fixedness or stability of geopolitical or cultural boundaries as the three essays in this section attest. Each case study highlights the movement of ideas and practices and their crossing of physical and social boundaries.

Section 1 closed with Hickey's deconstruction of the "two Buddhisms" typology, an analysis of how white privilege operates in scholarship on American Buddhism, and offered suggestions for more nuanced methodologies moving forward. This section opens with a historical case study that lends credence to the problems of rigid, either/or dichotomies in the study of US Buddhism. The Buddhist Churches of America, and North American Jodo Shinshu more generally, are often relegated to the category of "Asian American Buddhism." This typecasting of the tradition ignores the ways in which the community has engaged the broader American culture as well as cultural influences that are not Japanese American. In his essay, Michihiro Ama explores the life and work of Sunya Gladys Pratt, an English-born American woman and a Shin Buddhist convert. Such individuals crossing racial or ethnic boundaries draw attention to the constructed and permeable nature of categories of belonging.

Jeannine Chandler explores the ongoing "Dorje Shugden controversy." What began as a sectarian doctrinal dispute largely confined to the Tibetan community has become a global issue attracting active participation by Western converts and sympathizers. This participation is the result of both diasporic movement of Tibetans following the 1959 Chinese invasion of Tibet as well as the increasing ease of global communication, especially via the Internet. Western involvement in the dispute has had several consequences both for Tibetan Buddhism and Western understandings of Tibet.

Helen Baroni's contribution focuses on correspondence between Robert Aitken and students living at a distance. Based in Hawaii, Aitken is well known as a founding figure of US Buddhism, and his numerous books were extremely popular for a generation of new Buddhist sympathizers and converts. However, his career spanned a time when Zen communities were not widespread, and dozens of students sought him out via written correspondence from locations far and wide. These exchanges are the basis of Baroni's study and demonstrate the influence of one teacher beyond his local community.

FOUR

"First White Buddhist Priestess"

A Case Study of Sunya Gladys Pratt at the Tacoma Buddhist Temple

MICHIHIRO AMA

The April 25, 1936, *Los Angeles Times* headline read, "First White Buddhist Priestess Ordained," and was accompanied by a photograph taken at the Tacoma Buddhist Church in Washington. The caption read, "Mrs. Sunya Pratt, English-born resident of Tacoma, Wash., receiving ordination papers as first White priestess in Buddhist religion at ceremony in northern city. Bishop K. Masuyama is conferring the rites. . . . New priestess is mother of two children."[1] The Tacoma Buddhist Church (presently the Tacoma Buddhist Temple) is an affiliate of the Buddhist Mission of North America (BMNA; presently the Buddhist Churches of America), the mainland US branch of the Jodo Shinshu Nishi Honganji-ha Shin Buddhist denomination headquartered in Kyoto, Japan. Sunya Pratt (1898–1986) has received scant attention in the history of Euro-American women who contributed to the spread of Buddhism in the United States, standing in the shadow of more eminent people such as Helena Petrovna Blavatsky, Mary Elizabeth Mikahala Foster, Caroline Rhys Davids, and Beatrice Erskine Lane Suzuki.[2] By examining Sunya Pratt's life, this study explores how an early Euro-American woman negotiated with and established herself in an ethnic Buddhist order. It analyzes her commitment to and activities at the Tacoma Buddhist Church during a time of Shin Buddhist response to the growing popularity of Theravada Buddhism among Euro-Americans, as well as her adaptation to Shin Buddhist practice. Her involvement in the Tacoma Buddhist Church represents how a local Buddhist organization became translocal, transcending a sectarian boundary.

A BRIEF BIOGRAPHY OF SUNYA GLADYS PRATT

Gladys Pratt was born on February 6, 1898, in England and died on February 11, 1986, in Tacoma, Washington. Her father, Henry William Brice, introduced her to Buddhism when she was thirteen and encouraged her to choose her own religion. She moved to Seattle after marrying James Wesley Pratt, who was also born in England. He came to Canada in 1913 as a concert violinist, but after the outbreak of World War I, he joined the Canadian army, which sent him back to England. While working at an air force base, he met Gladys, who was working there as a typist. They married in 1917 at St. Martin's Church, in the parish of Chelsfield, Kent. After the war, Wesley brought her to Canada. They moved to Seattle and settled in Tacoma in 1931. For the next thirty-four years, they managed their family business, the Tacoma Button Company, until it closed in 1965. Their first daughter, Veronica, was born in 1918 and their first son, Patrick, in 1926.[3]

At the BMNA headquarters' suggestion, Gladys Pratt began to attend the Tacoma Buddhist Church. Robert Clifton, who was ordained in 1933 at the BMNA and became the leader of its English Department, read an article she wrote on Buddhism and became interested in her. When Bishop Masuyama Kenju and Clifton visited the BMNA's umbrella organizations in the Pacific Northwest in 1934, they met and asked her to help out at the Tacoma Buddhist Church. Since Masuyama wanted to introduce Buddhism to Euro-Americans, Pratt decided to volunteer by assisting Tacoma's Japanese resident minister, who needed the help of a native speaker in educating *nisei* (second-generation Japanese American) children through English lessons and Buddhist discussions. Without an official title, Pratt supervised the Tacoma Buddhist Church's Sunday school. Its enrollment increased so rapidly that she organized youth study groups on weeknights. Because of her success in Tacoma, the BMNA's regional organizations in Seattle and Portland asked her to operate similar sessions in their areas. Despite her community contributions, Pratt was not compensated for her activities, because the Japanese parents ignored the value of and the need for youth Buddhist education and were not forthcoming financially (Buddhist Churches of America 1974, 1:264–265).

Pratt was ordained at the BMNA as part of Masuyama's effort to increase the number of Caucasian Buddhist novices. He admitted a number of Euro-Americans: Francis G. Geske, Richard K. Prosser, and Robert Clifton in 1933; Julius Goldwater in 1934, who was a relative of Senator Barry Goldwater and who later played a significant role at the Los Angeles Honganji Buddhist Church; Frank B. Udale in 1935; and S. Alex White and Pratt in 1936 (Buddhist Churches of America 1998, 119, 172, 177, 178). Among them, Pratt was the only female postulant.

While Pratt was the first Caucasian woman in the United States to be recognized as a Buddhist priest by mainstream media in the 1930s, it is unlikely that local journalists during the 1930s knew much about the history of Euro-American Buddhist women in the United States, and the BMNA may have used the phrase "first White Buddhist priestess" as part of a broader propagation campaign that overlooked Pratt's predecessors. Clearly, Pratt was not the first Caucasian to be ordained by the BMNA. For example, Bishop Uchida had ordained a few Euro-Americans during the 1920s, such as Robert and Alice Clarke and Thomas M. Kirby. The Clarkes supervised the BMNA English Department after Kirby left for Hawaii, although their organizational commitment was brief.[4] In addition, there may have been Euro-American women outside the BMNA ordained by Asian Buddhist monks in the United States.

The practice and definition of female ordination in America also needs to be examined on the basis of its historical and global contexts. Forms of ordination for women vary depending on the specific tradition, and the reestablishment of higher ordination in Theravada lineages has been sought only recently (Numrich 1998, 153). In the case of the Shin Buddhist tradition, there are three steps in becoming a full-fledged minister: initiation/confirmation (*kikyōshiki*), novice ordination (*tokudo*), and Dharma teacher (*kyōshi*) certification. Pratt completed the second step, but it is unclear whether or not she was qualified as a Dharma teacher, and it was not until 1953 that she became an official minister of the Tacoma Buddhist Temple (Buddhist Churches of America 1998, 149). This may indicate that she was *not* the "first White Buddhist priestess" in America, but it is still fair to say that she was the first Euro-American woman who received significant media coverage in her home country when she was ordained.

After her ordination, Pratt became more active at the Tacoma Buddhist Church. In addition to helping the resident minister, who did not have a good command of English, and educating the *nisei* in Buddhist teachings, she began to initiate other Euro-Americans in Tacoma and Seattle under the *issei* (first-generation) ministers' supervision. Records show that Pratt held initiation services for six Caucasians in one year (possibly 1937) alone.[5] It appears she admitted more Euro-Americans prior to the outbreak of the Pacific War than after. Whenever initiating new members, she reported their names to the BMNA English Department.[6] During this time she successfully integrated into the ethnic community. One newspaper photo shows her wearing a kimono and dancing with young Japanese Americans at the Tacoma Buddhist Church's Bon festival.[7] She also grew as a leader of the *nisei* Buddhists. In 1941, when the BMNA convened its second national young Buddhist conference in Seattle, Pratt appeared as the keynote speaker.[8]

After the outbreak of World War II and the US government's evacuation of Japanese and Japanese Americans from the West Coast, Pratt remained as a caretaker of the Tacoma Buddhist Church. Japanese Buddhist ministers were the first to be taken away by the FBI. After the War Relocation Authority forced the *issei* and *nisei* residents to move to Camp Harmony, Pratt contacted and gained permission from the authority to serve the Japanese Buddhists there, particularly by conducting Sunday school, until the government further relocated the internees to permanent camps.[9]

Pratt continued to direct Sunday school at the Tacoma Buddhist Church after the war. The church celebrated her more than thirty years of outstanding contributions in 1969 (Buddhist Churches of America 1969). At her fifty-year testimonial celebration in 1984, a former Dharma school student sent her a letter of appreciation. Her message perhaps best summarizes the significance of Pratt's commitment to Buddhist education.

> . . . I would like to thank you by letting you how important you were to me as a role model during my Sunday School years. It was not particularly easy growing as a Japanese Buddhist girl during the 50's and 60's in a White Christian male-dominated world. When my generation was starting school,

> there was still a little more than lingering prejudice in Tacoma against the Japanese-Americans who had so recently returned from the relocation camps. Before the days of "Black is Beautiful" and "Yellow Power" it could be painful knowing that I was different than those who were in the majority.
>
> You changed my attitude, by your example and by your teachings. One long ago Sunday, when I was in early elementary school, I suddenly realized that the minister who was giving the flannel board story was different too. SHE was a White woman in Japanese Church. This was inspiring and made me realize that life is full of possibilities.
>
> Later, during the Sangha classes you taught for 9th Graders, you gave me another unforgettable lesson. You said there are as many as ways to become a Buddha as there are human beings in that enlightenment can be described as the fulfillment of each person's character. Again, I learned that it is natural to be different from everyone else and to be appreciative of each person's differences.[10]

For the Dharma school students, Pratt was a model for transcending racial boundaries and ethnic Buddhist practices. She used her favorite teaching instrument, the flannel board, to present cut-and-paste drawings of the histories and teachings of Śākyamuni and Shinran.[11]

Pratt was, however, sometimes difficult to deal with and was not necessarily liked by all the Dharma school students, especially during her later years. Her husband, who never became a Buddhist, died in 1977. Two years later on the anniversary of his death, their daughter Veronica died of stomach cancer. Pratt became depressed, stopped going to the temple, and began to receive psychological treatment. During this period, she daily called several temple members who supported her recovery, speaking with them for sometimes hours over the phone. Eventually, with their help, Pratt was able to resume her activities at the temple.[12] But as a heavy smoker, she failed to present herself as a role model, lighting a cigarette as soon as she left the altar after a service. Some of her students disliked her for bringing cats to the Dharma school classroom and letting them walk on the tables covered with plates.[13]

Despite some complaints from the children, Pratt's contributions overcame her negative image. In 1975, the BCA office presented a certificate of appreciation to her for "her many years of dedicated effort in teaching the young people the Buddha-Dharma and the Buddhist Way of Life." In May 1985, through a nomination to the regional office of Consulate-General of Japan, she received the Sixth Class of the Order of the Precious Crown from the Japanese government. After Pratt's death in 1986 at the age of eighty-eight, the Tacoma Buddhist Temple board named one of its facility rooms after her and established a "Reverend Pratt Fund" for Buddhist education. The Sangha Class made a tribute to her by rearranging the verses of the *gāthā* "*Sayonara*" (Goodbye). Pratt's grave is now at the New Tacoma Cemetery, with her husband and daughter.

THERAVADA BUDDHISM, SHIN BUDDHISM, AND UNIVERSAL BUDDHISM

Despite her commitment to her local Buddhist organization, Pratt was not initially interested in Shin Buddhism. This was also true for other Euro-Americans who became ordained at the BMNA. In *Why I Became a Buddhist*, a small booklet published by the BMNA, those ordained during the 1930s, such as Prosser, Goldwater, Pratt, Udale, and White, all agreed that the concepts of enlightenment, nirvana, wisdom and compassion, and karma were inspiring. In the case of Pratt:

> So why am I a Buddhist?—no other Path is there in my eyes—for I know that All is Buddha, that nothing in the Universe is not part of the great Oneness, that all sentient life is potentially Buddha, and that which I call "myself" cannot be otherwise. Therefore to me Buddhism is the true rule of life, to be understood, tested, and applied day by day. Within its teachings lies the secret of spiritual Peace and contentment, "the mind at Peace" undisturbed by the distractions of Samsara. (Buddhist Mission of North America, n.d., 9)

In her mind, the immanence of buddha-nature would lead her to experience Buddhism pragmatically, and upon the attainment of spiritual peace she would not be disturbed by any event. Neither in this booklet nor in any interview Pratt gave at the time of her ordination did she mention Shin Buddhism; nor did any of the other Caucasian ministers who had been ordained during this period by the BMNA.

The doctrinal orientation of Shin Buddhism differs from the basic teachings of Śākyamuni. Shinran (1173–1262), the posthumous founder of Jodo Shinshu, realized that it was impossible for him to sever blind passions and become a buddha in his lifetime. Therefore, he gave up the goal of awakening through ascetic practices and searched for an alternative. He came to entrust himself to the Primal Vow of Amida Buddha, believed to embrace all sentient beings in the Pure Land upon the recitation of his name. In Shin Buddhism, the practice to become a buddha by one's own meritorious effort is called self-power (*jiriki*), whereas the act of relying on Amida's compassion is considered other-power (*tariki*).

The Euro-American novices' lack of interest in Shin Buddhism raises questions about their motivation to become Buddhist priests at the BMNA and perhaps points to their reluctance to embrace the doctrinal orientation of the order with which they were going to be affiliated. During the nineteenth century, Western scholarship on Buddhism focused primarily on the Pali canon and early forms of Theravada Buddhism (see Hallisey 1995). As Tweed points out, mainstream Protestants and conservative Unitarians at that time were much more curious about the atheistic and nondualistic dimensions of Śākyamuni's philosophy than they were about Pure Land Buddhism, which they perceived as similar to a God-centered religion (Tweed 1992, 15–16). Although Zen, a form of Japanese Buddhism, came to be recognized somewhat during the early thirties, Shin Buddhism had not yet captured the attention of Euro-American Buddhist sympathizers (see Goddard 1938). The unpopularity of Shin Buddhism among Euro-American sympathizers may have also been due to the lack of Shin texts available in English at the time. So the question is: Why were some Euro-American Buddhist converts attracted to the BMNA?

From the very beginning, the BMNA headquarters chose to propagate Śākyamuni's doctrine, rather than Shin doctrine, to Euro-Americans. When Sonoda Shūe, the BMNA's first superintendent, founded the Dharma Sangha of Buddha in 1900 together with Euro-American sympathizers, he avoided sectarianism. The Dharma Sangha of Buddha's constitution stated that "the purposes for which it is formed are, to constitute a society to maintain churches and to propagate the doctrines of Gautama Siddartha, the Buddha Sakyamuni, as set forth in the sacred scriptures of His disciples, and to the end: 1st To teach the doctrines embraced in the generic term, Buddhism."[14] It was a trans-sectarian group, uniting a multiplicity of Buddhist traditions and practices by focusing on Śākyamuni's doctrine. Bishop Uchida Kōyū, whose tenure was between 1905 and 1923, followed in Sonoda's footsteps by distancing the BMNA from Shin. He encouraged the leaders of local umbrella groups to name their organizations *bukkyōkai* or "Buddhist Church" but not to include Honganji or Jodo Shinshu in their names (Uchida 1957, 5–6). The name "Buddhist Mission of North America" itself demonstrates a lack of both sectarian and national identity. Bishop Masuyama, whose term of office was between 1930 and 1938, continued this approach. In these ways, the BMNA office shifted the orientation of its propagation from Shinran to Śākyamuni.

The choice of Śākyamuni over Shinran corresponded to a larger movement, what I call here "Universal Buddhism." In the late nineteenth century, Henry Steel Olcott attempted to create an "International Buddhist League" by combining Theravada and Mahayana in Asia, as well as a "United Buddhist World" by bringing together Buddhists from both the West and East (Prothero 1996, 5–6). In *The Gospel of Buddha* (1894), Paul Carus presented Buddhism in a nonsectarian manner, essentially ignoring the diversity of Asian Buddhism (Snodgrass 2003, 239–240). During the early 1930s, the search for Universal Buddhism continued. For instance, Bishop Emyō Imamura and Ernest Hunt of the Honpa Honganji Mission of Hawaii responded to T'ai Hsü's call to work for a cosmopolitan form of Buddhism. Imamura and Hunt established a branch office of the International Buddhist Institute (IBI) in Honolulu and published an English journal, *Hawaiian Buddhist Annual*, from 1930 to 1934 (Moriya 2001, 125–127; Pierce 2000, 174–176). Hunt went beyond Imamura's trans-sectarian cooperation with his plan to replace Japanese forms of Buddhism in Honolulu with the ethical teachings of Theravada Buddhism (Tanabe 2005, 90). In the Universal Buddhism movement, Theravadin elements were deemed indispensable.

An example of the BMNA's integration of Theravada is observed in Pratt's ordination ceremony. Records from 1933 indicate that the BMNA modeled its ordination procedure for Euro-American novices after the Sri Lankan Theravadin ritual.[15] Pratt's liturgy, which diverged from Shin Buddhist tradition, was eclectic. A newspaper article covering Pratt's ordination reported:

Some 200 persons, the majority of whom were occidentals crowded the small auditorium of the Buddhist church and saw Bishop Masuyama, head of the order in North America; the Rev. J. Yutsawa [Yukawa] and the Rev. Julius Goldwater receive the neophyte into the brotherhood of the Gautama. . . .

Mrs. Pratt and her sponsor, the Rev. Goldwater, were preceded by a choir of 10 Japanese girls dressed in simple yellow kimonos. The ordination party was met at the altar by Bishop Masuyama in a brilliant red robe and insignia of his high office. Priests intoned a chant which was like a slow discordant wail, each long phrase of which was marked by a sharp in-taking of breath.

"This candidate desires ordination," said the Rev. Goldwater when the chanting ceased. "She asks this assembly for admittance. If they agree, let them remain silent."

Mrs. Pratt stood holding her yellow robes out before her. She addressed the bishop.

"In compassion for me, Lord take these robes," she said in a clear but halting voice. "Ordain me in the brotherhood of our Lord Buddha."

Bishop Masuyama placed a yellow stole about her neck and as the candidate touched a pinch of incense to her forehead and then dropped it into a burner of glowing coals he said in English: "I do hereby ordain you into the brotherhood of the sun [*sic*, but most likely *sangha*]."

As Mrs. Pratt left to don the yellow robes she will not again wear until her death, the choir stood and sang in English a hymn of which two verses are as follows:

How glorious is thy Dharma
O Buddha, Blessed Lord:
How wonderful thy Sangha

Which spread thy word abroad.
Thine infinite compassion,
Thy pure and holy life
At length shall lead the nations
From bloodshed, hate and strife.

> Returning, the candidate repeated three times the vow—"I take my refuge in Buddha. I take my refuge in Dharma. I take my refuge in Sangha"—and received the scroll from the bishop giving her the title of "Upasika Bhikuni," meaning "the utmost perfection of womanly virtue," and the new name of "Teium."
>
> "May the light of the Gautama guide your footsteps and may you find everlasting peace," was the benediction.[16]

Her ordination ceremony, and the ordination rites of Euro-Americans in general, is surprising, with Śākyamuni Buddha emerging as their spiritual authority rather than Amida Buddha.[17]

In Pratt's ordination ceremony, we find a mixture of Shin, generalized Mahayana, and Theravada elements. Masuyama, who wore bright red robes, acted as Pratt's teacher and gave her yellow robes. Ordinarily, Shin Buddhist initiates in Japan would wear black robes; Shin clerics can put on robes of various colors (*shikie*) later in their careers, depending on their rank. Pratt would have vowed to take the five or ten precepts, albeit unreported in the aforementioned newspaper article. Like the other Caucasian neophytes, Masuyama bestowed upon Pratt a Japanese Dharma name, Teiun (literally, "chaste cloud").[18] But rather than using Teiun, she substituted the Sanskrit word "Sunya" for her first name. It is unclear whether Masuyama gave it to her or if she chose it herself.[19] Celibacy was not required for the Shin clergy; hence, Pratt became a novice without having to divorce or abandon her children. She even remained unshaved.[20]

Pratt's unconventional ordination ceremony can be best explained through the concept of ritualization. Catherine Bell, defining it as a "strategic way of acting," states,

> When analyzed as ritualization, acting ritually emerges as a particular cultural strategy of differentiation linked to particular social effects and rooted in a distinctive interplay of a socialized body and the environment it structures. . . . [R]itualization is a strategy for the construction of a limited and limiting power relationship . . . one that simultaneously involves both consent and resistance, misunderstanding and appropriation. (Bell 1992, 7–8).

Pratt's ceremony represents at best an integration of two different traditions but at worst appears as a "hodgepodge" of rituals. Whereas power relationships for Bell involve social control and solidarity, in the case of Pratt's ordination it also suggests the mutual interests of Euro-Americans and Japanese clergy in creating a new liturgy that would fit the popular perception of Buddhism in the United States. It diverged from the Japanese tradition, yet did not completely replicate the Theravadin style, and even introduced a choir into the ceremony. In attempting to accommodate a Euro-American novice, the BMNA officials chose to make the ordination rite eclectic; it was both cross-cultural (American, Japanese, and Sri Lankan) and cross-traditional (Theravada, Mahayana, and Shin) and complicated the "distinctive interplay."

This selective ritual practice also raises important questions. How was the symbolic amalgamation of Theravadin and Shin elements justified on a doctrinal level? How did Euro-Americans ordained at the BMNA reconcile a broad range of concepts, such as the differences between *jiriki* and *tariki*, Śākyamuni and Amida Buddha, and emptiness and the materiality of the Pure Land? Or for that matter, how did they attempt to understand Shin Buddhist doctrine? These questions were left up to each Caucasian novice to answer, because the BMNA leaders themselves were unclear on how to reconcile the notion of self-power with that of other-power. In Japan, Buddhist leaders had championed their religion as the supreme form of Buddhism without developing relationships with Theravada or other Mahayana schools of Buddhism on the Asian continent. In the case of Shin Buddhists, they had considered the *tariki* path more accessible and attainable than the *jiriki* way based on Shinran's doctrinal exposition. Thus, when Shin clerics encountered and interacted with foreign Buddhists for the first time in the United States, they found a disparity between their mindsets and the realities of these other Buddhists. The great majority of *issei* Shin clergy was complacent and unprepared to reinterpret Shin doctrine in the light of transnational Buddhist practices.

The Caucasian ministers ordained at the BMNA during the 1930s initially ignored Shin Buddhism, with none of them making a lifetime commitment to it other than Pratt. Robert Clifton, who was in charge of the BMNA English Department, left the order in the early 1940s to pursue his interest in Theravada Buddhism (Buddhist Churches of America 1998, 171). Goldwater left the Nishi Honganji Los Angeles Buddhist Church after the war. Its board members sought a legal settlement of his alleged improper use of church funds during his service as the church's caretaker between 1942 and 1945. Other Euro-American ministers also left the BMNA either before or after the war for unknown reasons.[21] Ernest Hunt (1876–1967), who became the minister of the Honpa Honganji Mission of Hawaii during the early 1920s and led its English Department, changed his affiliation from Shin Buddhism to Soto Zen after the nationalistic bishop fired him in 1937.

Why then did Pratt continue to serve at the Tacoma Buddhist Temple and remain faithful to the BMNA until her death? Her local connections and gradual effort to understand Shin Buddhism seem important in this regard. First, unlike the other Euro-American novices, Pratt did not have a great deal of mobility. While the others visited Japan and participated in further ordination ceremonies at Nishi Honganji's head temple in Kyoto, Pratt remained in the Tacoma/Seattle area. She had, in fact, never visited Japan. Her husband ran a local family business with the help of Pratt and their children. Being responsible for its growth and her children's education, Pratt's activity was physically limited. The Tacoma Buddhist Temple was the only ethnic Buddhist group in Tacoma where she could play both local and regional roles by educating the *nisei* youth and helping the BMNA office admit other Caucasians in Seattle. She also had good relationships with *issei* ministers in need of a native speaker's assistance. Early records also show that she expressed an interest in Shin Buddhism after her ordination. During the late 1930s, Pratt corresponded with Nakai Gendō, a Nishi Honganji priest in Japan who had served as resident minister of Seattle Buddhist Church between 1902 and 1907, and obtained a list of Shin texts in English.[22] The Sunday school materials, distributed to her students in 1966, demonstrate that she was teaching the historical development of Buddhism through Shinran's perspective and according to Nishi Honganji doctrine. These accounts, however, do not sufficiently explain how she reconciled the differences between the basic doctrines of Buddhism in which Śākyamuni encouraged his followers to observe precepts and the orthodox Shin Buddhist position in which Shinran did not see moral conditions as necessary for birth in the Pure Land. Perhaps she was able to connect these two positions on a deeper, personal level following the deaths of her husband and daughter. She may have come to an understanding of the importance of entrusting oneself to something other, beyond the limited ego-self, namely, to Amida's compassion, which would have been in line with Shin teachings. Or, without speculating on any such possibilities, it may simply have been that the binary concept of self-power and other-power did not present her with any contradictions.

CONCLUSION

Sunya Pratt was an unusual Euro-American Buddhist minister. She was bound by neither parochialism nor sectarianism. The phenomenon of Universal Buddhism among Euro-American converts had reoriented the propagation goal of the Buddhist Mission of North America, making her service to the Tacoma Buddhist Church more suitable to the needs of the organization and her own interests. At the same time, despite the differences between the doctrine of Shin Buddhism and the basic principles of Śākyamuni Buddha to which she was initially drawn, she remained part of an ethnic Buddhist organization for the rest of her life. She understood the importance of an ethnic and Shin Buddhist heritage that her congregation had brought with them from Japan. She was one of the very few Caucasians who was able to help and interact with Buddhists of Japanese ancestry in the Tacoma/Seattle area, especially during the prewar and postwar periods.[23] Pratt even critiqued modernity and modern nation-states from a Buddhist standpoint. She explicitly stated that ignorance about oneself was the cause of hatred, anger, intolerance, and prejudice, which would affect the politics of a nation in the form of collective karma.[24] Such a stance, in addition to her connection to the Tacoma Buddhist Church, may have isolated her from her Euro-American neighbors, who would have been more in the mainstream of Protestant American culture. She might have struggled with them as much as the people of Japanese ancestry, who were suffering from racial and religious discrimination.

For the Buddhist Mission of North America, integration of Theravadin elements was necessary for drawing in Euro-Americans. Shin Buddhist leaders lowered the priority of propagating their sectarian teaching to Euro-Americans because of the latter's interest in Śākyamuni's basic doctrine. Pratt was a role model for Euro-American ministers for the BMNA as she made a lifetime commitment to a local Buddhist temple as well as the BMNA and was able to incorporate Shinran's teaching into her Sunday school program. Her presence at the Tacoma Buddhist Church demonstrates how a local Buddhist group balanced the needs of its ethnic community with the appeal of a more "universal" Buddhism.

NOTES

For assistance on this research, the author thanks Reverend Kōsho Yukawa, Reverend Kakei Nakagawa, Ted Tamaki, Tadaye Kawasaki, Toyoko Nakagawara, Yasuko Morita (members of the Tacoma Buddhist Temple interviewed on March 28, 2009), Patrick Pratt (Sunya Pratt's son), and Eiko Masuyama.

1. *Los Angeles Times*, April 25, 1936, Part I. Sunya Pratt's ordination was also reported locally; for instance, "Tacoman Is Ordained a Buddhist Priestess," *Tacoma Daily Ledger*, April 24, 1936; "Buddhist Priestess: Tacoman First White Woman to Take Vows in the U.S.," *Tacoma News Tribune*, April 23, 1936; and "To Be First U.S. Buddhist Priestess," *Tacoma Times*, April 22, 1936. *Time Magazine* also reported this event on May 11, 1936.
2. In the *Encyclopedia of Women and Religion in North America*, Lori Pierce mentions Sunya Pratt under the heading "Asian Buddhist Communities from China and Japan." This section, however, is separated from the discussion of other Euro-American Buddhist women under the heading "Euro-American Buddhists" (Pierce 2006, 636).
3. *Tacoma News Tribune* on April 7, 1984; Buddhist Churches of America (1974, 1:264–265); telephone interview with Patrick Pratt on February 22, 2009, and his response to the author on April 17, 2009; and the tomb marker for the Pratt family described in Patrick Pratt's letter to the New Tacoma Cemetery, dated April 19, 1986.
4. After Uchida returned to Japan in 1923, the BMNA lacked strong leadership, and the head changed frequently. When Masuyama took over in 1930, the Clarkes' names no longer appeared in the BMNA records.
5. Correspondence from Pratt to the BMNA English Department, dated February 16, 2503 (BCA Archives, Chronological Files, Box No. 1.01.04, Folder 1938–1939). Pratt seems to have used the year count based on Śākyamuni Buddha's death or his birth. After

analyzing the dates shown in Pratt's other letters, it seems likely that 2503 is the year 1937.

6. For instance, two individuals were admitted in February 2504 (possibly 1938) and another two in May of the same year (BCA Archives, Chronological Files, Box No. 1.01.04, Folder 1938–1939).
7. *Tacoma News Tribune*, August 16, 1937.
8. *Tacoma Times*, April 28, 1941.
9. Tacoma Buddhist Temple, "Temple History," http://www.tacom-abt.org.
10. Tacoma Buddhist Temple, *Myokyo: Tacoma Buddhist Temple Newsletter* (March 10, 1986).
11. Other Tacoma Buddhist Temple members also expressed similar experiences. For instance, according to Tetsuo Tamaki, Pratt helped him in preparing for an oratorical contest at the college he was attending during the late 1940s. After the speech lessons, they chatted over a "spot of English tea" and discussed Buddhism. She not only introduced him to Buddhism but differentiated Shin Buddhism from Judeo-Christianity and other forms of Buddhism (from Tamaki's speech given at Pratt's seventh memorial service on February 9, 1991). Toyoko Nakagawara recalls, "She always used to tell us when asked questions like 'Do you believe in God?' answer back, 'What is your interpretation of God?' She had many high school classes [students] come to this temple to answer their questions on Buddhism" (Toyoko Nakagawara's memory of Pratt, interview with the author).
12. Toyoko arranged for several Japanese ministers and Pratt's previous Dharma school students to visit and encourage her. These *nisei* cheered her up. Toyoko noted, "Instead of listening to her flannel board stories they waited for her to drop one of her pieces so they could jump up and retrieve the piece for her. This brought a big laugh from her and she said, 'Toyo, would you please pick me up to go to the Temple?'" Toyoko lived five minutes away from Pratt's house. She became her caretaker after her son, Patrick, moved to Minnesota and was unable to return to take care of her (Toyoko Nakagawara, interview with the author).
13. Author's interview with Toyoko Nakagawara and Tadaye Kawasaki on March 28, 2009.

14. "Constitution and By-Laws of the Dharma Sangha of Buddha," 1 (BCA Archives, Chronological Files, Box No. 1.01.01, Folder 1900).
15. "Ordination Ceremony" (BCA Archives, Correspondence Files, Box No. 1.02.07, Folder 1933).
16. "Tacoman Is Ordained a Buddhist Priestess," *Tacoma Daily Ledger*, April 24, 1936.
17. When Goldwater was ordained on June 17, 1934, he faced a statue of the Buddha "sitting cross-legged" on the altar at the Nishi Honganji Los Angeles Buddhist Church. "Buddhists Ordain American, S.A. Goldwaite [*sic*] Enters Priesthood Here," *Los Angeles Times*, June 18, 1934, Part II. Traditionally, the object of worship (*honzon*) in Jodo Shinshu is not the statue of a sitting Buddha but a statue or figure of a standing Amida Buddha.
18. A Shin Buddhist receives a *hōmyō*, although a precept name (*kaimyō*) is common in other denominations.
19. "To Be First U.S. Buddhist Priestess," *Tacoma Times*, April 22, 1936. The article states that she dropped the name Gladys in 1934. According to *The Golden Lotus* 20 (April 1963), "In addition to the honor of being ordained by Bishop Masuyama, she was given the name 'Sunya.'"
20. For female Shin Buddhist novice candidates in Japan, tonsure is not compulsory, though it is compulsory for males. The history of Shin Buddhist women's ordination needs further research.
21. There are no records of Prosser's activities after he returned to the United States from Japan in 1936, nor are there any of White's involvement at the BMNA after 1941. Although Udale officiated at non-Japanese services at the Buddhist Church of San Francisco during World War II, his whereabouts after 1945 are unknown (Buddhist Churches of America 1998, 119, 177–178).
21. This letter is kept at the BCA Archives (Chronological Files, Boxes No. 1.01.04, Folder 1938–1939).
23. According to the members of the Tacoma Buddhist Temple, Grace McLeod also participated in the Seattle Buddhist Church and interacted with Pratt.
24. *Northern California Bussei Guide*, conference booklet (1941), 36.

FIVE

Invoking the Dharma Protector

Western Involvement in the Dorje Shugden Controversy

JEANNINE CHANDLER

Since the 1960s and 1970s, the involvement of Western converts in Tibetan Buddhism has initiated the transformation of the Tibetan Buddhist world. The mere participation of Westerners in Tibetan Buddhism and, subsequently, the Tibetan independence issue (or vice versa) has allowed for Western influence in the affairs of the Tibetan diaspora. The explosion of the Dorje Shugden affair in the West exemplifies the convergence of several phenomena: globalization, advancements in modern communication technology, translocalism, diasporic politics, and religious sectarianism. Since Westerners have become involved in the unfolding of the Shugden controversy, the debate has been transformed and internationalized. As the conflict has been exported overseas and across cultures, the issue has assumed a new dynamic as a set of novice, non-Tibetan Buddhists has become involved in an age-old, Tibet-specific religious feud. This blight on the exposed underbelly of Tibetan religious politics highlights the translocality of Tibetan Buddhism as it straddles two different cultures.

Dorje Shugden ("Powerful Thunderbolt") is a *dharmapāla*, or wrathful protector deity, in the Tibetan Buddhist pantheon. These doctrinal guardians are usually depicted in an angry or demonic aspect and are described as violently subduing Buddhism's adversaries, be they mental obstructions to one's personal practice or actual human beings (Nebesky-Wojkowitz 1998, 4). Shugden is believed by some to be the embodiment of a vengeful spirit of a monk who was once a rival in popularity to the Fifth Dalai Lama (1617–1682), who is often considered a controversial figure himself due to his participation in non-Gelug practices.[1] Shugden was frequently deemed responsible for plagues, deaths, and destruction, acts he allegedly inflicted on those who blended the traditions and teachings of the different schools, particularly punishing those Gelug practitioners who dabbled in Nyingma practices. The malignant presence was later subdued and co-opted by leaders of the Tibetan government and ruling Gelug religious sect and, in this manner, became a spiritual protector of the Gelug school, a guardian of its monasteries, and defender of its doctrinal purity (Nebesky-Wojkowitz 1998, 135–136). Although Shugden is considered by his detractors to be a mundane protector (even an evil spirit), he is regarded by his devotees as a high-level worldly deity, one who may soon transcend samsara.

In the early 1900s, the controversy surrounding Shugden's status was reinvigorated by Pabongkha (1878–1941), one of the most powerful Gelug lamas of the twentieth century. His conservative interpretation of Buddhist teachings and his later antagonism to Nyingma doctrine coincided with a lifelong devotion to Dorje Shugden. Pabongkha was a charismatic teacher who inspired many loyal disciples. Shugden worship thus endured through the latter half of the twentieth century and into exile and enjoyed some powerful sponsorship, as Pabongkha's leading disciple, Trijang Rinpoche (1901–1981), became the junior tutor of the Fourteenth Dalai Lama (Dreyfus 2005).

The recent phase of the Dorje Shugden conflict began after the Dalai Lama, the Tibetan religious elite, and the Tibetan government escaped into exile. The 1950s marked a colossal transition in Tibetan history as the Chinese invaded and occupied Tibet and tens of thousands of Tibetans followed the young Dalai Lama into India in 1959. The fledgling government in exile was forced to deal with a plethora of new circumstances, including a large, disparate refugee community in need of basic services, as well as a virtually unknown modern political world. Following a period of adjustment and acclimation, social relations and religious practices stabilized and familiar age-old disputes returned to the fore.

In 1973, Zemey Rinpoche (1927–1996), a senior Gelug lama, distributed a publication privately among the Tibetan exile community in Dharamsala. This tract, known as "Sacred Words of the Able Father" (or colloquially as "The Yellow Book"), was based on oral teachings Zemey had received from his guru and Shugden devotee, Trijang Rinpoche.[2] "The Yellow Book" detailed a list of Gelug lamas who had allegedly been harmed or punished by Dorje Shugden because of their involvement in non-Gelug practices (usually those of the Nyingma), or who had insulted Shugden in some way. The distribution of this collection was a thinly veiled warning to Gelug scholars to not practice the teachings of other schools or else they would anger Shugden and perhaps suffer the consequences (Dreyfus 2003, 300–301). Despite his past participation in the Shugden practice, the Dalai Lama denounced the treatise, and in 1976 he began to discourage the worship of Shugden.

With the Dalai Lama's 1976 pronouncement, the issue was generally confined to the Gelug community. The Shugden dispute at that time was virtually unknown outside the refugee community, much less within the Western Buddhist movement, which was still in its infancy during the 1970s. Within a few decades, however, Tibetan Buddhism had acquired quite a following in the West, particularly in America, as Hollywood celebrities publicly endorsed Tibetan Buddhism and the Dalai Lama. By the mid-1990s, the Dalai Lama's reputation as a Nobel Peace Prize–winner and the international face of Tibetan Buddhism had successfully attracted media attention and sympathizers to the Tibetan struggle for independence, in addition to potential converts to the Tibetan religion. The Dalai Lama's popularity peaked at the same time that the Shugden conflict erupted on the global stage.

The Dalai Lama's initial discouragement of public and official Shugden propitiation in the 1970s and 1980s became virtual proscription in the spring of 1996. Citing Shugden's divisive and sectarian tendencies, the Dalai Lama declared that the continued propitiation of Shugden contributed to the degeneration of Tibetan Buddhism into "spirit worship" and constituted a threat to his life and to the interests of a free Tibet.[3] Despite the government's insistence that the Dalai Lama's decree does not constitute a "ban," as argued by his critics, it is important to note that those who choose to worship Shugden against the wishes of the Dalai Lama and mainstream Tibetan society become virtual outcasts. Those who continue Shugden practice are acting in defiance of the Dalai Lama, the spiritual and political leader of all exiled Tibetans. Those adherents who further choose to receive empowerments from the Dalai Lama while upholding Shugden worship are not only acting in opposition to the Dalai Lama but are also perceived by the larger society to be putting his life in danger. For Tibetans, perhaps one of the worst acts that one may commit is the forsaking or harming of one's guru, and this is compounded when that guru is the Dalai Lama, considered to be the embodiment of Tibet (see Barnett 2001). As the Dalai Lama and Tibet are so equated in the minds of many Tibetans, to go against his wishes is also to sabotage the cause of Tibetan independence (see Chandler 2009). The exile community is closed and tight-knit. To transgress the bonds of that community by essentially repudiating one's leader, one's nation, and one's religion places one decidedly outside the bounds of mainstream society. One is thus, in a sense, exiled from exile.

With the Dalai Lama's decree in 1996, tension and hostility erupted in India, as Shugden worshipers, accusing the Dalai Lama of religious persecution, founded pro-Shugden organizations in India and elsewhere around the world. In February 1997, the violent killings of three Buddhist monks in Dharamsala were attributed to Shugden supporters, and these murders drew more international attention to the Shugden dispute. The spread of the controversy resulted in the Dalai Lama's international reputation being called into question, and he was derided for being a religious despot.[4]

Although the publicizing of the Dharamsala murders garnered some international attention to the Shugden controversy, Western students of Tibetan Buddhism and Tibet sympathizers became aware of the dispute primarily through Tibetan lamas who lived in and/or traveled to Europe and the United States. In the late 1990s, several pro-Shugden Tibetan teachers traveling in the West helped to disseminate the controversy, hoping to generate support from Westerners in opposing what they perceived to be religious persecution.[5] Some lamas already positioned in the West, upon hearing the Dalai Lama's declaration, simply refused to comply. Other individuals in exile traveled to the West in order to continue their Shugden worship unfettered. Once settled in the West, many of these pro-Shugden lamas made their views on the Shugden issue public via their own websites and/or newspaper and magazine interviews and thus facilitated the transmission of the controversy.

The Shugden-worshiping group with the greatest impact in the West has been the New Kadampa Tradition (NKT). Shugden worship is a central component of New Kadampa Buddhism. Its founder and guru, Geshe Kelsang Gyatso, a conservative teacher originally of the Gelug tradition, has become quite popular and successful among Westerners. Since the mid-1990s, Western activist organizations such as the Shugden Supporters Community (SSC) and the Western Shugden Society (WSS) have joined the NKT in publicly criticizing the Dalai Lama regarding his stance on Shugden worship. The Dalai Lama has countered the perspectives of these groups and pro-Shugden lamas like Kelsang Gyatso by reiterating his position and actively discouraging Shugden worship through his teachings in the West as well as on his affiliated websites.

Western involvement in the Shugden conflict has been influenced and defined by the unique characteristics of Tibetan Buddhism as it has developed in the West. The global evolution of Tibetan Buddhism outside of Tibet has long been affected by Western romanticization of Tibet, Tibetans, and Tibetan Buddhism. The enduring influence of the Shangri-La myth and the attractions of Buddhist modernism have obscured traditional Tibetan Buddhist teachings and Buddhist theory in general (Lopez 1998; cf. Wallace 2001). The guru-disciple bond has particularly suffered under Western projections or expectations, having been wrenched from its Asian context and grafted onto the Western historical, social, and psychological framework. The American cultural context in particular, with its emphasis on individualism, equality, and democracy, has had varying success in accommodating the hierarchy and monasticism of Tibetan Buddhism. Many Westerners are baffled by the teacher-student bond, and this confusion often manifests in two diametric forms: those who render the guru irrelevant to their Buddhist practice and those who are all too willing to blindly devote themselves to their gurus. At one end of the spectrum, Westerners are frequently criticized for their casual adoption of the religion and their tendency to "pick and choose," jettisoning aspects of Buddhism they find unpalatable (Wallace 2001). One such aspect is the centrality of the lama to the student's pursuit of enlightenment. At the other extreme of the guru-disciple relationship scale, some teachers have exploited and abused their students, and students have looked upon their teachers as godlike father figures. Georges Dreyfus has stated that Tibetan lamas tend to infantilize their Western students. Many Tibetan teachers view Westerners as "nice kids" but not fully mature or trustworthy. According to Dreyfus, the cultural gap between Tibetans and Westerners, as well as the nature of the organization of Tibetan Buddhism in the West, places Tibetans at the top of the hierarchy.[6]

I submit that the ambiguities regarding the Tibetan guru-Western disciple relationship is at the core of the Shugden controversy, fueling the increasing Western involvement in the conflict. Westerners who render the guru irrelevant to their religious practice may inadvertently fuel sectarianism among conservative Tibetan Buddhists who believe in the traditional role of the guru. The Western misunderstanding of the guru-disciple relationship has exacerbated sectarian tensions in the Tibetan Buddhist community. As noted earlier, Western confusion regarding the role of the guru has led some Western converts to see the lama as a "father figure" and form an unhealthy attachment that has sparked exploitation and intensified sectarian affiliation. Robert Barnett has noted this guru idolization among NKT members and claims that Westerners involved in the conflict do not know enough about Tibetan Buddhism, the NKT, or Dorje Shugden to make any informed judgments about this issue. Due to the misunderstandings and confusion inherent in Tibetan Buddhism as imported to the West, Western students often have no context from which they can understand the specifics of the Shugden debate.[7] They do, however, have an uncritical and unconditional obedience to Kelsang Gyatso and his beliefs. In this way, many Westerners have become involved in the conflict due to their devotion to their lamas. This devotion has often manifested in the form of sectarianism among Western converts to Tibetan Buddhism.

Sectarianism has also been fueled by the increased activity and relative saliency of the Tibetan lamas, their centers, and their satellite branches throughout the West. This has resulted in more teachers and groups in close proximity to one another, which has subsequently initiated competition for converts. This competition has manifested in sectarian behaviors, and contemporary Tibetan Buddhist controversies, like the Shugden affair, have highlighted base sectarian attitudes among both Tibetan teachers and their Western disciples. Just as the competition among the monastic colleges in traditional Tibet helped the monks build a cohesive school-based sectarian identity (Hopkins 2001, 261), guru devotion and sectarian/factional competition in the West have provided the means for some Western converts to showcase their Buddhist affiliations. In America, in particular, the fusing of American values (including its obsession with competition) with the hierarchy of Tibetan Buddhism has helped entrench sectarian conflict. The American cultural context has intensified the traditional sectarianism and factionalism of Tibetan Buddhism, as American converts "choose sides" in disputes about which they know little, primarily because doing so solidifies their self-identification as (Tibetan) Buddhists. The Shugden issue showcases the manifestation of what I have termed "conspicuous compassion," as Western adherents of Tibetan Buddhism attempt to demonstrate that they are the "most Buddhist" by (often blindly) supporting and defending their lama or group (Chandler 2009, 86–98). The price is harsher sectarian divisions. Sectarianism in Tibetan Buddhism in the West has also sharpened the boundaries between the four schools of Tibetan Buddhism on a global level, as Western sectarian consciousness reflects back on the Tibetan Buddhism of the Western-influenced exile community. The Shugden conflict provides evidence that, despite a surface commitment to ecumenism in the exile Tibetan community as a whole, sectarian consciousness has actually become more entrenched among Tibetan Buddhists in the West.

Westerners have transformed the Shugden conflict in several important ways. First, whereas in traditional Tibetan society this issue regarding Shugden would have been a private matter (confined to a small group of religious elite), since Westerners have become involved, the international press has begun to pay more attention to the controversy, and the Internet has become a primary forum for debating this issue.[8] Further, Western participation in the dispute has often been viewed as "interference" by some Tibetans in the diaspora and, as such, has implications for Western-Tibetan relations and the development of Tibetan Buddhism in the West. With the spread of Tibetan Buddhism around the globe, the religion, including its attendant controversies, is now beyond Tibetan control. Therefore the involvement of Westerners in the Shugden issue has resulted in a Tibetan backlash against Westerners. For example, following the outbreak of tensions in the 1990s regarding this controversy, in a letter to the Western-run SSC (Shugden Supporters Community), Karma Gyaltsen, the president of the Capital Area Tibet Association of Washington, D.C., noted:

> We are pleased that you are concerned about the future of Tibet. But, as Tibetans, we would like to state categorically, leave it to the Tibetan people to decide what sort of future we want. You do not have to impose your views on us. The Tibetan people need international support. What we do not need is action [*sic*] of people like yourselves who try to think that they know more about Tibet than us the Tibetan people.[9]

With regards to the Shugden controversy, many Tibetans are unhappy with those Westerners who have protested the Dalai Lama over Shugden, as they feel that Westerners do not understand the issue or the Dalai Lama's position in the debate. Some have reiterated that this is a Tibetan issue and Tibetans will resolve it, without Western interference.[10]

The introduction of Western views and values into the Shugden affair has further hastened the transformation of the dispute. Westerners have influenced the Shugden controversy by fueling the perpetuation of the conflict, specifically via inflammatory rhetoric on the Internet. Activists (on both sides), Western media, and Tibetan lamas (and their followers) in the West have complicated this issue in their manipulations of language and casual use of loaded terminology. Analysis reveals that both sides of the Shugden conflict have co-opted inflammatory language and "hot-button" terms to their own ends, especially on the Internet. It is these latter two points that I explore next.

As noted earlier, the injection of Western attitudes and morals into the Shugden dispute has inexorably altered the development of the conflict. In America, *democracy* and *freedom* (of speech, of religion, of assembly, etc.) are extolled by the government, educational institutions, and the media as the underlying themes of America's establishment, history, and policymaking. The cultural and political weight of these terms in contemporary American society cannot be overstated (especially considering their now nebulous definitions and casual overusage). The use of these ideals in the Shugden battle is particularly interesting in light of the Western transformation and portrayal of Tibetan religion and history. Buddhism in the West is generally characterized as an inclusive, egalitarian, *democratic* religion, in which anyone may take part, in any manner and to any extent he or she wishes. Mike Wilson notes that "people in the West, especially America, are likely to be receptive to . . . claims of religious repression, whether true or not, because of Western values and history that emphasize religious diversity" (Wilson 1999, 33). However, as Stephen Batchelor notes, Buddhism has never identified itself as a democratic tradition. Tibetan Buddhism defies this definition even more so, with its fusion of politics and religion, and myriad hierarchies of lamas, deities, and lineages (Batchelor 1998). Despite this fact, as Donald Lopez states, many Americans view the Dalai Lama's refusal to "tolerate the intolerant" with regards to the Shugden issue as somewhat baffling,[11] and this is reflected in the involvement (and corresponding rhetoric) of Westerners supporting Shugden worship.

Activists (on both sides of the Shugden conflict), Western media, and Tibetan lamas (and their followers) in the West have complicated the issue with their use of Western rhetoric to support their respective positions. The Dalai Lama has increasingly made efforts to associate himself (and thus Tibet and its religion) with the reason, logic, and demythologized qualities of Buddhist modernism and modern science and concurrently (whether intentionally or not) disassociate himself and Tibetan Buddhism from the esotericism and complexities of deity worship, particularly in the eyes of the West. In his talks to Tibetans on the Shugden controversy, he emphasizes the history of the conflict in the context of traditional religious and cultural beliefs in his endeavors to convince others of his position: lineage relationships, examples of unfortunate encounters with Shugden, as well as deity visions in his own dreams.[12] While speaking to Westerners, however, his reasons are more often stated simply and without much reference to the existence of deities at all. He argues against Shugden propitiation because (1) he must follow the historical precedents set by Dalai Lamas before him (as the Fifth and Thirteenth Dalai Lamas placed restrictions on Shugden worship); (2) he promotes nonsectarianism, not only among the four schools of Tibetan Buddhism but among all religions (and therefore opposes Shugden's divisiveness); and (3) he cautions that with the continuation of the Shugden practice, Buddhism is in danger of deteriorating into "spirit worship."[13] Thus, to a Western audience, in opposing the supplication of Shugden, he not only emphasizes historical precedence but also world peace and a back-to-the-basics Buddhism stripped of cultural specificities and characterized by logic and reason.

Each side of the Shugden dispute has made use of the highly polarizing, stereotyped imagery and labels associated with previous and continuous conflicts around the world to lend credence to their claims. Similar to the Dalai Lama, Kelsang Gyatso has also appropriated Western values, language, and associated imagery to accentuate his position on the Shugden issue. In one interview, he compared anti-Shugden activities reported to be taking place in India to the violence and oppression of the Mao-era Cultural Revolution, a sensitive issue for many Tibetans (and Chinese for that matter) and a period generally characterized as the epitome of Mao's tyrannical rule and the antithesis of Western values such as democracy and freedom.[14] Elsewhere, he has used Western civil and legal language to make his point, as shown in Kelsang Gyatso's open letter (published in an open Internet forum) to the Dalai Lama (and a Western audience) regarding the Shugden issue. "Your ban on the practice of Dorje Shugden is a direct attack on religious freedom. This is against the UN 'Universal Declaration of Human Rights,' and also against the law *in democratic countries such as the United States*. You are also engaging in Deity discrimination, which breaks the constitutional law of India."[15] This passage illustrates Kelsang Gyatso's use of loaded terminology in order to garner support for his position on Shugden.

Kundeling Rinpoche, a Shugden-supporter, has compared the alleged persecution of Shugden worshipers by the Dalai Lama and the exile government to Nazi atrocities and accused the Dalai Lama of inciting the spring 2008 protests in Tibet to hide his "apartheid policy" of dealing with Shugden believers.[16] Both sides have made use of the post-9/11 culture of fear in America, the attendant prejudice against Islam, and the history of perpetual conflict in the Middle East in order to give weight to their arguments. In a booklet handed out at protests by the Western Shugden Society, in an article entitled "21st Century Buddhist Dictator: The Dalai Lama," the Dalai Lama is accused of being a "Saffron-Robed Muslim" (supposedly having been born into a Muslim family) and a falsely recognized incarnation. The author(s) seemingly imply a connection between evil and Islam (a prevalent linkage in parts of American society) and use that image to show that the "real nature" of the Dalai Lama is "cruel and very evil."[17] Geshe Dragpa Gyaltsen, a Shugden supporter, noted in a *Newsweek* interview that the escalating violence and discrimination against Shugden followers will ultimately cause them to become the "Jews of Tibetan Buddhism." Oddly enough, in the same article, Western Buddhologist Robert Thurman characterizes Shugden believers as the "Taliban of Tibetan Buddhism."[18] This use of inflammatory language—labels with particular meaning and history in the Western cultural context—has exacerbated tensions in the Shugden conflict.

Westerners have also influenced the Shugden controversy by fueling the perpetuation of the conflict, specifically via inflammatory rhetoric on the Internet. Modern technology and globalization via the Internet have allowed the Shugden debate to persist and fester years after the major events took place in the mid-to-late 1990s. With the spread of the debate to the Internet, the Dorje Shugden controversy has slipped out of the hands of the Tibetans into the anonymous and inflammatory chat rooms of cyberspace. Online discussion groups, blogs, and forums offer an unprecedented level of anonymity in social interaction and, as such, allow people to express thoughts and criticisms they would not normally share with a peer, much less a teacher. Some Westerners have reportedly resorted to using Tibetan names in discussion forums in order to lend legitimacy and credence to their posts and comments and grant the illusion of Tibetan support for their opinions.[19] An examination of these sites reveals more about the nature of the rivals than facts of the rivalry itself; yet the structure and content of these Internet debates highlights the impact of Western involvement in the Shugden controversy.

Geshe Kelsang Gyatso, the New Kadampa Tradition, and other Shugden-worshiping groups (on one side) and the Dalai Lama, the Tibetan government in exile, and their international supporters (on the other) have made this issue the focus of several websites, discussion forums, and message boards. The major search engines of Yahoo! and Google both maintain discussion groups devoted to the New Kadampa Tradition and the Dorje Shugden affair.[20] YouTube has a host of videos produced by both sides of the argument detailing the history of this conflict. Both Facebook and Twitter have pages devoted to the deity.[21] Dorje Shugden even has his own "Free Dorje Shugden!" MySpace page.[22] Other websites, namely Phayul, E-sangha, and Wikipedia, have also committed significant time and space to the Dorje Shugden issue.

Phayul ("fatherland") is a website committed to providing "news and views on Tibet" to the exile community and the diaspora at large. While the message forums are obviously tailored to the Tibetan community, it is apparent from postings that Westerners sympathetic to Tibet and Tibetan Buddhism have chosen to promulgate their opinions there as well. The Buddhist message forum has more than twenty topic areas dedicated to the discussion of Dorje Shugden. Topic headings include "New Kadampa Tradition," "Free Dorje Shugden," and "A topic on a ghost only creates negative thoughts in our minds." Another discussion forum ("What is wrong with Tibetan society," started by a Westerner) became quite heated as debate of the Shugden issue quickly degenerated into anti-Western invective. One irate participant remarked to the Westerner who instigated the thread: "The so-called non-Tibetan 'Buddhist Practitioners' like you create havoc in our society. I have not known sectarian conflict in my life until castaways like you started making mess in our community. . . . Mind your own business and let us alone."[23] This statement implies that Westerners have intensified the Shugden conflict through their involvement. As evidenced by these discussions on Phayul and other websites, the Dorje Shugden controversy creates an intersection of sectarian, nationalistic, and cultural debate.

In contrast to Phayul, the E-sangha website (defunct since 2009) touted itself as "an established Buddhism portal" and, in essence, attempted to create a virtual *sangha* through its discussion forums, blogs, and message boards. In its time, E-sangha was controversial for its willingness to tackle provocative issues in the modern Buddhist community, while at the same time banning or silencing groups or members that were not deemed compatible with the website's stance toward certain issues, such as the Shugden controversy. Thus, E-sangha's debate over the Dorje Shugden issue assumed a somewhat different format than that of Phayul. As opposed to the latter, E-sangha did not align itself with a particular ethnicity or sect; rather, it aimed to provide "a place where Buddhists are able to meet on the Internet to discuss all matters relating to Buddhism."[24] Therefore, while Phayul is intent on providing an Internet site for Tibetans of the diaspora (and thus the focus, first and foremost, being on an exclusive sense of national, rather than religious, identity), E-sangha aspired to present an inclusive, nonsectarian Buddhist discussion forum, where posters may debate Dharma topics, investigate gurus, and (often) mull over various Buddhist scandals. As such, E-sangha members were culled from all over the world and provided a transnational cyber window into the world of globalized Buddhism. That being said, the site was not impartial, as the E-sangha administrator posted the following announcement as "required reading" for all guests and potential posters before proceeding into the Buddhist forums: "These few 'Buddhist' schools of thought are not recognized by E-sangha. No links to their websites, their books, or their followers' websites are allowed: New Kadampa Tradition (NKT) and all other proponents of Dolgyal/Shugden, Dark Zen, True Buddha School, Aro Ter / Flaming Jewel Sangha."[25] Thus E-sangha clearly chose sides in the Shugden dispute.

Wikipedia furnishes perhaps the most interesting cyber debate concerning the Dorje Shugden issue. The website publicizes itself as "the free encyclopedia that anyone can edit."[26] According to Wikipedia's entry on itself, "the authors need not have any expertise or formal qualifications in the subjects which they edit, and users are warned that their contributions may be 'edited mercilessly and redistributed at will' by anyone who so wishes."[27] In light of these Wikipedia policies, the "Dorje Shugden," "New Kadampa Tradition," and "Kelsang Gyatso" entries (among others related to this issue) have become contentious territories, where both sides of the debate are attempting to amend the articles to reflect their versions of history. "Edit wars" are common on the "discussion" sections of these entries, as Shugden and NKT supporters argue for a balanced characterization of their protector deity, guru, and organization, and followers of the Dalai Lama (along with some ex-NKT members) conversely cite documents, speeches, and articles (from the Tibetan government in exile and the Dalai Lama himself) that present a less flattering view of NKT, Kelsang Gyatso, and Dorje Shugden. The two sides debate a number of issues in the discussion forum, including whether or not the Dalai Lama "banned" outright Dorje Shugden worship; whether or not Dorje Shugden, Kelsang Gyatso, or the Dalai Lama are emanations of the Buddha; and (naturally) whether or not propitiating Dorje Shugden is a "legitimate" Buddhist practice. What follows is a posting from a Shugden supporter regarding the content of the Dorje Shugden entry:

> User: Kt66 is not fit to edit any article concerning the Buddhist Deity Dorje Shugden, the New Kadampa Tradition, its founder Geshe Kelsang Gyatso, or its lineage gurus. I move to seek a ban on this editor contributing further to these topics. He has made no secret of his identity, so it is not "outing" him here to refer, as evidence supporting my position, to his numerous blogs, websites and forum contributions across the www [World Wide Web] promoting his view on this topic. He has stated his intention to "warn" the world about the evils of this cult/these practices/these individuals. It is clear, therefore, that he has *no interest in contributing simple, factual content to these topics in this encyclopedia*—his aim is solely to promote his own POV [point of view]. The sheer volume of his highly opinionated and selectively-referenced work throughout the www undermines his claims to neutrality and provides some evidence for a charge of obsession on his part.[28]

This statement gives an example of the ongoing debate in cyberspace regarding the Dorje Shugden practice and also showcases the issue that many critics have regarding Wikipedia in general, that anonymous individuals with their own agendas are writing supposedly neutral articles on topics awash in controversy and historical revisionism.

Examination of these websites reveals that the Dorje Shugden conflict can serve as a mirror, reflecting the diverse viewpoints of Tibetan Buddhists (both ethnic Tibetans and Westerners). The cyberspace medium further illuminates how the Shugden controversy functions as a lens through which one may grasp the transcendence of Tibetan Buddhist sectarianism through the boundaries of the Tibetan diaspora.

The current incarnation of the Shugden conflict is so significant and complex because of the combination of the circumstances in exile and the involvement of Westerners in the dispute. The different cultural context of liberal Western society has added a new dimension to the debate, as each side has co-opted Western "foot soldiers" to support their perspectives. The Western interpretation of the guru-disciple relationship in Tibetan Buddhism has not only complicated the development of Tibetan Buddhism in the West but also exacerbated sectarian conflict among the four traditions, both in the West and in Asia. These elements have influenced the evolution of the Shugden conflict. The use of Western rhetoric in the dispute and the proliferation of inflammatory websites among the cyber *sangha* have also fueled the intensification and perpetuation of the issue. The spread of the Shugden controversy in the West and the influence of Westerners on the course of the dispute has, therefore, transformed the stakes of this conflict. The resolution of the Shugden dispute is essential not only for the future of solidarity within the Tibetan community but also for the global development of Tibetan Buddhism.

NOTES

1. Georges Dreyfus, "The Shuk-den Affair: Origins of a Controversy" (retrieved from the website of the Tibetan government in exile, www.tibet.com, April 6, 1999); see also Dreyfus (2005, 174).
2. Zemey Rinpoche, "The Yellow Book," post #567, posted by "Henry" in the E-sangha Tibetan Buddhism forum under the subtopic heading of "New Kadampa Tradition," April 18, 2005 (retrieved from the Buddhist website E-sangha, www.lioncity.net/Buddhism, November 30, 2006).

3. "Points of the Kashag's Statement Concerning Dolgyal," May 31, 1996 (retrieved from the website of the Tibetan government in exile, www.tibet.com, on January 7, 2006). See also "His Holiness the Dalai Lama's Response to Media: A Question on Shugden at the Press Conference in Indianapolis," August 16, 1999 (retrieved from the website of the Tibetan government in exile, www.tibet.com, January 7, 2006).
4. Tibetan Studies Press Office, "Background Reports: Tibet in Exile" (retrieved from www.tibet-internal.com, October 26, 2005).
5. John Goetz, "On the Outs," *NOW* 17, no. 21 (1998) (retrieved from the website of *NOW* magazine, www.nowtoronto.com, April 25, 2005).
6. Georges Dreyfus, interview with the author, January 27, 2006.
7. Deepak Thapa, "It's Dalai Lama vs. Shugden," *Himal South Asia Magazine* (September 1996) (retrieved from the website of *Himal South Asia Magazine*, www.himalmag.com/96sep, February 3, 2008).
8. Ibid.
9. Ibid.
10. Amalia Rubin, interview with the author, February 6, 2006.
11. Colman Jones, "Spiritual Split," *NOW* 17, no. 21 (1998) (retrieved from the website of *NOW* magazine, www.nowtoronto.com, April 25, 2005).
12. Tenzin Gyatso, H.H. the Fourteenth Dalai Lama, "Concerning Dholgyal with Reference to the Views of Past Masters and Other Related Matters," speech, Dharamsala, October 1997 (retrieved from the website of the Office of the Dalai Lama, www.dalailama.com, June 27, 2006); Tenzin Gyatso, H.H. the Fourteenth Dalai Lama, "Speech by His Holiness the 14th Dalai Lama to the Second Gelug Conference," Dharamsala, December 6, 2000 (retrieved from the website of the Office the Dalai Lama, www.dalailama.com, June 27, 2006).
13. "His Holiness the Dalai Lama's Response to Media: A Question on Shugden at the Press Conference in Indianapolis," August 16, 1999 (retrieved from the website of the Tibetan government in exile, www.tibet.com, January 7, 2006).
14. Don Lattin, "Feud Divides Tibetan Buddhists: Dalai Lama Angers Deity's Devotees," June 6, 1997 (retrieved from the website of the World Tibet Network News, www.tibet.ca, January 26, 2006).

15. Italics mine. Geshe Kelsang Gyatso, "Open Letter to H.H. the Dalai Lama," December 9, 1997 (retrieved from the website of CESNUR, Center for Studies on New Religions, www.cesnur.org, October 26, 2005).
16. TibetInfoNet, "Sowing Dissent and Undermining the Dalai Lama," May 21, 2008 (retrieved from the website of TibetInfoNet, www.tibetinfo.net, July 24, 2008).
17. "21st Century Buddhist Dictator: The Dalai Lama," from a booklet handed out at demonstrations protesting the Dalai Lama in April 2008 entitled *The Tibetan Situation Today: Surprising Hidden News* (p. 14). The booklet is available online at http://www.westernshugdensociety.org/files/tibetan_situation.pdf.
18. Tony Clifton, "Did an Obscure Tibetan Sect Murder Three Monks Close to the Dalai Lama?" *Newsweek*, April 28, 1997 (retrieved from the website of CESNUR, Center for Studies on New Religions, www.cesnur.org, October 26, 2005).
19. Colman Jones, "Spiritual Split," *NOW* 17, no. 21 (1998) (retrieved from the website of *NOW* magazine, www.nowtoronto.com, April 25, 2005).
20. http://groups.yahoo.com/group/Kadampa-Buddhism-Forum; http://google.groups.com/groups/alt.religion.buddhism.nkt.
21. www.facebook.com/wisdombuddha; www.twitter.com/wisdombud dha.
22. "Free Dorje Shugden!" (retrieved from www.myspace.com/dorjeshugden, November 18, 2006).
23. "Disrobed?" Posted by "Youlo," April 8, 2004, in Buddhist message forum, "What Is Wrong with Tibetan Society?" (retrieved from www.phayul.com/forums, January 15, 2006). I have edited this quotation for grammar and spelling mistakes to make for easier reading.
24. E-sangha homepage, www.e-sangha.com.
25. "Announcement: ALL MEMBERS READ—New Rules Effective 02-02-09," posted by "Dorje Shedrub" (Founding Member/Contributor) on the E-sangha homepage under "Messages for Guests and Visitors," www.lioncity.net/Buddhism/index (retrieved February 20, 2009).
26. Wikipedia, main page, http://en.wikipedia.org/wiki/Main_Page. Wikipedia has been the subject of its own controversy in recent years. The fact that anyone can edit the encyclopedia entries has

resulted in some minor scandals. This topic has been discussed in depth on the H-Asia list-serve by scholars, professors, and teachers of Asian history. See H-Net's December 2005 thread "Further Comment on Wikipedia," http://h-net.msu.edu/.

27. "Wikipedia" entry, http://en.wikipedia.org/wiki/Wikipedia.
28. "Atisha's cook" regarding "Kt66 POV" on Wikipedia: "Talk: Dorje Shugden" discussion forum, January 16, 2009, http://en.wikipedia.org/wiki/Talk:Dorje_Shugden (retrieved February 20, 2009). I have edited punctuation and spelling errors in this quotation in order to facilitate ease of reading.

SIX

Zen at a Distance

Isolation and the Development of Distant Membership

HELEN J. BARONI

In his portrait of Buddhism in America in the nineteenth and early twentieth centuries, Thomas Tweed quoted from a letter written by a young American Buddhist convert living in Vermillion, South Dakota, to a Buddhist priest in San Francisco: "You cannot know how utterly alone I have felt during the past years . . . knowing of no other person in America attempting to follow the teachings of the Lord Buddha, and how I desire to be of service to his cause." Tweed observes that this young man was perhaps among the most isolated of American converts or sympathizers at that time, since most of the others lived in a few urban areas (Tweed 1992, 44). Approximately ninety years later, in 1988, a woman living in a remote region of Wyoming wrote to Robert Aitken asking his advice regarding her practice. She explained that she had attempted to practice *zazen* on her own for twenty-five years without the benefit of a teacher or a *sangha*. She had recently read *Taking the Path of Zen* (1982), Aitken's most popular book, and found it quite helpful for her practice. She continued: "In all the time spent pursuing the idea of Zen, which seems to ideally suit my mind type, I have yet to meet face to face another human being who is of the same bent. My family and acquaintances are all Mormons or Baptists or don't seem to give a damn." It would almost seem that little had changed for American Buddhists and Buddhist sympathizers living outside the same few urban areas.

Despite the rapid growth in Zen centers and smaller meditation groups that characterized the development of Zen in America during the last three decades of the twentieth century, isolation remains an issue for many Buddhist sympathizers and solo practitioners in America. Distant correspondents who wrote to Robert Aitken, founder of Honolulu Diamond Sangha (hereafter, HDS),[1] throughout the same time period continued to raise concerns about their feelings of isolation from a Zen group or teacher. This chapter first identifies the major causes of this isolation, which go beyond simple geographical considerations and include factors such as physical disabilities, limitations caused by financial and family constraints, as well as self-imposed forms of isolation. It then discusses Aitken's programmatic response to the problem of isolation, which he experienced in the early years of his own Zen practice and which he regarded as a critical issue for the growth of Zen in America.

The chapter argues that Aitken experimented with possible solutions to the problem of isolation, developing styles of response that suited both the particular circumstances faced by individual correspondents as well as the changing landscape of Zen in America. Throughout his professional career as a Zen teacher and into retirement, Aitken carried out a letter writing program, a Zen ministry by mail. One of Aitken's primary goals for this program was to facilitate the transition of his correspondents from isolated sympathizers or solo practitioners to active members, affiliated in some capacity with a Zen center or group, not necessarily HDS. The chapter describes Aitken's experimentation with different forms of distance teaching, which eventually led him to propose a fully developed pattern of Distant Membership designed to suit the majority of isolated correspondents.

This chapter is part of a larger study of the correspondence between Robert Aitken and his Distant Correspondents.[2] The letters used for the study are found in the Robert Baker Aitken Papers, an archive housed at the Hamilton Library at the University of Hawaii.[3] These letters reveal the beliefs and practices of American Buddhist sympathizers and solo practitioners.[4] The category of "Distant Correspondents"[5] used here includes individuals introduced to Zen through means such as publications and university classes, who have little or no direct experience practicing with a Zen community or with a teacher. It also includes individuals who previously practiced at a Zen center with a teacher but now practice Zen on their own. The larger study explores the concerns that these individuals bring to bear in their letters written to a recognized American Zen teacher, the understanding of Zen practice and the image of the "Zen master" implicit in their letters, and the responses the letters elicited from Aitken himself. In this chapter, I am only concerned with the issue of isolation raised by Distant Correspondents and how this problem contributed to the creation of an alternative form of Zen affiliation in America that I call Distant Membership.

DISTANT PARTICIPATION IN TRANSLOCAL BUDDHIST NETWORKS

In describing the development of the term "translocal" in historical studies of non-European cultures, Volker Gottowik explains that scholarly usage of the term places the emphasis "not on crossing national boundaries [as the term transnational implies], but on overcoming spatial differences. In this context, it is stressed that there are many borders, inside and outside the nation state, which are likewise important. There is rather a multiplicity of borders, which are not necessarily political, but economic, social, religious, etc." (Gottowik 2010, 180–181). Buddhist solo practitioners and sympathizers, represented here by Aitken's Distant Correspondents, encounter numerous borders to be crossed before they can engage in the style of Buddhist practice that they would find appropriate. As Gottowik intimates, the borders include economic, social, and religious factors that may present themselves as obstacles to the actors involved.

Not all borders are crossed physically. The Distant Correspondents made their initial crossings via the written word through published materials and the exchange of letters. Through their reading and experimentation, they participated in a translocal movement of Buddhism as presented in popular writings about Zen. Aitken, for his part, made an effort to build bridges across these same borders, first through his published writings and then through his letters. He invited his correspondents to participate in the developing network of Zen practice centers and thus experience the benefits of affiliation with a living *sangha*. If nothing else, he offered them the tenuous connection as Distant Members in the growing network of Honolulu Diamond Sangha and affiliated centers.

ROBERT AITKEN AND HONOLULU DIAMOND SANGHA

Robert Aitken founded Honolulu Diamond Sangha, in 1959, as a small Zen meditation group without a resident teacher. In the early years, Aitken and his wife Anne acted as "first among equals," leading a small group of interested individuals for biweekly *zazenkai* (seated meditation meetings). Throughout the first fifteen years of HDS's history, the Aitkens invited a series of Zen teachers from Japan to visit, lead *sesshin* (intensive meditation retreat), and provide guidance in *kōan* practice. In some cases, teachers stayed for an extended period of time, and, in other cases, more prominent teachers came to guide a single *sesshin*, usually in transit between Japan and the mainland of the United States. In these early years, Aitken continued to pursue his own Zen training, both in Hawaii and during extended visits to Japan.

Matters changed significantly for HDS in 1974, when Aitken received permission to teach independently from Kōun Yamada, then the leader of Sanbōkyōdan, a lay Zen movement headquartered in Kamakura, Japan. Aitken later received full designation as a Dharma heir and Zen master from Yamada in 1986. Under Aitken's leadership, HDS flourished throughout the 1980s and 1990s and began to establish a number of affiliated groups located on the mainland United States, as well as in Australia, New Zealand, and Latin America. HDS remained affiliated with Sanbōkyōdan until 1995, when it became an independent American Zen lineage. Most of the HDS-affiliated groups likewise split from Sanbōkyōdan and are now regarded as independent centers within Aitken's Diamond Sangha lineage.

As an offshoot from Sanbōkyōdan and later as an independent lineage, Honolulu Diamond Sangha developed as a part of a transnational and translocal movement of Zen. HDS served as a pivot point, bringing together Japanese Zen teachers with individuals from all over the world who came to join in *sesshin* in Honolulu. Aitken himself embodied the translocal process of spreading Zen outside of Asia, first by traveling between Hawaii and Japan for training and later by visiting far-flung Zen communities in the United States, Australia, and New Zealand as a teacher in his own right. His writings widely extended Aitken's outreach beyond the confines of established and nascent Zen centers to individual Buddhist sympathizers living throughout the English-speaking world.

Aitken's second major book, *Taking the Path of Zen*, appeared in 1982, and quickly became popular among Zen students and sympathizers. Presented as a guide for beginners in Zen meditation, it came to be used by countless Zen practitioners and sympathizers as the basis for experimentation and exploration of the practice of *zazen*. Hundreds of these individuals wrote to Aitken to request his advice.

ISOLATION FROM A TEACHER OR *SANGHA*

During the last decades of the twentieth century, America experienced a rapid growth in the number of Zen centers and smaller meditation groups. The first enduring Zen institutions in the United States were founded in Hawaii in the early twentieth century to serve growing communities of Japanese and Japanese American Buddhists. Between 1900 and 1969, a total of twenty-two Zen temples and centers were established. The data displayed in table 6.1 show the growth in the number of new Buddhist centers from 1970 through 1997. This growth matches the increase in the number of letters that Aitken received from Distant Correspondents over approximately the same time period, shown in table 6.2. While one could surmise that the growth in Zen centers would reduce the problem of isolation faced by solo practitioners, as many as 40 percent of the Distant Correspondents continued to regard isolation as a serious concern well into the 1990s.

TABLE 6.1. Zen Institutions in the United States

Years	*New sites*	*Percentage of total sites by 1997*	*Cumulative number of sites*
1900–1969	22	10%	22
1970–1974	31	14%	53
1975–1979	22	10%	75
1980–1984	28	13%	103
1985–1989	40	18%	143
1990–1994	51	24%	194
1995–1997	23	11%	217

TABLE 6.2. Distribution of Letters through Time

Years	*Number of individuals writing letters*	*Percentage of total letter writers by 2001*
1968–1974	6	2%
1975–1979	30	12%
1980–1984	48	19%
1985–1989	69	27%
1990–1994	67	26%
1995–2001	31	12%
No date	7	3%

Some of Aitken's Distant Correspondents seem to have written simply to make contact with an actual living Buddhist. Many of them, like the woman from Wyoming, had never had the opportunity to meet a practicing Buddhist, let alone a teacher. They appear to have been seeking the encouragement of human contact. In December 1987, a man from Texas wrote in his second letter to Aitken that although he had been reading about Zen for four years, he never had "any contact with anyone actually practicing it before [receiving] your letter." He found it tremendously encouraging "just knowing someone is out there." Aitken responded warmly with advice about locating a meditation group in his area and invited him to continue writing. "I have a huge correspondence, but I get to each letter eventually."

While only thirty of the 261 Distant Correspondents explicitly discussed problems arising from a sense of isolation from a Zen teacher or from a community of like-minded practitioners, the issue seems to be lurking just beneath the surface in many more of the letters. Isolation appears to have been a factor, for example, in an additional thirty-three cases in which the Distant Correspondent requested assistance in finding a possible teacher or *sangha* within a specific geographical area or requested permission to become Aitken's student and relocate to Hawaii. When one considers additional factors, such as the circumstances faced by Buddhist prison inmates (eighteen cases) and the sometimes self-imposed isolation of former members of Zen centers (twenty-two cases) who wrote to Aitken before they were ready to accept a new teacher, the number of "isolated" individuals grows to 106, nearly 40 percent.

The most common reason that Distant Correspondents said they felt isolated was their geographical distance from a Zen center or meditation group. Forty-five individuals mentioned either their physical distance from a teacher or Zen center or requested information about a teacher or center in their general vicinity. In some regions, the situation changed over the years, and new possibilities opened up where none had existed previously. In 1977, for example, Aitken remarked to a man living in Fort Worth, "Texas is a wasteland for Zen activity." A decade or so later, he would begin recommending that his correspondents get in touch with Rubin Habito at Maria Kannon Zen Center in Houston and Pat Hawk, one of his own Dharma heirs, then at Empty Sky Zen Center in Amarillo.

In a few cases, correspondents revealed that their apparent proximity to a Zen center based on simple distance in miles was rendered irrelevant by other factors such as the quality of the roads and the weather. A man living in Leavenworth, Washington, reasonably close to Seattle in good weather, explained that his mobility was limited for much of the year because "for 7 months of the year we have 8–10 feet of snow. We get our mail by walking with snow shoes for 2½ miles." An individual living in the mountains near Taos, New Mexico, described a similar experience of isolation during the winter months.

Nor is it always practical for individuals living in less remote areas to travel relatively short distances to the nearest big city or town to attend weekly *zazenkai*. Several Distant Correspondents indicated that they were limited in their ability to travel due to their own physical or emotional disabilities (five cases), their responsibilities for caregiving to children or ailing family members (four cases), or for financial reasons (five cases).

Several of the Distant Correspondents discussed problems of isolation resulting from physical or emotional disabilities. A woman living in New Mexico indicated that she had been practicing Zen for about seventeen years and in recent years usually sat alone. Since reading *Taking the Path of Zen* two years previously, she had taken up the Mu *kōan*, still working without a teacher. She requested Aitken's "guidance for my practice. I know the student usually goes to the *roshi*, but I have MS." Her first question related directly to practice: "Does one concentrate on Mu or on the question, 'Does a dog have the Buddha Nature?'" Aitken responded, "I was moved to learn that you are persevering with *zazen* despite your poor health and chronic pain." He encouraged her to "remember you are sitting with earnest Zen students everywhere" and assured her, "The relief you feel on experiencing no-self is an unmistakable clue that you are on the right road. Persevere. Breathe MU."

Another case of a man living in rural England seems to combine various forms of isolation including geographic limitation, caregiving, and other emotional concerns. He identified himself as a publisher who had practiced Zen for approximately twenty years. He originally traveled regularly to participate in Zen meetings and *sesshin*, but this caused friction in his marriage, so his participation dwindled. His life eventually became more constrained because his wife suffered from bouts of depression and more recently cancer. He felt that he could no longer leave her even for brief periods to pursue his practice. Eventually, he found himself struggling with his own depression and alcoholism and facing a new sense of urgency to practice. "I was desperate for understanding of why we are born? why we die? In the midst of this I was totally isolated, utterly alone, and in need, and still am of spiritual company." Having joined AA, he stopped drinking and was able to engage in *zazen* once again, up to thirty minutes daily. "Just sitting doesn't seem to be helping me get the answers I want. What am I doing wrong? What do I need to do? I have considered founding a group and bringing in a teacher. There is no one here who could fulfill the role of master." Aitken's reply unfortunately is not preserved in the file, although the man's subsequent note of thanks indicated that he found whatever advice it contained quite helpful.

Several Distant Correspondents planned to take matters into their own hands to alleviate their sense of isolation. Some asked Aitken's advice on how to proceed with founding a Zen group on their own. Numerous others indicated that they were determined to relocate in order to be near a Zen teacher and center, requesting permission to move to Hawaii or asking for recommendations for teachers on the mainland. One man writing from Alaska indicated, "What would be helpful now would be some specific direction in conducting *zazenkai* for our little group. I feel the need for a little more structure and ritual in my practice, and that might be a start." Aitken sent him a copy of the sutra booklet used for chanting at HDS and suggested that they "could undertake a project as a way of giving yourselves definition as a *sangha*, such as prison visitation, hospice work, or whatever seems appropriate to your place and time." He recommended that they could also undertake a study project, reading Zen books that appealed to them and discussing them. To a young man writing from Miami, he affirmed, "You can form a *sangha* with one Zen friend." He recommended that they should agree on the length of time to sit and then use a kitchen timer so they would not need to watch the clock. He added that they could recite the Four Great Vows and read from a book such as *Zen Wave* (Aitken 1978) as part of their ritual.

A few individuals expressed a sense of isolation for reasons that appear unique to their situation; these cases may nonetheless reflect similar experiences of other solo practitioners. A woman writing from Texas in 1977 explained her preference for "mail-study" of Zen in the following terms: "I am considered a minority because of race; therefore, it seems important at this time for me to practice quietly-alone causing only personal vibrations. . . . Later, hopefully, I will gain more courage." Membership at most Zen centers, as at other non-ethnic Buddhist centers in the United States, was predominantly white at that time. Indeed, pictures from the period show that this was true even at HDS, located in perhaps the most racially diverse place in the United States, where Euro-Americans represent less than 30 percent of the population. As James Coleman (2001, 20) notes, this racial demographic is "a matter that has been of considerable concern to Buddhist leaders." This woman's hesitancy may indicate that there is more interest in Zen among minorities than membership numbers indicate. It would seem probable that other individuals would likewise feel uncomfortable joining and participating in an overwhelmingly white *sangha* and prefer instead to practice alone.

A clinical psychologist employed at a university in Arkansas as a student counselor faced a professional dilemma. He wrote to "seek advice or counsel on my practice, which is two 25-minute periods each day of breath counting. I know it is better to sit with others, but the problem here is that there are no Zen or even meditation groups in town, only contemplative prayer. I hesitate to start a group myself, since it could interfere with my work." He worried that some students would perhaps want to have contact with him outside of therapy, which could potentially cause problems. For others, his involvement with Zen could confuse them, "since Zen is so foreign in the Bible belt." While this situation may appear to be unique to this clinical psychologist working at a university in a region without a Zen center, it is suggestive of related types of professional and personal limitations experienced by other Zen solo practitioners and sympathizers. Among the Distant Correspondents, for example, a few Protestant ministers expressed concern that members of their congregation would be put off or even scandalized to learn of their minister's interest in practicing Zen. Several Distant Correspondents, especially prison inmates and people living in the so-called Bible Belt, indicated that there was still a stigma attached to practicing a religion other than Christianity well into the 1990s. As Jeff Wilson's essay (chap. 2 in this volume) demonstrates, American Buddhism is characterized by regionalism. Even today, despite the relative receptivity to Buddhism in many parts of American society, public participation in Zen practice can still entail too high a personal cost to be worth the benefits of communal practice.

A few of the Distant Correspondents who identified a sense of isolation as a difficulty in their practice mentioned their unhappiness with the options that existed nearby. A woman wrote from Cologne, Germany, that she was determined to improve her English so that she would be able to practice outside of Germany. She had been practicing Zen for twenty years with several well-known teachers, but she still felt a kind of isolation. She wished to meet with Aitken, either in Europe or the United States, to "get clear about that what I call Zen within me and I am at variance with." She explained that her Zen teachers in Germany were all priests and nuns, "and although they are kind father confessors, they do not correspond with Zen within myself and what I encounter in the sutras, Mumonkan and Biyanlu."[6]

A physics professor from a major research university in New Orleans described the Zen teacher he encountered at his local Zen center as "a hard-core Soto type," who belittled his desire for *kenshō* (an initial awakening experience) as contrary to the bodhisattva ideal.

> Is it wrong to want *kensho*? My question to you is, is it so wrong for me to focus at this stage on achieving some kind of opening? What should my (beginners) attitude towards my practice be after I have the more basic things down?
>
> I would like to know if you have any advice on how to find a compatible teacher. How should I balance my own unenlightened gut feelings with submission to the guidance of someone with so much more experience? How can I know,

> as an unenlightened person, if this lack of emphasis on kensho is just a different perspective, or is it just covering a lack of realization.

Thus, while some Distant Correspondents lived in cities with an existing Zen center, they did not necessarily find that the local option suited them, and American cities supporting multiple Zen centers remain a rarity.

While numerous Distant Correspondents made it clear that they could not afford to travel to Hawaii (or California, or Sydney, etc.) for *sesshin*, a handful mentioned that they could not even manage a visit to a Zen center in a neighboring region of the country. There are hints of this type of limitation in other letters in the archive, including those sent by Aitken's students not included in this study. Indeed, Aitken himself raised the issue of financial limitations far more often than did his Distant Correspondents. I suspect this is based on his long experience with the genuine financial struggles faced by many of his students.

Financial limitations rarely emerge in scholarly discussions of Zen practitioners in the West, and it appears that practitioners are generally assumed to be relatively wealthy. Coleman's research on what he calls "New Buddhism" in the West indicates that members of Buddhist centers do in fact enjoy above-average income levels (2001, 20). My research with the Distant Correspondents, on the other hand, suggests that one of the factors contributing to solo practitioners' sense of isolation relates to financial constraints. Monetary concerns may hinder a certain segment of the Buddhist solo practitioner and sympathizer population from ever joining a *sangha*, especially when combined with even minor geographic isolation. While individuals with sufficient disposable income find the travel necessary to maintain a form of Zen practice that includes regular *sesshin* in more or less distant locations within their financial reach, those with more limited income may be priced out of the market. Aitken himself raised the issue of financing one's practice quite often, warning people that they would need "a good cushion of dollars" if they planned to visit Hawaii for any length of time. In many cases, he had reason to doubt that his correspondents could afford even the modest price of a "corresponding membership" in HDS, much less the plane fare to participate in *sesshin* in another city.

CORRESPONDING MEMBERSHIP

Aitken understood that many would-be practitioners of Zen had no access to a Zen teacher. He therefore offered "counseling by mail" from the beginning of his teaching career. In 1974, newly designated as an independent teacher, he extended his first explicit invitation, offering this service along with his mailing address in the article "The Zen Buddhist Path of Self-Realization" (Aitken 1974). At about the same time, Aitken created the category of "Corresponding Membership" for HDS as an alternative for individuals who could not personally visit HDS but who wished to receive HDS publications and audio recordings and to consult with a Zen teacher.

In a letter composed in June 1977, Aitken described Corresponding Membership to a woman requesting "private instruction by mail" in the following manner:

> Corresponding membership, which includes the bulletin with my talks every other month and personal letter writing, is $20/year. For an additional $15, you get tapes periodically, about once a month—also *teisho*. . . . The measure of commitment expected is nil. The measure of commitment that you will need to get anywhere is something more than that. Positive possibilities of mail study are that I will answer your letters. Negative possibilities are that we can't strike the sparks at a distance that we can nose to nose in the interview room.

Aitken routinely waved the $20 membership fee for "personal letter writing" for individuals whom he judged could not afford the expense. In most of these cases, he offered to continue writing to them as a "Zen friend." On a few occasions, he took a further step and asked the HDS staff to provide complementary subscriptions to their newsletter and periodical publications.

Aitken eventually decided to abolish the "Corresponding Membership" category sometime around 1982. He explained his reasoning in a letter to a high school teacher who enquired whether or not the offer for "counseling by mail" that he saw in *What Is Meditation?* was still available seven years after the publication date. Aitken replied, "We discontinued the Corresponding Membership category because I wrote people whether or not they were members. Please write as often as you wish. I'll respond eventually." As his promise suggests, the decision to discontinue the membership category had no negative impact on his maintaining an extensive correspondence program.

Aitken consistently encouraged his Distant Correspondents to find a group, affiliate with a Zen center, and accept the guidance of a trustworthy Zen teacher, the same message found in *Taking the Path of Zen*, often in the same words. His constant refrain is that it is best to practice with others. As he wrote to one correspondent, "The real point of the practice is that the other is no other than myself. This is hard to realize if your practice is exclusively alone." He advised many correspondents that they could form their own tiny *sangha* with one Zen friend and reap the benefits of mutual support and greater motivation to maintain the practice.

Aitken's advice about joining a meditation group developed somewhat through time, as conditions changed in the broader society. In the early years, when Zen groups were few and far between, Aitken sometimes suggested that meditating with another kind of meditation group could also be beneficial. In a 1978 letter to a man living in the Philippines, for example, he distinguished the types of yoga meditation styles that could form "a good basis for later Zen practice" from those that would be "confusing" and best avoided. Such suggestions disappear from Aitken's letters after about 1985, when many more options for practice with a Zen group existed. He did, however, continue to recommend to individuals who practiced using the *kōan* Mu, typical of both Sanbōkyōdan-related groups and Rinzai groups, that sitting with a Soto Zen group, where *kōan* are less often used, could be beneficial.

While Aitken sought to support individuals who had no option but to practice Zen without a community or teacher, he nevertheless maintained that true practice requires the direction of a teacher. A high school teacher from Texas asked him about the viability of maintaining a solo practice and wondered what difference a teacher could make. "If everything is illusion, why bother?" Aitken responded firmly:

> There is no way anyone can study Zen without a teacher. You can learn to sit quietly and to reach a pleasant place in the inner world, but from my point of view, that is not true practice. As to the world being delusion, so why bother, the world

> is not delusion. The world is ephemeral. We are deluded when we think otherwise. . . . Only through zazen can the truths of the Dharma be realized.

Holding true to his conviction that Zen practice requires a teacher, Aitken sought to match his correspondents with possible Zen centers. Whenever possible, he conveyed specific suggestions for contacting a teacher or Zen center in the individual's general vicinity, complete with names, addresses, and phone numbers. In the earliest period, when few centers existed, he often recommended that Distant Correspondents subscribe to the publications and newsletters of several distant centers, including the Honolulu Diamond Sangha, Zen Center of Los Angeles, and San Francisco Zen Center, while simultaneously scoping out the possibility that a local meditation group already existed. He recommended contacting an academic Department of Religion or Department of Philosophy at a nearby university or college, since professors who teach about Buddhism often have information regarding local meditation groups, many of which meet on or near college campuses. Aitken eventually began to recommend HDS-affiliated groups as well as his own Dharma heirs. Some well-known teachers and centers are conspicuously absent from his list of recommendations. Aitken stated in a few letters that in good conscience he could only recommend those teachers that he personally knew and trusted.

Aitken regarded solo practice as difficult at best, although he recognized that for some individuals it remains the only viable option, at least for periods of time. For these individuals, Aitken sought to minimize their sense of isolation with the encouragement that, even when they sit alone, they should bear in mind that they sit *zazen* with all living beings. As he said to a man living in rural Oklahoma, "When you sit, remember you are sitting with everyone here at Diamond Sangha, and everyone in the whole world. There is no such thing as isolated practice." To a woman limited by a physical disability, he remarked, "Remember you are sitting with earnest Zen students everywhere."

In the early years, Aitken experimented with the possibility of conducting *dokusan*-style exchanges via conventional mail. He undertook one such relationship with a geographically isolated Distant Correspondent in November 1975. The student appears to have made some significant progress in his practice and had passed at least one or two *kōan* cases.[7] After a year of exchanges, Aitken called off the experiment.

"Mail and the written word just don't do it. Not your fault or mine. Your experience will keep. I suggest that you continue with Mu—this is my koan too, after I have completed koan study. Only Mu." Aitken continued to correspond with the student for many years, but thereafter they only undertook *dokusan* face to face when they met at *sesshin*. A year later, Aitken informed another correspondent, "I have experimented with doing *dokusan* (personal interviews) by mail, and somehow it doesn't work."

Aitken clearly recognized the limitations in conducting counseling via written exchange alone. He sometimes expressed his written recommendations in tentative terms, explaining that without the benefit of personal contact to back up his impression of a situation, he could not speak with full confidence. When writing to a woman experiencing serious physical manifestations of violent shaking during *zazen*, for example, he suggested that she experiment using a focus, such as breath counting. He then explained that he was "not making this as a firm suggestion, because we are not working face to face." In another case, he closed his letter to a correspondent seeking "a new way to practice and a new teacher" with an apology. "All this is counseling at long distance. I am not able to look at your face and eyes, so I may be in error. If so, please forgive me. I do hope you can find ease of mind and body."

DISTANT MEMBERSHIP

Aitken's advice for individuals living and practicing in isolation eventually became standardized, as is exemplified by the following exchange from 1995. The Distant Correspondent, an individual from Alabama who had maintained a solo practice for ten years, asked, "1. How can I sustain my practice in this situation? 2. Can I modify my practice in a way to increase its efficacy?" Aitken responded,

> 1. Sit down with the consciousness that you are sitting with everyone and everything everywhere. 2. Attend *sesshins* with good teachers when you can. The nearest to you is Pat Hawk in Amarillo . . . [provides telephone number]. Call him and get a schedule. Don't write, it will take too long. 3. Read some each day. Widen your reading of Zen books by browsing in a good bookstore or library and choosing those that interest you.

Although the student asked only two questions, Aitken added the third point about reading, an item he routinely included on his agenda of recommendations for improving one's Zen practice.

I have chosen to refer to this form of Zen affiliation as Distant Membership, because Aitken sometimes encouraged isolated correspondents to regard themselves as "distant members of Diamond Sangha." The label Distant Member likewise suits the pattern of long-distance affiliation that Aitken came to recommend for solo practitioners with the freedom and financial means to travel. The pattern Aitken recommended came to invariably include the following suggestions: (1) The Distant Member should continue to practice *zazen* as regularly as he or she could manage, preferably at least once a day. (2) The individual should seek out communal support somewhere in their immediate geographical vicinity and attend group meditation sessions, ideally once or twice a week. Aitken routinely commented that in some cases this would entail finding a single "Zen friend" with whom to sit with once a week. (3) The Distant Member would need to establish a teacher-student relationship with a qualified teacher whom they could trust. (4) Finally, a Distant Member would need to travel to attend *sesshin* with their teacher at least once a year.

CONCLUSIONS

Concerns related to isolation stand out as the most critical problem identified by the Distant Correspondents as a limiting factor for their ongoing practice. Their concerns in this regard provide a significant counterpoint to many previous studies of Buddhism in America. By stressing the rapid growth of interest in the tradition in the late twentieth century, existing studies create the impression that most if not all Americans enjoy access to a Buddhist community and teacher. The Distant Correspondents testify that this is not the case. In addition, the present study highlights related problems such as financial constraint and family obligations that compound geographical distance in limiting access for many sympathizers and solo practitioners to ordinary affiliation with a Buddhist community—issues that have previously received little attention.

It is possible that steadily growing access to the Internet has ameliorated the sense of isolation expressed by many of the Distant

Correspondents in their now old-fashioned paper letters. In the last decade, more and more people feel comfortable participating in "virtual" interactions with like-minded people. Anyone with Internet access, however isolated, can participate in any number of virtual Buddhist communities on sites such as Second Life. Some individuals seem now to regard membership in a virtual community as an adequate substitute for participation in face-to-face interactions. In light of these changes, it would be fascinating to see whether or not concerns related to isolation continue to be raised in email exchanges with Buddhist teachers. Would one find clearer generational differences, for example?

It would likewise be fascinating to learn if innovative practices such as "doku-phone" taken up by some of Aitken's successors since the late 1990s are proving to be more effective than Aitken's early experiments with *dokusan* by mail. Although I have not confirmed that they are using video technology, one can imagine that some Zen teachers are conducting *dokusan* via Skype, thus allowing for visual contact and nonverbal means of expression. As we progress through the early decades of the twenty-first century, Zen teachers and practitioners may need to redefine what they mean by "face-to-face encounters."

NOTES

1. The group now officially known as Honolulu Diamond Sangha has had several names throughout the years. In the early days, it was named simply Diamond Sangha, although people often referred instead to one or the other of its primary sites of practice, Koko An Zendo, located in Honolulu, and Maui Zendo. In recent years, Diamond Sangha refers to the whole network of affiliated Zen centers in the United States and abroad, while the name Honolulu Diamond Sangha was adopted for the sites on Oahu, including Koko An (before it closed) and the new temple located in Palolo Valley.
2. Please see my full-length study, Baroni (2012).
3. The full collection comprises all written materials saved by Aitken over several decades, including extensive personal correspondence, HDS records from his tenure as director and teacher, HDS newsletters, drafts of Aitken's unpublished sermons and talks, as well as copies of his published materials.

4. Tweed (1999) suggests the inclusion and importance of this category for the study of Buddhism.
5. The category of "Distant Correspondent" was not created by Aitken himself but by the author. In defining the larger study, I made a distinction between the extensive correspondence Aitken maintained with his students, colleagues, family, and personal friends and his correspondence with individuals who wrote to him as strangers. Aitken referred to this latter category of correspondence as part of his "writing program." I refer to it here and elsewhere as his Zen ministry by mail.
6. The correspondent refers here to two famous collections of *kōan*, the *Mumonkan* (Ch. *Wumenguan*) and the *Biyanlu* (Jpn. *Hekiganroku*). They are not sutras but classical texts from the Zen tradition in China.
7. It is impossible to be more specific, because the file has been edited to remove the successful *dokusan* exchanges. Aitken submitted his entire archive unedited except in the rare cases such as this when *kōan* work was conducted via mail.

SECTION III

FREE-FLOATING DHARMA DISCOURSES

Scholars have long noted that Buddhism has permeated the broader American cultural landscape; there have been fewer direct studies of these types of movement. Each of the contributions to this section highlights the manner in which Buddhist ideas have become either partially or fully emancipated from a Buddhist institutional context.

Richard Hughes Seager discusses developments in the art world resulting from Buddhism's permeation into broader popular culture. He explores the use of Buddhist ideas and iconography by both Buddhist and non-Buddhist artists, highlighting the ways in which Dharma images are used in different manners by Buddhist practitioners within Buddhist communities, on the one hand, and contemporary American artists on the other. The latter draw on what he calls "free-floating Dharma discourses" or "eclectic, free-floating, book, art, and culture-generated discourse about Buddhism and others Asian religions." These Dharma discourses circulate in popular culture, independent of practice communities, and underscore the ability of Buddhist ideas to become unmoored from specific religious social settings to be appropriated by individuals in the pursuit of self-expression.

Kimberly Beek examines the production of an emerging Buddhist literature in the United States, which she argues may be fruitfully viewed as a new American literary genre. It can be distinguished from other American literary forms that may include Buddhist elements by the centrality of Buddhist themes. This emergent literature underscores the growing influence of Buddhist ideas in American culture.

In her contribution to the section, Mira Niculescu focuses on a Buddhist practice that has been emancipated from the category of "Buddhism" altogether. Once domesticated and secularized in the broader US culture, "mindfulness" meditation could be appropriated into Jewish traditions where, she argues, it has taken on a new form, divorced entirely from Buddhism. This work further pushes the boundaries of our subject of study and asks us to reimagine the category of Buddhism itself.

SEVEN

Dharma Images and Identity in American Buddhism

RICHARD HUGHES SEAGER

The critical study of American Buddhism has been taken up by scholars in a number of disciplines in religious studies. These include Buddhologists trained in textual studies in one or another Asian tradition, Americanists working out of the historiography of the religious history of the United States, and social scientists who approach Buddhism primarily in terms of the dynamics of immigration. This diversity of academic points of view makes for a rich, if uneven, body of critical literature, most of which focuses on new organizations within Euro-American or Asian American communities and how Buddhists are adapting Asian traditions to the West. While the study of Western and American Buddhism remains a new field of inquiry, academics and other observers have developed an increasingly nuanced understanding of its institutional and ideological landscape over the last two decades.

In this essay I step back from a tight focus on religious groups to take a more panoramic look at the use of Buddhist and Buddhism-inspired images. Dharma images have been used frequently in advertising, popular media and the arts, and in and around Buddhist practice communities. But as far as I know, there has been little sustained interpretation of what role these images play in the movement of Buddhism beyond its original Asian borders. I explore this question by sketching in an argument about the distinctive ways in which images function in two different American communities. In particular, I am interested in how Dharma images are used by practitioners, on one hand, and by creative artists, on the other, and what the contrast in their respective uses may suggest about what it means to be a Buddhist in contemporary American society.

Briefly stated, my central thesis is that a useful distinction can be made between those Americans who use Dharma images for religious practice in community and those who use them as vehicles for artistic self-expression. For the first group, Buddhist images are markers of religious identity. In the second, they signify creativity and individuality expressed in the production of art. Mary Douglas's *Natural Symbols* is helpful here (Douglas 1970). Among both Asian American and Euro-American practitioners, Dharma images resemble what Douglas calls "condensed symbols." Condensed symbols communicate highly complex religious and philosophical data that are readily understood within cohesive communities. Their meaning need not be self-consciously articulated because they are embedded in a "restricted code," a discourse grounded in communities that share basic assumptions about meaning, social organization, and spiritual aspiration, in this case immigrant and convert Buddhist practice groups. In contrast, artists tend to treat Dharma images as what Douglas calls "diffuse symbols." These are also data-rich but require considerable interpretation—an "elaborated code"—because they are highly personalized and are produced in more loosely jointed social groups, in this case the art world.

To begin to develop my argument, I need to take the discussion back five or so decades before the number of American Buddhist organizations began to grow rapidly around 1970, when Buddhist institutions were still largely confined to old-line Chinese and Japanese immigrant communities. Among Euro-Americans, Buddhism had been trickling into the United States for over a century by way of texts such as Paul Carus's *The Gospel of Buddha* (1894) and Dwight Goddard's *A Buddhist Bible* (1938). Many Americans also encountered Buddhism, particularly Zen, through literary expressions such as the *haiku*, practices such as martial arts and the tea ceremony, and through interest in Asian architecture and the fine arts. At that time, Buddhism was usually understood within a generalized image of Asian or oriental religions. Permeable boundaries existed among traditions like Hinduism, Buddhism, and Taoism and their practices and arts, which fostered a kind of pan-Asian spirituality in the West with a long and complex history. Much of this earlier interest in Asian religions reflected the influence of Romanticism with its emphasis on spiritual selfhood as expressed in philosophy, literature, and art.

This eclectic, free-floating, book, art, and culture-generated discourse about Buddhism and other Asian religions reached a kind of culmination in the literary output of Jack Kerouac, Allen Ginsberg, Alan Watts, and others now associated with the Beat generation. For a time, the Beats, despite their eclectic orientation, were understood to be the quintessential expression of American Buddhism. But as Beat gradually morphed into Hip, the situation changed rapidly. Over the course of the 1970s and 1980s, many counterculturists began to take up the practice of Buddhism in face-to-face relations with Asian teachers from different nations, cultures, schools, and lineages. Among these mostly Euro-American seekers, the generalized Asian image began to wane as their knowledge increased about Zen schools, Vajrayana lineages, *vipassanā* meditation techniques, and other elements of Asia-based sectarian systems. The earlier, eclectic Dharma discourse began to give way to a new one grounded in Euro-American Buddhist practice communities. Around the same time, the new immigration also fostered the flourishing of Buddhist immigrant organizations grounded in a wide range of sectarian and regional traditions. In both communities, the process of Buddhist institution building was well underway by 1990, even as terms like "Asian religion," "Buddhism," and "Zen" continued to possess a powerful, but highly generalized, spiritual cachet in Western and American popular culture.

It is against this background that I want to develop a two-part argument about the use of Dharma images and other traditional forms drawn from Asian Buddhist traditions. The first part of my argument is that Buddhists in both Asian American and Euro-American communities display a comparable regard for images. Wendy Cadge has argued that there is an ongoing convergence between these two communities despite fundamental differences between them in terms of worldview, tradition, demographics, and institutional history. For instance, converts have begun to adopt paraliturgical rituals to enhance seated mediation, while immigrants have incorporated meditation into their congregational practice. Both communities tend to appeal to an educated clientele, emphasize the leadership role played by laypeople, and increasingly conduct both the religious and administrative business of the community in English (Cadge 2005).

I suggest that the essentially religious use of images is another convergence between the two communities, even if immigrants and converts approach Buddhist visual culture from very different directions.

In Asian American communities, the use of images is directly related to the traditional immigrant strategy of transplanting myths, rituals, aesthetics, and institutions to the United States to re-create the ethos of the homeland, a complex social process that spans generations. Temple architecture and decoration, ritual paraphernalia, Buddha statues and images, and graphics in community publications are often highly articulated and reflect the styles and forms of sectarian and regional traditions in Asia. The essentially conservative nature of this task was central to the old argument against immigrants as a source of an authentic American Buddhism.

In contrast, most Euro-Americans were first exposed to generally Asian and specifically Buddhist forms and images in the free-floating, book, art, and culture Dharma discourse that prevailed through the early 1960s. Originally the object of spiritual curiosity and aesthetic appreciation, Dharma images took on new meanings as converts began to use them in practice and to embellish their new institutions. Over the course of a few decades, Buddha and bodhisattva images, *gohonzons*, *tangkas* and mandalas, *stūpas* and *kuṭīs*, and a wide range of ritual implements from *oriyoki* bowls to butter lamps became both cherished and commonplace in Euro-American home altars and Dharma and retreat centers.

As Cadge's emphasis on the continuing distinctiveness of these two communities suggests, Asian forms and images may signify substantially different content to immigrants and converts. There is, moreover, a range of ways in which these Dharma images function for different people within each of these communities. Both Asian and Euro-American Buddhists may regard images as devotional objects, road maps for contemplation, or simply aesthetically pleasing. Of importance here, however, is that images, whether elaborate or minimalistic, are generally understood within both communities to be an integral, if not indispensable, part of practice whether an individual understands that practice in spiritual or therapeutic terms.

The essentially religious character of this use of Dharma images is underscored when contrasted to the different role they play among contemporary artists. In the art world, Dharma images are highly personalized, sometimes abstract, and often make no visual references to Asian Buddhism. Often conceptual in nature, these images are embedded in elaborate codes insofar as they are grounded in a loosely jointed community and significant explanation is needed to make their

Buddhist significance apparent to observers. For some artists the concept of Dharma practice itself is transformed by its reinterpretation in terms of participatory, installation, and performance art.

To develop the second part of my argument, I turn to the Awake consortium, an informal association of some thirty artists, scholars, writers, museum curators, cultural critics, and meditation practitioners. They gathered together in a two-year consultation held over eight weekend sessions from April 2001 to February 2003 at the San Francisco Zen Center's Green Gulch Farm, convening under the title Awake: Art, Buddhism, and Dimensions of the Mind. Their mission was to explore the "common ground between creative mind, perceiving mind, [and] meditative mind." Their goal was to reveal "to the American public threads of Buddhist influence that run through the fabric of contemporary culture and [the] potential for satisfying aesthetic experience engendered by an open, aware state of mind."[1] The outcomes of Awake were disseminated to the public in affiliated shows and, more particularly, in two publications, *Smile of the Buddha: Eastern Influences in Western Art from Monet to the Present* (Baas 2005) and *Buddha Mind in Contemporary Art* (Baas and Jacob 2004).

SMILE OF THE BUDDHA

In the first text, *Smile of the Buddha*, Jacquelyn Baas revisits the role of the visual arts in the free-floating Dharma discourse noted earlier and revisions it in a number of important and ingenious ways. Essentially, she expands the cast of artists she sees as having contributed Buddhist content to the fine arts canon. Some are predictable if overlooked in the past, such as Isamu Noguchi. Others have only in the past few decades become incorporated in the study of spirituality and the arts, such as Wassily Kandinsky. Some are pop or hip figures like performance artists Yoko Ono and Laurie Anderson. Others are familiar figures in the art canon from Odilon Redon to Georgia O'Keefe, whom Baas interprets with a new East/West twist. Throughout *Smile of the Buddha*, Baas's arguments for Buddhist influence vary from specific and concrete to speculative, suggestive, and ingenious. At times, she seems to be reaching but does so in an engaging if not entirely persuasive manner.

More significantly for her interpretation of Buddhist influence in contemporary art, Baas shifts the fulcrum of the discussion from an older emphasis on figures in the East-West modern canon like Claude Monet and Frank Lloyd Wright to postmodernists such as Marcel Duchamp and John Cage. This shift to a postmodernist perspective also enables Baas to shift the ground for the discussion of what constitutes Buddhist influence in modern art.

Given Cage's well-known affinity for Zen, Baas is on solid ground in her discussion of his work (Bass 2005, 164–177). Her take on Cage's drawings of the famed dry garden at Ryoanji as a visual expression of emptiness and on his interest in chance as reflecting Buddhist ideas about non-ego and indeterminacy is both familiar and persuasive. So, too, is her interpretation of Cage's musical composition *4'33"*—four minutes and thirty-three seconds of silence framed by the opening and closing of a piano—as a ritualized performance that signifies emptiness and silent meditation.

In contrast, Baas's discussion of Duchamp, who figures significantly in her arguments about Buddhism and the postmodern, are more oblique and tentative (Baas 2005, 78–95). Baas draws many of her insights from Tosi Lee, an art historian and Duchamp scholar, who rests his historical case for Buddhist influence on the assertion that Duchamp worked at a time when an interest in Buddhism pervaded Paris arts circles (Lee 2004, 124–138). More specifically, Lee notes that one of Duchamp's signature pieces, *Bicycle Wheel*, bears a visual similitude to the Sāñcī Dharma wheel that Kandinsky could have readily seen on display at Paris's Musée Guimet. In Lee's view, *Bicycle Wheel* marked the commencement of Duchamp's new path in art. It was, in effect, his own turning of the wheel of Dharma that set in motion a new age in the history of art.

Throughout much of the discussion of Duchamp by both Baas and Lee, arguments for Buddhist influence rest on a kind of implied analogy between art theory and the Dharma, which they tease out with reference to concepts drawn from general Buddhist philosophical vocabulary. For instance, Baas and Lee see Duchamp's well-known ready-mades as seeking to teach viewers to see things encountered in daily life—whether bicycle wheels or, more famously, urinals—in and of themselves without preconceived notions. This in turn evokes a Buddhist analogy: Duchamp aims to foster "visual or 'retinal' indifference," a nonattachment of the eye to things and conventional ideas about them. He sought to "replace sensual perception with absolute apprehension," a notion that suggests to Baas a mode of encountering the world informed by Buddhist philosophy and meditation.

The point here, however, is not to question one or another aspect of Baas's arguments about Western art from the perspective of Dharma and postmodernity. More significant is her shifting of the discussion from concrete Asian influence on modern Western art to postmodernist arguments that rest on visual similitude and analogy. This gives a new twist to a century-old question of how to identify Asian religious influences in Western art. As in art commentary written in the past, Baas moves too easily between the specifically Buddhist and the generally Asian as the juxtaposition of "Buddha" and "Eastern" in the title of her book suggests. As a consequence, she sees Buddhist influences in art that could just as well be said to be Taoist or generically Asian or to owe their genesis to Western Romanticism. Such evocation of Asian influence is perennial and orientalist, which is not to say it does not play an important role in Buddhism coming West. On the contrary. *Smile of the Buddha* is another iteration in a long tradition in which Dharma and Dharma-like ideas and images are understood not as elements in religious practice but as expressions of the creative imagination of artists. In other words, *Smile of the Buddha* is a twenty-first-century expression of the kind of free-floating Dharma discourse that helped to shape Euro-Americans' initial reception of Buddhism in the West.

BUDDHA MIND IN CONTEMPORARY ART

Buddha Mind in Contemporary Art, coedited by Baas and Mary Jane Jacob, more persuasively builds a case for concrete Buddhist influences in the arts, even as it explores the often nuanced ways in which the Dharma informs both the production of art and the formation of Western Buddhist identities. Equal parts biography, interview, portfolio, and critical review, *Buddha Mind* explores the work of installation and performance artists, all of whom have some link to Buddhism. A few were raised Buddhist. Others have professional connections to Asian Buddhist communities. Some practice the Dharma. Common to them all, however, is a conceptual link between Buddhism and art and the view that the production of art itself is a kind of Dharmic activity.

Three sketches suggest the varied ways, often imaginative and quite stunning, in which the Dharma figures in the contemporary art world in terms of both the production of art and the articulation of Buddhist identity.

A practicing Buddhist with an eclectic spiritual orientation, Ernesto Pujol is an installation artist raised in the Cuban exile community. He attended art school before becoming a novice in Mepkin Abbey, a Trappist monastery in South Carolina in the early 1980s. After leaving the monastery, he entered the New York arts scene and eventually converted to Buddhism. One piece Baas and Jacob profile in *Buddha Mind* is *(Mapping with Chairs) Water Table*, his installation at the Spoleto Festival 2004 in Charleston, North Carolina. In this piece, there are no visual references to Asian Buddhism. Instead Pujol uses brilliant blue chairs to draw the viewer's gaze into the natural and industrial landscapes associated with rice cultivation in coastal South Carolina, touching in the process both contemporary environmental issues and the history of slavery.

In a fairly direct way, Pujol articulates both the Dharmic dimension of his art and the way Buddhism figures in his identity. He understands art such as *(Mapping with Chairs) Water Table* to be meditative installations, what he calls "staged moments of wakefulness." Life is about suffering, and art—like spirituality—is about the transcendence of suffering. Pujol now understands himself as having been a Buddhist for decades, even though he never had a name for it. Prophetic aspects of Roman Catholicism remain important to him, but he writes that as both artist and Buddhist, "I pursue the notion of the humble bodhisattva, quietly pointing ways to freedom from suffering through wakefulness" (Baas and Jacob 2004, 196–202).

Born in Belgrade in former Yugoslavia, Marina Abramovic expresses her own Dharmic sensibilities and Buddhist identity through installation and performance art. Since 1979, she has been associated with Tibetan monastics in India and spent a number of years working as a choreographer for lamas, assisting them in their effort to translate traditional dance and chant into performance pieces suited for a Western context. The Buddhist content is explicit in Abramovic's *At the Waterfall*, one of several of her pieces profiled in *Buddha Mind in Contemporary Art*. It is a video installation consisting of images of the heads of 108 monks and nuns from different Tibetan orders each chanting their root mantra, which is placed before twelve deck chairs. The viewer sitting before it experiences a cacophony of voices that eventually distills into a waterfall of light and sound, creating in the process a meditative space.

The Buddhist content in a second piece, *House with the Ocean View*, is more indirect and thoroughly conceptual. A built environment signifying a cell from which there is no escape, Abramovic lives within it for twelve days, fasting and engaging in purification and self-mortification. Throughout her stay, viewers can observe her through a telescope to study her intently, or they may casually drop by, in either case sharing vicariously in her personal performance of suffering.

Abramovic articulates both the Buddhist content of her art and her own sense of what it means to be a Buddhist more obliquely than Pujol. She presents *House with the Ocean View* as a performance of timeless silence, stillness, vulnerability, suffering, and nonattachment, which is communicated between artist and viewer through their mutual gaze. She does not think of herself as a Buddhist artist per se. She cannot meditate either in her daily life or in a monastery but does so only inside her performance. "There I am most connected to Buddhism." Abramovic understands art in terms that evoke both the Western ideal of service and the Buddhist bodhisattva. The moment that you produce work "it is your responsibility to share it with society. You are the servant of the society in which you live. . . . That is how I see my function. That's how Buddhism works in my own life" (Baas and Jacob 2004, 186–195).

Born in Los Angeles, Sanford Biggers expresses his own understanding of the Dharma in the context of an Afro-American-Dadaist-Asian synthesis that has informed his art since the 1990s. For instance, in *Om II*, he created in performance an urban graffiti-styled AUM using the production techniques of the Tibetan sand mandala. For a performance piece, *Hip Hop Ni Sasagu (In Fond Memory of Hip Hop)*, which he mounted in a Soto Zen temple in Japan, Biggers forged a ceremonial bell by melting down silver jewelry, a process he saw as "distilling bling-bling materialism out of contemporary hip-hop." Biggers then placed sixteen bell-playing performers in the sanctuary in four concentric circles. After sitting *zazen* for fifteen minutes under the direction of a temple master, performers rang their bells in a lightly scripted sequence, creating in the process an improvisational, non-egoistic meditative space.

Biggers evokes the Dharma in terms reminiscent of language used in the 1950s by Beats to characterize Zen. It is improvisational like jazz. It is a window into emptiness, like the music of John Coltrane.

Referencing Buddhist lingo popular in the 1980s and 1990s, Biggers sees Buddhism as a movement "into the void" or into the zone. Of the three artists under consideration here, Biggers expresses his own sense of being Buddhist most tentatively. "Maybe I *am* a Buddhist," he recalls thinking at the time of the temple performance as he contemplated the sequence of events, the law of cause and effect, which brought him to Japan. This is "something that I never really talked about or felt comfortable with before. This was probably the first time I ever thought about it like that" (Baas and Jacob 2004, 204–211).

In *Mandala of the B-bodhisattva*, Biggers pushes the limit on the conceptual relationship between the Dharma and performance art. For this installation piece Biggers created sixteen-foot-square breakdance slipmats used in competitive dancing on which he painted mandala forms. He then videoed viewer-participants at The Battle of the Boroughs Breakdance Competition at Bronx Community College in 2001, inviting them to break in on the dance, to create art rather than merely observe it, to become b-boy bodhisattva-like figures moving in the void while devoid of egoist intent. This video formed the basis for a gallery installation.

In the second part of my argument, I am suggesting that the publications of the Awake consortium are evidence of the use of Dharma images and the formation of Buddhist identities of a sort quite different than those found within Asian American and Euro-American practice communities. The artist's approach to the use of Dharma images is characterized not by the practice of Buddhism in cohesive social groups but by the imaginative deployment of Buddhism in the service of self-expression by creative individuals at work in the art market and world. This use of the Dharma image does not necessarily foster a Buddhist religious identity per se but rather a sense that being Buddhist in America and the West is more an outlook on the world inflected by ideas and sentiments that in some sense can be said to be Buddhist.

CONCLUDING THOUGHTS

There are three summary points that I want to make by way of conclusion. First, religious practice with Dharma images and the imaginative use of them as vehicles for creative self-expression are two distinct social-emotional processes. One can interpret them in a unitary perspective as performance, for instance, which would require a more sophisticated theoretical lens. It should also be acknowledged that practice, self-expression, and art are often seen as intimately related, if not quite conflated, by some Buddhist modernists. But it seems to me that if one's goal is to understand the different kinds of dynamics at work in the complex landscape of American Buddhism, it is more productive to make a clear distinction between them. Piety in practice and creativity in the production of art play distinct roles in the formation of American Buddhism and American Buddhist identities and can be analyzed as such. At the same time, to distinguish them is also to designate a clear starting point for interpreting the considerable overlap that often exists between them both within and outside of practice communities.

Second, the creative, self-expressive use of Dharma images is tied up with an Asia-inspired book, art, and culture free-floating Dharma discourse that in the 1950s and early 1960s formed the substance of Euro-American Buddhism. As increasing numbers of Americans made a turn East, this discourse operated as a kind of big tent of oriental spirituality in which curious seekers encountered a wide range of philosophies, practices, and teachers representing Hinduism, Buddhism, Taoism, and other traditions of Asia, great and small. Once inside, many seekers pursued the serious study and practice of the Buddhadharma in particular, which by about 1970 was resulting in the creation of new Euro-American practice communities. Seen as part of a dynamic historical process, this free-floating Dharma discourse set the stage for the rapid growth of practice groups in the 1980s and 1990s that became the engine behind the institutionalization of Euro-American Buddhism. Baas and Jacob's work attests to the fact that this interplay between Dharma and art continues today in postmodernist performance and installation modes, which further suggests that new variations on the art-Dharma theme can be expected to surface in the future, perhaps to serve other important ends. At any rate, it seems likely that such free-floating Dharma discourses have played a significant role in the widespread diffusion of general knowledge about Buddhism among people in the United States (Wuthnow and Cadge 2004, 363–380).

Third, the problematic dimension to the imaginative deployment of Dharma and Dharma-like images must be noted. This free-floating Dharma discourse and its art products are, almost by definition, orientalist projects insofar as they are imaginative appropriations of Asian cultural material by the West to serve its own ends, which are often far removed from original intents. There are many nuanced interpretive questions here. Biggers's b-boy bodhisattva, for instance, while engaging and conceptually brilliant, is significantly removed from the bodhisattva ideal as it is practiced in Asian, Asian American, and Euro-American Buddhist communities. Because projects such as these cannot escape orientalist critiques, it may be more useful and satisfying to see artists like Pujol, Abramovic, and Biggers in a different interpretive light as producers of hybrid images in an age in which multilateral cross-fertilization among cultures is amplified by economic globalization.

Whatever the case, it is my own sense that the long-term viability of a uniquely American Buddhism rests with the people who practice the Dharma in strong, disciplined religious communities, whether Asian or Euro-American. Still, free-floating discourses about Asia, Dharma, and art and its products lend a splendid and inventive aura to American Buddhism. It is part of Buddhism's appeal to Western audiences, a skillful if indirect means of promulgation. It also works in profound, if sometimes obscure, ways to tone and shape the process of adapting the Dharma to the ethos and culture of the United States.

NOTES

1. The Awake website is no longer online. For some critical information on the project, see Klein (2005) and Finucane (2006).

EIGHT

TELLING TALES OUT OF SCHOOL

The Fiction of Buddhism

KIMBERLY BEEK

The emergence of any new genre of literature signals a new collective outlet for human expression. This chapter presents "Buddhist fiction" as a new form of creative literary discourse that recontextualizes Buddhism in the West. Buddhist fiction is a popular genre of novels and short stories that is nascent in the world of Buddhist literature and not yet fully recognized in the realm of English literature, emerging in tension between change and continuity. A brief introduction of this popular fiction genre will highlight the significance of its emergence within the contexts of Buddhist literature and Buddhism as it is developing in the United States through both Asian American and convert efforts. As a small case study, excerpts of Amy Tan's Asian American novel *The Kitchen God's Wife* (1991) will be juxtaposed with Keith Kachtick's Buddhist novel *Hungry Ghost* (2003) to illustrate the interdiscursive tension that relates these two genres. Some reviews that serve as reader-reception material of these particular novels point to an interdiscursive tension of the genres, a space for questioning the category of "Buddhism" itself. By examining the emergence, contexts, juxtaposition, and reception of two exemplary works, we can see how the emerging genre of Buddhist fiction tells tales out of school, outside of established genres, providing new trajectories for imagining the domestication of Buddhism in globalized, contemporary contexts.

EMERGENCE

Anne Donovan's debut novel *Buddha Da* (2004) lures potential readers combing the fiction aisles in bookstores with a cover sporting a picture of a smiling Buddha face hovering over a man who is sitting on a park bench. *Buddha Da* is the story of a Glaswegian father or "Da" named Jimmy whose foray into Buddhist meditation causes a commotion with his life, family, and friends. Dan Zigmond's review of *Buddha Da* in *Shambhala Sun* magazine relates, "We are witnessing an explosion of Buddhist fiction in the West."[1] He lists several more novels that could fall into this popular genre, including Keith Kachtick's novel *Hungry Ghost*. A portion of the novel *Hungry Ghost* was published in Wisdom Press's short story anthology *Nixon Under the Bodhi Tree* (Wheeler 2004), named after the O. Henry award–winning story of the same title by Gerald Reilly. The anthology's title also notably includes *And Other Works of Buddhist Fiction*. Kachtick is the editor of a second Wisdom Press anthology of short stories published in 2006, *You Are Not Here and Other Works of Buddhist Fiction*.

As a genre, Buddhist fiction cuts across many literary categories. Buddhist fiction could fall under the umbrella category of "genre fiction," a somewhat elastic term used to group works sharing similarities of character, theme, and setting (Saricks 2009, 6). Some recognizable popular genres of fiction would be adrenaline genres like adventure and thrillers or landscape genres such as fantasy or historical fiction (Saricks 2009, vii). *Buddha Da* and *Hungry Ghost* represent romantic suspense stories—not necessarily love stories but the typical romance pattern of a hero on a journey. They are generally stories of the challenges of Buddhist converts trying to live as Buddhists in our contemporary world. Similar to these works are novels like *Where Do We Go from Here*, by the famous German film director, producer, and author Doris Dörrie (2001), and *Sitting Practice*, by award-winning Canadian author Caroline Adderson (2003). Buddhist fiction also comes in the form of adventure and detective stories, such as John Burdett's popular Thai detective mystery series that started with *Bangkok 8* (2003); Eliot Pattison's political thriller series that started with *The Skull Mantra* (1999), set in Tibet and based on the Chinese detective Shan Tao Yun; anthropologist-turned-fiction-author Liza Dalby's novel *Hidden Buddhas: A Novel of Karma and Chaos* (2009), set in present-day Japan but brimming with well researched history; or acclaimed author Mark Salzman's book *The Laughing Sutra* (1991). These last four novels are written by Westerners in the voices of Asian characters. Under the emerging genre title of "Buddhist fiction" we could also include the work of the award-winning author, professor, and activist Charles Johnson. The plots of the novels *Oxherding Tale* (1985) and *Middle Passage* (1990) are founded on and developed out of Buddhist doctrines, yet these works are most often placed in the genre of African American literature because the author himself is African American and because his work also deals so thoroughly with race issues. Johnson's novels and short stories can also fall into the genre of literary fiction[2] compared to the more popular works of Buddhist fiction mentioned earlier; Johnson's writing style is highly intellectual, and Buddhist concepts are not overtly denoted in his earlier works.

A chapter in John Whalen-Bridge and Gary Storhoff's edited volume *The Emergence of Buddhist American Literature* (2009) was dedicated to the work of Charles Johnson, who also provided the afterword for this landmark collection. This volume of essays on contemporary Buddhist literature in America, edited by two English literature professors, highlights a field of study made fertile from the marriage of modern Buddhist experience and expressions of it in poetry and fiction. While the majority of the volume focuses on poetry and the work of the Beats, the last third of the collection is made up of essays that examine the work of fiction authors of color who are also Buddhist. Interestingly, the genre title "Buddhist fiction" was not used in this collection, even to refer to Johnson's work. Johnson himself, however, recognizes Buddhist fiction in the foreword to what he deems "the world's first volume of 'Buddhist fiction'" collected in the short story anthology *Nixon Under the Bodhi Tree and Other Works of Buddhist Fiction* (Johnson 2004, ix).

For a richer description of Buddhist fiction, we might turn to some thoughts from the editor of *Nixon Under the Bodhi Tree*, Kate Wheeler. A former Buddhist nun, she has twice been awarded the O. Henry Prize for best short story. In the anthology, both Johnson and Wheeler describe Buddhist fiction as a "dramatization of the Dharma." Buddhist fiction is not the Buddhist story we're used to—not *jātaka*s or *avadāna* stories, nor Chinese or Japanese miracle tales, described by Wheeler as great stories "meant to seduce us toward a moral" but still regarded as "lower" than Buddhism's "instructions, either textual or oral," which she says "point beyond the existence of anything like a solid character. However wonderful that may be, it's a little different when we read stories for their own sake" (Wheeler 2004, xiv–xv). Perhaps this is because fiction is a confrontation with life as it is, just like the Dharma. Ferguson says that Wheeler suggests "western literature often remains mired in the first Noble Truth, depicting the suffering we endure without delving into the third and fourth Noble Truths, the all-important way forward. . . . Buddhist fiction might point to our ability to liberate ourselves from our suffering, to face it, feel it, and loosen our attachment to it."[3]

CONTEXTS

Based on the descriptions of Buddhist fiction thus far, we might tentatively define Buddhist fiction as an emerging genre of fiction, written in English, in the form of short stories and novels. It has major Buddhist themes, Buddhist characters, or Buddhist-influenced plot structures. Regardless of presentation through other fiction genres such as adventure or romance-suspense, there is generally a strong element of globalization and mobility in Buddhist fiction. Given these characteristics, earlier fictional works like *Siddhartha* (1922) by Herman Hesse, or works by the Beats such as Jack Kerouac's *Dharma Bums* (1958), can be identified as predecessors of Buddhist fiction. As well, and most important for this essay, the genre of Asian American literature is similar in that it also often presents globalized and mobile experiences of Buddhism. But the defining characteristic of Buddhist fiction is a storyline that hinges on or is structured by distinctly Buddhist experience.

Static descriptions of Buddhist fiction tell us a little about the forms it takes, and the people who write it, but not much about the context out of which Buddhist fiction is emerging. In her work on genres, Amy Devitt proposes a theory of genre that is dynamic. She purports that we must shift our thinking about genre from a formal classification system to a rhetorical and essentially semiotic social construct (Devitt 1993, 573). Devitt argues that contemporary analyses of genre are based on the ways that people themselves classify texts into genres. This classification is based on the participants' or users' recognition of a genre and what distinguishes it from another (Devitt 2004, 8). Simply by noting the ethnicity of the names of Buddhist fiction authors herein, clearly most authors of Buddhist fiction are Buddhist converts, and some are Buddhist sympathizers. The genre is very contemporary and began to flourish in the 1990s at the same time that convert Buddhist temples and communities in North America and the United Kingdom were dramatically increasing in number. Authors, journalists, book reviewers, publishers, and readers label and list works of literature as Buddhist fiction.[4] These literati become a social grouping of individuals who recognize Buddhist fiction as a distinct form of fiction, a form that is Buddhist from their perspective. This is because genres such as fiction will change historically, and new genres, such as Buddhist fiction, will emerge over time and space such that "what appears as 'the same' generic form at one level," for example, the level of the novel, "has recognizably distinct forms in differing social groups," such as among Buddhists or Buddhist sympathizers (Kress 1987, 42). It is no surprise, then, that Buddhist fiction is not the only contemporary Western genre with Buddhist elements. Asian American literature contains Buddhist elements, too.

Whalen-Bridge and Storhoff (2009) recognize such Buddhist elements in the work of Maxine Hong Kingston, one of the most acclaimed and notable authors of Asian American literature and a professor at the University of California, Berkeley. Hong Kingston's book *The Woman Warrior: Memoirs of a Girlhood among Ghosts* (1975)[5] popularized the "talk-story" narrative technique in Western literature. Talk-story is a narrative form used in oral traditions in Asian cultures and has been combined with English literature narrative styles for use in novels and short stories. The phenomenal popularity of Amy Tan's works is testament to the success of this narrative form.

The work of Hong Kingston and Tan typically fall under the genre of Asian American literature, a genre that generated a subfield in the area of English literature approximately forty years ago. The field emerged at universities in California in the late 1960s. It was bolstered by feminism and evolved out of activist attempts to increase our capacity to live with difference, as Stuart Hall would say (1993, 359). So stories of Asian American literature turn on the immigrant and refugee experiences of Asians in the United States, and the academic subfield itself deals with the many challenging issues of race and ethnicity faced by Asian Americans.

Since Asian American literature encompasses a diverse array of cultures that have been influenced by Buddhism, from Chinese and Japanese to Indian, Korean, and Vietnamese cultures, it is not surprising that Buddhism is present in this literature. But while both Asian American literature and Buddhist fiction could fall under the umbrella of Buddhist literature as delineated by Whalen-Bridge and Storhoff (2009), they are distinguished as different genres of Buddhist literature in the West. Literary and cultural theorist Tzvetan Todorov describes genres as institutions: "Like any other institution, genres bring to light the constitutive features of the society to which they belong" (Todorov 1990, 16). Here we can begin to understand the difference between Asian American literature and Buddhist fiction, an emerging genre that amplifies the rising voice of a sociocultural group related to Asian American culture through Buddhism. As we can tell from the backgrounds of the authors who write Buddhist fiction, this emerging genre mainly represents Buddhism as imagined by convert Buddhists and Buddhist sympathizers.[6] Further to this, Todorov reasons that genres develop "from other genres. A new genre is always the transformation of an earlier one, or of several: by inversion, by displacement, by combination" (Todorov 1990, 16). This is not to suggest that Buddhist fiction developed out of Asian American literature. On the contrary, these genres are related not by genealogy but through tension, through the stretching and balancing of various cultural elements.

The tension between the so-called two Buddhisms has been well covered by Hickey in chapter 3 in this volume. As she points out, this tension was highlighted by the comments of Helen Tworkov (1991) in a *Tricycle* magazine editorial when she suggested that well-educated, middle-class whites were the spokespersons of American Buddhism, dismissing the longer history of Asian American Buddhists. Indeed, Tworkov's rash assumption does not ring true in consideration of developments in popular fiction where, by the early 1990s, Asian American literature provided a deep, rich voice for Asian Americans and the Buddhisms they practice. Buddhist fiction, on the other hand, was not yet a recognizable genre. Thus, the tension between Asian American and convert American Buddhists highlighted by Tworkov's comments is paralleled in the tension between Asian American literature and Buddhist fiction. It is in this tension that the genres are discernible. It is this tension that creates the interdiscursivity of these genres.

JUXTAPOSITION

Examples from both Asian American literature and Buddhist fiction will help illustrate the interdiscourse of the two genres. Considering plot events concerning death from Tan's Asian American novel *The Kitchen God's Wife* and Kachtick's Buddhist novel *Hungry Ghost: A Novel* amplifies how each novel, in its own way, is highly representative of its genre. A portion of Kachtick's novel was republished in the anthology *Nixon Under the Bodhi Tree and Other Works of Buddhist Fiction* and was thereby recognized as Buddhist fiction by a community of authors who write Buddhist fiction. Amy Tan is arguably the most recognizable author of Asian American literature in the United States, particularly after the success of her novel *The Joy Luck Club* (1989).

In *The Kitchen God's Wife*, Tan uses both contemporary narratives and talk-story narratives. The storyline in the novel is outlined even in the title. As we learn from the story, the "kitchen god's wife" refers to a woman in Chinese mythology who cared for a selfish man. The man became a minor god, but the wife was forgotten. In Tan's novel, the title points to the early life of the main character, Winnie Louie. Most of the novel is narrated by Winnie in talk-story form as she tells her daughter Pearl the sad, secret-filled events of her life on a small island outside Shanghai in the 1920s up until the desperate events in Shanghai that led to Winnie's coming to America in 1949.

Winnie's story is framed within contemporary family events set in California, so that we get to meet most of the characters in their American contexts first through Pearl's narrated perspective. One instance of a family event in the opening of the novel is the funeral of Grand Auntie Du, who is actually not a blood relative but so close to Winnie that she is considered family. Pearl, her husband, and her young daughters travel to Winnie's community in the heart of a California Chinatown to attend the funeral. Since Pearl grew up in America with her mother Winnie and her father Jimmie, a Christian minister, Pearl is not fully acquainted with Chinese cultural traditions. This adds an interesting perspective to the funeral as described from Pearl's view.

> Through the haze of the incense-blurred light, I can barely see my mother. She's gesturing for us to come sit with her . . . we walk quickly down the aisle, past what must be only a dozen or so mourners—Mary, Doug, and their children, some people from the church, all Chinese.
>
> [Pearl makes her way to the casket] . . . I look at Grand Auntie in her casket. Her mouth looks caved in, her thin face like that of a wizened bird. She is so still, yet I feel like we are

> all waiting for something to happen, for Grand Auntie suddenly to transform and manifest herself as a ghost. . . . Above the casket, a white banner made out of ten feet of butcher paper is stuck to the wall with masking tape. . . .
>
> "What does that say?" I ask my mother quietly. "'Hope your next life is long and prosperous.' Nothing too special," my mother replies. "I didn't write it. This is from people with the Kwong family association. Maybe Helen gave them a donation." . . . [Pearl notices that Uncle Henry turns on a spotlight and starts filming Grand Auntie Du.] . . . The next moment, I hear hollow wooden knocking sounds, followed by a persistent ding-ding-ding, as if someone were impatiently ringing for the bellhop in a hotel lobby. These sounds are joined by two voices chanting a tune that seems to consist of the same four notes and syllables. It repeats so many times I'm sure it's a record that has become stuck. But now, emerging from the left alcove are two Buddhist monks with shaved heads, dressed in saffron-colored robes . . . chanting "Ami-, Ami-, Amitaba, Amitaba" . . . they drone, and now the old ladies in the old style jackets begin moaning and wailing, waving their arms up and down, overcome with grief, it seems. Uncle Henry turns the camera toward them.
>
> "Are they Grand Auntie's good friends?" I ask my mother. She frowns. "Not friends, maybe Chinese people from Vietnam. They came early, later saw we didn't have too many people to mourn Grand Auntie. So they talked to Auntie Helen, she gave them a few dollars. And now they're doing the old custom, crying out loud and acting like they don't want the dead person to leave so fast. This is how you show respect." I nod. Respect. "Maybe these ladies can do two or three funerals every day," my mother adds, "earn a few dollars. Good living that way. Better than cleaning house." (Tan 1991, 27–31)

Shortly after the funeral, Pearl learns that she has been willed a gift from Grand Auntie Du. The gift is an altar for the kitchen god's wife. The novel ends with a good measure of reconciliation between mother and daughter, and Winnie creates a figure of a kitchen god's wife for Pearl to use in the altar.

From the very opening of Pearl's view "through the haze of incense-blurred light," surrounded by family, friends, and "people from the church," we get a sense of globalization and the translocal, of situating Chinese traditions in contemporary American culture. According to James Watson, traditional Chinese funerals were collective and public events that required the cooperation of family and community in order to create what amounted to a performance. Thus, the pasting up of banners and wailing are the means by which a family gives public notification of a relative's death (Watson 1988, 12). Tan has given this element of performance a modern twist. In keeping with Chinese tradition, there is a banner at Auntie Du's funeral, and Chinese women from Vietnam have been hired to ensure the requisite wailing, all of which are videotaped for posterity by Uncle Henry.

By developing Pearl's character as the modern "outsider" to her own Chinese culture, Tan is able to narrate a funeral scene that shows how tradition is simultaneously maintained and transformed in this family and community. Tan's wailing mourners who were hired to "perform the old custom" are particularly well drawn, especially in contrast to the fictional depictions of mourners from the modern classic Chinese novel *Jia* ("Family"), by Ba Jin (1931). In her article "Translator, Traitor; Translator, Mourner," Rey Chow examines Ba Jin's depiction of a mournful wailing scene that takes place at a funeral in 1920s China. Chow asserts that this scene is a "tonally derisive portrayal of mourning" and argues that Ba Jin's use of third-person narrative voice to render the wailing scene "stages the mourning women as a spectacle of nonsense, [and] is caught up in an implicit act of (cultural) reflexivity" (Chow 2008, 566–567). Chow posits that because of the embeddedness of wailing in Chinese cultural history, the scene of ritualized mourning is "consciously (re)presented and mocked as a farce . . . indicative of a culture trapped, as it were, in a kind of premodern barbarity" (Chow 2008, 567). Tan's depiction of wailers does not read as derisive but more as an attempt to maintain tradition: proper respect needs to be shown for Auntie Du.

Clearly Buddhist aspects of this scene are most recognizable with the appearance of the monks. According to traditional Chinese funeral customs, the family pays money to ritual specialists, such as Buddhist monks, so that the corpse can be safely expelled from the community and the spirit sent off on its journey to another world (Watson 1988,

12). In his article on conflicting themes of salvation in late and early modern imperial China, Cohen notes that "unlike the ordinary realm of ancestors, which mirrors this world in most ways, the Pure Land is desired for ways in which it differs from this world" because it is not inhabited by relatives but by the Buddha Amitābha (Cohen 1988, 185). In the case of Auntie Du, the other world is the Western Paradise or Pure Land (*jingtu*) of Amitābha Buddha. Buddhist funerals across Asia were designed so that the living could help expedite a loved one's safe passage over death's threshold toward an auspicious future destiny (Cuevas 2004, 379). By casting Pearl as an outsider to her own family traditions and culture, Tan is able to teach her reader how Pure Land Buddhism seamlessly blends with Chinese traditions, even in a California setting.

Hungry Ghost presents the reader with something very different. In this novel, Kachtick tells the story of Carter Cox, a thirty-nine-year-old photographer living the life of a postmodern, globe-trotting, materialistic, womanizing bachelor who is a fictional example of the second noble truth, that *dukkha* stems from craving and clinging. What makes Carter an interesting protagonist is that he is aware of many of his worst traits and, in his own faltering manner, is attempting to change his ways by following a form of Tibetan Buddhism on a bodhisattva path to uncover his "Buddha Nature." But Kachtick provides his reader with his reason for using this narrative technique when Carter's character states: "Your heart is your Buddha Nature, you remind yourself. It's the voice speaking to you right now, reminding you that karma is in play at all times, in all places. Karma does not punish. It does not reward. But it always leads to another pain or joy" (Kachtick 2003, 45). Kachtick employs this narrative technique in an attempt to give a voice to Carter's precarious awareness of a need for conscience and compassion, or, as he calls it, his Buddha Nature, his potential to wake up.

At a Buddhist retreat, Carter meets Mia, a twenty-six-year-old Catholic and academic who also practices Buddhist meditation and has vowed to remain a virgin until she is married. Perhaps because she is a challenge, or perhaps because Carter sees in her a lovingkindness and compassion that he hopes is in himself, he befriends Mia and then invites her to assist him at a photo shoot in Morocco so that he can try to maneuver his way into her life. Carter's spiritual journey drives the plotline that leads to two different endings: one that is a crash-and-burn scenario for Carter's attempts at a relationship with Mia and any level of enlightenment, and one in which he gets his girl and learns a thing or two. In the first scenario, Mia leaves Morocco on her own, and Carter finishes his assignment, returns to New York, wallows in self-pity, chokes on his own food, and dies alone in his apartment building hallway. What follows is a return-from-death experience into Buddhist *lokas* wherein Carter's dead Dharma teacher, Christopher, is the guide. Carter finally begins to realize that he is dead as he is being ushered into the Buddhist intermediate state and Christopher explains why he is the guide: "I'm only here to remind you of what you already know. Since you *persist* in interacting with the universe dualistically, you're stuck with yours truly: the embodiment of your Buddha Nature packaged, as it were, in the interactive form of one of the few folks in your decidedly self-centered life to whom you opened your heart and shared" (Kachtick 2003, 244). Before dropping off Carter in the hungry ghost realm, Christopher explains that "karma has propelled you—*you*—this awareness—through the Bardo of Dying and the Bardo of Becoming, the transitional stages between death and rebirth. . . . To cut to the chase, my karma-heavy friend, you're obliged to spend some time ridding yourself of the extra baggage you've accrued" (245). Finally, Christopher leaves Carter in the hungry ghost realm with these parting words:

> Yes, this is the Hungry Ghost realm. Here in this wasteland you'll find there's no water fit to drink, though there's an endless supply of gnarled and leafless trees, bent and crimped, semi-petrified in perpetual autumn. . . . Sorry. If it's any consolation, the only thing that suffers here is the ego. In the Hungry Ghost realm you're reborn, alive but not alive, dead but not dead. Though you've entered this realm without a body, you'll feel physical sensations—in your instance, mostly unquenchable thirst. Dehydration up the wazoo. Parched lips, cracked tongue, endless edentate smacking—that sort of thing. . . . No, relax—*relax*—if you don't fight it, it won't drive you so batty. And that stench is from—well, you see them.
>
> Ooh—be careful—those are pointy.
>
> By virtue of the weight of your accrued karma, you're due to stay here for one third of a minor *kalpa*: approximately three hundred years. Not a good hand to be dealt, I admit. Bleak as a midnight scourge. But remember: when you realize

> the nightmare you're stuck in is an illusion, the nightmare dissolves. Easier said than done, I'll grant you, but that's pretty much the brass ring.
>
> I *know* your lips are dry, but use your *loaf*, man—it's *salt* water.
>
> Listen—*you* know what to do. Be patient with yourself. Be generous to your heart. And whenever you need some sound advice, you know where to find me. Until then, Cheers. (Kachtick 2003, 246–248)

"But that's not what happens," is the first line of the next chapter, and the novel continues without explanation for the hungry ghost realm episode and launches into a second version of the events in Morocco, with a much happier ending.

A look at a Tibetan *bhavacakra* will reveal that hungry ghosts reside in a realm of intense craving. They are depicted with enormous stomachs and tiny necks to reflect their insatiable desires in this *kāma-dhātu* or desire realm. In the "Gaki-zōshi,"[7] the hungry ghosts are painted in a state of perpetual thirst, licking drops of spilled water in cemeteries. We can only imagine that decaying bodies are the source of the stench in Kachtick's description.

Carter's experience of the hungry ghost realm is reminiscent of Tibetan *délok* narratives. As Bryan Cuevas relates, the central protagonist of the return-from-death account is called in Tibetan *délok* (*'das log*, "passed away and returned") and is "usually an ordinary person who dies, enters the *bardo* (Tib. Bar do; Skt. *antarābhava*)—the intermediate state between death and rebirth—tours the netherworld, and returns to report his or her afterlife experiences" (Cuevas 2007, 297). These same types of "return from death" Buddhist narratives are found in popular medieval Japanese literature as "hell-tour tales" (Kimbrough 2006). In an article on Japanese hell imagery, Caroline Hirasawa provides a genealogy of Japanese "hell-tour tales" from Chinese stories about journeys into the six realms led by Enma (Skt. Yama), stories generated by the whole and intact absorption of Indian cosmologies in China (Hirasawa 2008, 11). The Indian Buddhist cosmologies are outlined in the *Abhidharmakośa* attributed to Vasubandhu (fourth century). *Hungry Ghost*, then, can be read as a contemporary rendition of a classic Buddhist narrative mode.

RECEPTION

Literary reviews for these two novels give us insight into the tension that relates Asian American literature and Buddhist fiction. Reviews of *The Kitchen God's Wife* were based on Tan's writing abilities. One reviewer stated, "Where Ms. Tan writes about contemporary Chinese-Americans, her portraits are often witty and complex. You want to know more about people like Uncle Henry Kwong, who insists on videotaping the funeral of a relative."[8] Another reviewer most appreciated Tan's abilities in narrating the talk-story portions of the novel, calling the contemporary framing of Winnie's story an obstacle to a smooth read.[9] These reviews are an indication of the depth of the genre of Asian American literature and the breadth of the discourse created by the intersection of Western literature and Asian modes of storytelling. They also indicate the expectations of the reader for this genre as a custodian of Asian culture, in Tan's case, Chinese culture, within the contexts of Western society. Tan's novel, as representative of the genre of Asian American literature, reflects Todorov's explanation of how new genres are generated through displacement of aspects of earlier fiction genres—think of the Chinese novel *Jia*—as well as the combination of modes of storytelling from Asian culture and Western culture, such as the talk-narrative. This displacement and combination is the very foundation of Asian American literature.

In *The Kitchen God's Wife*, Tan does a particularly skillful job of showing the symbiosis between Buddhism and Chinese culture in Auntie Du's funeral scene, to the extent that the Buddhist aspects do not really stand out, and the presence of Buddhist monks is not questioned at a funeral attended by family and friends who are Christian. Reviewers did not notice either. It would seem that Western readers are readily accepting of descriptions of Buddhism in Asian contexts. But would authors of Asian American literature label their work Buddhist? Hong Kingston makes very clear the fact that she does not think her book *The Woman Warrior* is "a Buddhist book" (Whalen-Bridge and Storhoff 2009, 182). Very much like Tan's novel, while there are Buddhist ideas, settings, and even minor themes in Hong Kingston's work, these are not central to the plotline or character developments. Buddhism is often a component, but not an integral component, in the genre of Asian American literature.

In comparison, some reviewers of *Hungry Ghost* did not always appreciate the Buddhist elements in Kachtick's story. One reviewer suggested that the hungry ghost episode was a bizarre plot run—perhaps a nightmare or hallucination—and thought shoppers could buy the book where "budding Buddhists would get the in jokes."[10] Another reviewer wrote that the alternate ending was rather a "downward turn" to an otherwise "engaging chronicle of Calvin Klein–clad soul-searching."[11] A third reviewer recognized Buddhist elements in the novel but said that the "preaching about Buddhism drags the narrative down in spots."[12] Perhaps these reviewers did not appreciate the Buddhist narrative modes employed by Kachtick because these were displaced outside of any Asian context.

Pico Iyer, the famous travel writer, essayist, and himself a story contributor to a Buddhist fiction anthology, reviewed *Hungry Ghost* and thought that "its shrewdest irony, which catches the strangeness of the times, is to suggest that the best Buddhist teacher of all may turn out to be a devout Catholic who spends much of her time quoting Aquinas and St. Paul."[13] Kachtick's story situates Buddhist narrative modes and plot events in globalized, modern settings that do not convey the Asian origins of Buddhism. These origins are reflected in the mode of storytelling itself, not the setting. In light of Todorov's ideas about emerging genres, Kachtick's novel represents Buddhist fiction, or fiction that is Buddhist, as a genre displaced from Asian settings. And perhaps we could go as far as to say that this displacement of Buddhist modes of narration into Western settings is an inversion, a reversal of the usual, especially when Buddhist fiction is juxtaposed with Asian American literature. Perhaps it is Kachtick's combination of Buddhist and Western modes of storytelling—displaced, inverted, and therefore sometimes unpopular with reviewers—that best exemplifies the labeling of this emerging genre.

Buddhist fiction and Asian American literature are interdiscursive in as much as they both narrate stories with Buddhist elements. However, both of these genres raise issues of authenticity regarding the category of "Buddhism." The term "authenticity" is here used as an adjective for something of "undisputed origins." As we have seen from literary reviews of Tan's novel, it may be easier to recognize that something is Buddhist when the Buddhist characteristic in question is contextualized in Asian culture and tradition. This recognition does not, however, ensure that any and all works of Asian American literature can be subsumed under the category of "Buddhism," as shown in the case of Hong Kingston's novel *The Woman Warrior*. The religious and/or cultural identification of any author as Buddhist or Asian does not wholly translate into the identification of their creative works as Buddhist. Asian American literature is a combinative genre that narrates continuity and hybridity for Asian immigrants and ensuing generations, and these narratives do not necessarily include Buddhism.

The emerging genre of Buddhist fiction is held in tension with Asian American literature in its capacity to narrate change. We might wonder if the genre title "Buddhist fiction" is in any way a claim of authenticity, since the Buddhist elements of this fiction may not be narrated in Asian contexts, as in *Hungry Ghost*. After all, the majority of authors of Buddhist fiction are Buddhist converts and sympathizers, and mainly, but not exclusively, Caucasian. But as Thomas Tweed reminds Buddhist studies scholars, we will repeatedly run into problems in our research and scholarship if we "continue to draw on an essentialist-normative definition of religious identity, those that construct a core or essence of right practice or belief and measure all historical expressions against it" (Tweed 1999, 79), because religious identity in our contemporary world is never developed in isolation. The genre title derives its connections to Buddhism by way of extending modes of Buddhist narration into contexts that are not necessarily Asian. These modes of Buddhist narration may have traditional antecedents, as exemplified in Kachtick's return-from-death scene. Then again, the mode of narration may be something new, something changed, such as Kachtick's second-person narration, or Carter's "Buddha Nature." In this way, stories of Buddhist fiction provide a Buddhist orientation more so than an undisputed, definite origin.

CONCLUSION

All Buddhist literature, including Buddhist fiction, helps to "provide the conditions, as Benedict Anderson has argued newspapers did for modern nations, for the formation of a Buddhist imagined community" (Whalen-Bridge and Storhoff 2009, 3). Including Buddhist fiction under the umbrella of Buddhist American literature broadens this imaginary community. The emerging genre of Buddhist fiction presents clear and vivid images of Buddhism as a religious orientation, tethered to Buddhist tradition through literary devices that simultaneously communicate the sociohistorical contexts of the publication. We need to pay attention to the ways in which Buddhism is represented and imagined in literature, not because what is imagined will be realized but because what is imagined is derived from a context. Buddhist fiction does not tell stories with a nostalgia for tradition; Buddhist fiction extends a Buddhist mode of storytelling into our contemporary world. In this way, for better or worse, Buddhist fiction takes part in reconstructing Buddhism in the West.

NOTES

1. Dan Zigmond, "Buddha Da," *Shambhala Sun* (January 2005) (retrieved from http://www.shambhalasun.com/index.php?option=com_content&task=view&id=2639, July 15, 2005).
2. Saricks defines literary fiction as "critically acclaimed, often award-winning, fiction. These books are more often character-centered rather than plot-oriented. They are thought-provoking and often address serious issues . . . these are 'complex, literate, multilayered novels that wrestle with universal dilemmas'" (Saricks 2009, 177–178).
3. Erin Ferguson, "State of the Art Encounter: Interview with Kate Wheeler," *Dharmalife* 23 (Summer 2003) (retrieved from http://www.dharmalife.com/issue23/encounter.html on March, 25, 2006).
4. Journalist Kimberly French provides an excellent introduction to Buddhist fiction in her article "Sitting, with a Good Buddhist Novel," *UUWorld* magazine online (retrieved from http://www.uuworld.org/ideas/articles/158180.shtml). See also her bibliography of Buddhist fiction, "Guide to Buddhist Fiction," *UUWorld* magazine online (retrieved from http://www.uuworld.org/ideas/articles/162391.shtml).
5. Note that this "memoir" is in many ways fictional, and its fictional character raised a great deal of controversy for the author within the Asian American writing community.
6. This is not to say that the genre boundaries between Asian American literature and Buddhist fiction are not blurred by Asian American authors. Certainly there are elements of the Dharma and

Buddhist principles in many Asian American works. For example, it is not difficult to see the workings of a Vietnamese Buddhist understanding of karma in the plotline of Lan Cao's novel *Monkey Bridge* (1997). But identifying story elements as Buddhist and labeling an entire novel or short story anthology as Buddhist are generically different matters. It is interesting that most of the surnames of authors writing Buddhist fiction are distinctly Euro-American names such as Wheeler and Kachtick.

7. Kyoto National Museum, "Gaki-zoshi (Scroll of the Hungry Ghosts)" (retrieved from http://www.kyohaku.go.jp/eng/syuzou/meihin/kaiga/emaki/item03.html, November 10, 2010). The scroll dates to the Late Heian period (late twelfth century).
8. Christopher Lehmann-Haupt, "Book of the Times; Mother and Daughter, Each with Her Secret," *New York Times Books* (June 20, 1991) (retrieved from http://www.nytimes.com/1991/06/20/books/books-of-the-times-mother-and-daughter-each-with-her secret.html, February 3, 2010).
9. Robb Forman Dew, "Pangs of an Abandoned Child," *New York Times Books* (June 16, 1991) (retrieved from http://www.times.com/books/01/02/18/specials/tan-kitchen.html, February 12, 2010).
10. Christine Perkins, "Review of Hungry Ghost," *Library Journal* 128, no. 8 (May 2003): 156.
11. Jeff Zaleski, "Review of Hungry Ghost," *Publishers Weekly* 250, no. 17 (April 28, 2003): 48.
12. Joanne Wilkinson, "Review of Hungry Ghost," *Booklist* 99, no. 15 (April 1, 2003): 1378.
13. Pico Iyer, "Is the Pope Buddhist?" *New York Times Book Review* (July 27, 2003) (retrieved from http://www.nytimes.com/2003/07/27/books/is-the-pope-buddhist.html).

NINE

Mind Full of God

"Jewish Mindfulness" as an Offspring of Western Buddhism in America

MIRA NICULESCU

In a large room surrounded by trees, a dozen Caucasian people of both genders, aged between twenty and sixty-something, are sitting quietly. Their eyes are gently closed and they are "watching their breath." This is a daily scene at a silent meditation retreat in a Buddhist center in California. Only this is not Buddhism. This is "Jewish mindfulness."

"Jewish mindfulness" is a new hybrid practice that incorporates the Buddhist concept of "mindfulness" into the belief and practice system of Judaism. This phenomenon thus presents us with a case of Buddhism gone twice "beyond borders" as a result of its integration in America: beyond its own symbolic borders, as well as beyond the borders of a local religious tradition.

The practice of "Jewish mindfulness" appeared in the mid-nineties in America and has since spread all across the English-speaking Jewish world, from Israel to Canada, and now England. This new religious label is not only widespread geographically but also culturally: "Jewish mindfulness" can be described as a nondenominational movement within Judaism that gathers individuals from all Jewish backgrounds, from orthodox to secular, including Reconstructionist and Renewal.

The impact of an encounter between Buddhism and a traditional Western religion is not specific to Judaism, as demonstrated by the emergence of the prolific field of Buddhist-Christian studies, as well as by the introduction of an academic journal by the same name. Yet the integration of Buddhism within Jewish practice in America, as well as the fascinating questions it raises in terms of its causes, its modalities, and its significance, has barely been addressed in Jewish studies. The few articles (Gez 2011; Obadia 2004, 2013; Vallely 2008) and the only book (Linzer 1996) published on the encounter between Buddhism and Judaism have focused on the individualistic phenomenon of the "Jewish Buddhists." No study has yet been dedicated to the systematization and integration of Buddhist practice and philosophy within Jewish practice and theology and its institutionalization under the new label of "Jewish mindfulness."

Yet the phenomenon of Jewish mindfulness offers a particularly rich case study, not only to examine Jewish strategies of adaptation in cases of encounter with other cultures and the remaking of Jewish tradition but also to examine in real time the process of "religion-in-the-making" in the context of religious globalization within postmodern Western societies. No academic work has tackled this phenomenon. Currently the only article on this new form of "Jewish meditation" denies any borrowing from Buddhism but instead describes Judaism as a form of "mindfulness" (Sautter 2002). In contrast, I describe Jewish mindfulness as an appropriation of Buddhism to form a new hybrid product in which Buddhism itself has disappeared. I use three criteria to detect religion-in-the-making: the building of a lineage of teachers, the crafting of a practice, and the coining of a theology. These elements will be examined successively in terms of how "Jewish mindfulness" makes use of Buddhism while simultaneously moving away from it.

RELIGIOUS GLOBALIZATION IN THE WEST AND THE GENEALOGY OF JEWISH MINDFULNESS

Jewish mindfulness cannot be understood without unraveling the history that made it possible. Only the deep cultural transformations of Jewish identity induced by Western modernization and by the Westernization of Buddhism can explain how such hybridization occurred.

The Jewish-Buddhist Encounter

The appropriation of Buddhism in the context of Judaism is somewhat surprising. First, Judaism is a non-proselyte, monotheistic nation-religion. It can be defined, using Simmel's typology of social groups, as an "organic solidarity" community (2003, 113). Such communities define themselves by blood links. Consequently, they tend to form minorities within broader groups and as such are often persecuted. As Simmel accurately observes, their cohesion is continually maintained by permanent external existential threats. This is the case with the Jewish community. Over six thousand years, Judaism has survived diasporas and persecutions through policing its symbolic boundaries. It has done so by closing up hermetically to the world, behaving in the manner of what French anthropologist Roger Bastide calls "canned religions" (1967): religious groups that use a strategy for self-perpetuation that relies on tradition rather than cultural borrowing.

Of course in practice, Judaism has been, like any culture, widely informed by others. It has successively absorbed elements of Babylonian mythology, Greek philosophy, Islam, and, in the crafting of Hassidism,[1] Christian mysticism. But the guiding principle has been closure. In the absence of a country, Judaism has perpetuated itself through its people. This is why Jewish institutions are very careful about keeping the tradition alive through individual members. Consequently, they tend to be particularly preoccupied with the secularization and assimilation that have accompanied Western modernization in the Jewish community. In this perspective, any departure from the group is seen as a "betrayal"—and this indeed has been the case for Jewish Buddhists (Kamenetz 1994; Niculescu 2014).

Even more so, on a religious level, the presence of Buddha statues and the practice of bowing seem to directly contravene the central Jewish prohibition of *Avodah Zarah* (idolatry), proclaimed in the beginning of the Decalogue. This reluctance, however, can be tempered by seeing Buddhism as a secular philosophy rather than a religion.

Buddhism can be seen as religious (mainly in Asian Buddhism) or as secular (mainly in Western Buddhism). The practice of Buddhism has been transmitted in a secular manner among converts in the West; it is portrayed as a primarily individual enterprise proposed by Siddhartha Gautama to emancipate us from suffering. In this nontheistic context, statues are not idols, and bowing is not a devotional practice. It is not even a Buddhist precept from this viewpoint but an Asian cultural practice of salutation; through bowing, respect is shown to one's teacher, to fellow participants, and to one's own practice (incarnated by one's meditation cushion).

More broadly, important incompatibilities between Judaism and Buddhism have been erased: first, with the secularization and Western enculturation of both Judaism and Buddhism, which created a cultural common ground for such an encounter; and second, with the crisis of modernity of the mid-twentieth century. In this historical context a whole generation of countercultural Americans turned to Buddhism. In their first ranks were post-*Shoah* Jews.

The "Jewish Buddhism" Phenomenon

In the middle of the twentieth century, Buddhism and other Eastern spiritualities appeared as a new "salvation" for American youth in light of the perceived failure of Western modernity. Countercultural Jewish Americans were looking for alternative meaning systems that were markedly different from their upbringing. Before the Westernization (and, perhaps, its trivialization) of what was soon to become "Western Buddhism" (Prebish 2002, 66), they "went East" *en masse*, either physically through traveling or symbolically with the adoption of Buddhism.

As post-Holocaust Jews, these American hippies found Buddhism particularly attractive: The teachings of the Buddha addressed the notion of suffering but left "God" out of the equation. They offered a spiritual alternative to their followers that presented neither theological nor historical conflicts with Judaism, unlike Christianity or Islam. For this reason, from the late fifties on, many Jewish-born Americans started practicing Buddhism. They were soon called "Jewish Buddhists" (Kamenetz 1994). By the nineties, although they represented only 2.5 to 6 percent of the Jewish American population, Jewish Buddhists represented up to a third of the new Western Buddhists (Coleman 2001, 192; Kamenetz 1994, 7). Remarkably, they constituted the vast majority of American Buddhist teachers.

This wave of departure from Judaism alarmed many in the Jewish community. It seemed to threaten the future of Judaism, but this time from the inside. Jewish orthodoxy began reacting to this trend in the early seventies by sending charismatic emissaries to reach out to Jewish individuals "gone East," while "rehabilitation" centers were created to "bring them back to their senses" (Linzer 1996). When Jewish Buddhists began returning to Judaism (Vallely 2008), they laid the groundwork for the development of a new Jewish spirituality, first through the

"Jewish renewal" movement and later through the advent of "Jewish mindfulness."

From Jewish Renewal to Jewish Mindfulness

The Jewish renewal movement got underway in the seventies. Its main founder, Rabbi Zalman Schachter-Shalomi (1993), advocated for an unprecedented level of openness. He drew inspiration from other traditions (especially Buddhism)—but only insofar as they brought inspiration to the Jewish path.

Three decades later, Jewish mindfulness took a step further. Incorporating the Buddhist practice of mindfulness within Judaism met the needs of many Jewish individuals to practice meditation and yoga, but within a Jewish framework. As such, while the Jewish Buddhist phenomenon represents a departure from Judaism by placing the individual *in between* two traditions (Obadia 2004), Jewish mindfulness incorporates Buddhist meditation *within* a Jewish foundation. It enriches Jewish practice by integrating Buddhist teachings, satisfying the desire to benefit from Buddhism's bounty while remaining firmly within Judaism. The choice to import rather than "immigrate," so to speak, is another sign that Judaism is an "organic solidarity community"; even the most atheistic Jewish individuals keep very strong cultural and emotional links with the community.

FROM VIPASSANA TO JEWISH MINDFULNESS: MINDFULNESS AND COSMOPOLITAN CULTURE

Two processes have played key roles in the interfaith encounter between Buddhism and Judaism and, ultimately, in Buddhist-Jewish hybridization: mindfulness became separated from its Buddhist framework by means of the Vipassana movement, and American Jewish identity became cosmopolitanized. The appropriation of an exogenous meaning system was made possible through an intermediary object, a shared element that served to bridge the two communities. "Mindfulness" served as this element. By the time many Jewish people (both religious and secular) started to meditate, Buddhism had sufficiently penetrated Western culture to the point of becoming secularized. Meditation had already become a religiously "neutral" practice. American culture became the common ground between Buddhism and Judaism, and through the domestication of "mindfulness" meditation became not an exotic Eastern curiosity but a Western cultural good.

From the Westernization of Vipassana to Mindfulness

Of the three main Buddhist schools that have been adopted by Americans from non-Buddhist backgrounds, it is Vipassana that has most deeply penetrated Western culture.[2] Touted by followers as closest to the original message of the Buddha, Vipassana has expanded transnationally with the model of free ten-day silent retreats started by Indian teacher S. N. Goenka, who hails from the lineage of Burmese teacher U Ba Khin. Goenka's Vipassana has had great success in the West, due in no small part to his presentation of Vipassana using secular and largely religiously neutral concepts but also by means of its introduction by American teachers trained in Asia. Vipassana was brought to the West by a group of young Jewish Americans trained in Thailand, India, and Burma in the sixties. In 1975, they founded the first Western Vipassana retreat center in America, the Insight Meditation Society (IMS). Through them, *vipassanā* was translated as "insight meditation," and teachings were made accessible to an American audience by focusing on the concept of mindfulness of one's thoughts and actions. "Insight meditation," says the IMS website, "is the simple and direct practice of moment-to-moment mindfulness."[3]

IMS greatly contributed to Buddhism's secularization and Westernization, and individuals of all backgrounds, secular and religious, soon attended the center. When asked in a Jewish online newspaper, "Why isn't meditation a religious practice?" Sharon Salzberg replied: "I look out in the hall and there are rabbis and Trappist monks. . . . The common purpose is greater understanding."[4] Today the center is still one of the most prominent in America.

Salzberg, one of the first Vipassana teachers in America, defines the core Buddhist concept of "mindfulness" as simply "fullness of attention."[5] It can therefore be seen not only as a Buddhist concept but also simply a universal principle of wisdom, a commonsense, pragmatic attitude. This is why mindfulness became a major vehicle for introducing Buddhism in the West: it became a separate concept from

Buddhism proper and could therefore be appropriated outside of Buddhism. It was first largely used in the Western psychotherapeutic field before entering Western historical religions (Judaism and Christianity) as a tool to enhance religious experience.

From Secularized Mindfulness to "Jewish Mindfulness"

Vipassana has been assimilated so well because its original form was altered. While some scholars attribute the success in creating a new form to "religious individualism" (Fronsdal 1998, 169), I suggest, in accord with Seager (2002, 112), that it is precisely because it was not presented as a religion but as a secular life-improvement "technique" that Vipassana-originated "mindfulness" became the most widespread meditation practice in America. Simply put, it fit within both secular and religious lives, improving the efficiency of preexisting practices.

This "secularized and psychologized" Buddhism has been described by Martin Baumann as a "postmodernist Buddhism" (2002, 57). But for many practitioners, it is not Buddhism as such anymore. In its therapeutic applications, such as the Mindfulness-Based Stress Reduction of Jon Kabat-Zinn and the Non-Violent Communication of Marshall Rosenberg, the word "Buddhism" has disappeared from the equation altogether. It has been replaced by "mindfulness."

The process of extracting teachings from their cultural frame seems to be a general tendency in today's religious scene; Judaism has not been spared in this regard, as shown by the recent developments of mainstream Kabbalah. In this new religious commodity, the mystical teachings of Judaism have been divorced from their Jewish frame. In Kabbalah Centers now present all over the world, American and former entrepreneur Rav Berg takes some principles of Kabbalah, which he then isolates from their Jewish context, secularizes, and universalizes under the form of a costly self-help method (Einstein 2008). Just as mindfulness was made available outside of Buddhism, Kabbalah was also made available outside of Judaism while offering the world a life-enhancing "spirituality."

Through the Kabbalah Center, what was for centuries the esoteric core of Judaism became a secular life-actualization tool. Not only is Kabbalah now offered to everyone, including non-Jewish individuals, but many visitors are unaware that what they are practicing is a modified form of Judaism. This dynamic mirrors the fate of "mindfulness" in the West, in that many "mindfulness" practitioners ignore that what they are practicing, when they are practicing "mindfulness techniques," is really a Westernized version of Buddhism. "*Vipassanā*-derived mindfulness practices," says Fronsdal, "are taught in hospitals, clinics, prisons, and schools without any hint of their Buddhist source," so much so, he concludes, that "the biggest influence *vipassanā* practice will have on American society may eventually be in such non-Buddhist applications" (1998, 164–165).

Reducing religion to "well-being" practices is characteristic of postmodernity. In such a context, the traditional function of religion—purveying answers and expressing emotion—is now provided by nonreligious institutions. According to Zygmunt Bauman, "post-modern cultural pressures, while intensifying the search for 'peak experiences,' have at the same time uncoupled the search from religion-prone interests and concerns, privatized it, and cast mainly non-religious institutions in the role of purveyors of relevant services" (1998, 70). This is certainly applicable to the cases of Buddhism and yoga in the West. But Christian mindfulness (Coff 1991) and Jewish mindfulness seem to contradict this theory: they are appropriations of meditation and yoga outside of Buddhism or Hinduism by *another religion.* It appears, then, that rather than religious institutions fading away in postmodernity, they remain relevant.

Moreover, this phenomenon inverts the usual dynamic between the religious and the secular. Prior to secularization, religion in the West overlapped with other spheres of society; but the importation of mindfulness and yoga as therapeutic methods into Western religious practices shows that, today, secular practices can nourish the religious sphere. Furthermore, differentiation between the religious and the secular is now blurred. Western Buddhism, in typical postmodern fashion, transcends symbolic boundaries, becoming what Seager (in chap. 7 in this volume) calls "free-floating Dharma," a mobile meaning system.

The Cosmopolitanization of American Jews

Through the secularization of mindfulness, the Dharma could reach out to broader swaths of the American population, including those who already maintained strong, non-Buddhist religious identities.

These identities were already becoming more porous as a result of globalization. Under the influence of cosmopolitanism, religious identities could be maintained without being seen as exclusive. This development allowed Jewish mindfulness to emerge.

This transfer of a practice from one institution to another can be visualized as follows:

Vipassana Buddhism → Insight meditation → mindfulness → Jewish mindfulness

Or, put more simply:

Buddhism → meditation → Jewish meditation

Over the course of this process, "mindfulness" crossed over from one religion (Buddhism) to another (Judaism) via the secular.

In addition to developments in mindfulness and Vipassana in the United States, Buddhist ethics and aesthetics have been increasingly integrated within secular Western society since the seventies. They became part of a Western cultural ethos, which can be defined, in the current context of globalization, as cosmopolitan. Hence, post-countercultural Jewish Americans have grown up in a world wherein Buddhism, yoga, and mindfulness were part of a common American vocabulary. They didn't have to "reach out East" and leave their own culture to benefit from "Eastern spiritualities." Asian religious practices and beliefs had already been translated, integrated, and made available in Western culture. It was part of their cosmopolitan heritage.

In globalized contemporary Western societies, cosmopolitans do not need to travel to be described as such. Their local identity is already in itself hybrid. As Stuart Hall notes, "They are irrevocably the product of several interlocking histories and cultures" (1992, 310). Western cosmopolitans build their identities in the form of subjective *bricolages*, picking among all the cultural resources available. Within the margin of freedom allowed by their cultural and social determinations, they craft a tailored universe of meaning and of practice that is the most adjusted to their needs. This is why "cultures of hybridity are one of the distinctly novel types of identity produced in the era of late modernity" (Hall 1992, 310).

Of course, as Thomas Tweed reminds us, all cultures are hybrid (2002, 19). But the novelty of postmodern hybridizations is that, carried by the new information and communication technologies, they occur and proliferate quickly. They are also simultaneous, multicultural, and mostly virtual. In this new cultural context, cosmopolitanism is not even a choice or "a mode of managing meaning," as Hannerz describes it (1990, 238). It is simply the given of contemporary Western identity. For Kevin Robins, this type of identity can be defined as the imperative of "translation" versus "tradition": In a context where "the continuity and historicity of identity are challenged by the immediacy and intensity of global cultural confrontations, the comforts of tradition are fundamentally challenged by the imperative to forge a new self-interpretation based upon the responsibilities of cultural translation" (1991, 41). This thesis echoes Bastide's older typology of "canned" versus "living" religions (1967). We have seen earlier that Judaism has built and maintained itself as a community according to the "canned" religion model, namely, around tradition. As a proper hybrid, it shows an alternative to Bastide's and Robins's models as it is a religion that makes use of translation to keep the tradition.

"JEWISH MINDFULNESS" AS A NEW RELIGIOUS LABEL

Sociologists still struggle to define "religion." For some, the criterion is transcendence; others insist on social rituals and extend the definition to secular contexts. French sociologist Danièle Hervieu-Léger (1993) defines it as "chains of memory" or "lineage"; in other words, as "tradition." However, I consider this criterion alone insufficient. I retain three structural criteria to contend that Jewish mindfulness has features of a new religious practice (even if it hasn't created a new religion outside of Judaism but another Jewish trend within an already diverse American Judaism): a lineage of teachers, the institutionalization of a practice, and a theology to support both.

A Lineage: From Buddhist Teachers to Jewish Mindfulness Grassroots Communities

The founders of the IMS (Sharon Salzberg, Jacqueline Mandell, Jack Kornfield, and Joseph Goldstein) represent the first generation of teachers of "mindfulness" in America and are still the dominant figures in this field. Sylvia Boorstein, cofounder of the West Coast counterpart of the IMS in 1987 in the San Francisco Bay Area, Spirit Rock Meditation Center (SRMC), was their student. Trained in America by American teachers, she represents the second generation of Western mindfulness teachers. But, more importantly, she stands as the symbolic "mother" of Jewish mindfulness.

After years of practicing and teaching Buddhism, Boorstein suddenly found meaning in Judaism (Boorstein 1997). She resumed attending synagogue and soon was teaching mindfulness to her rabbi. Thus, she may be the first to have detached "mindfulness" from Insight Meditation for the purpose of renewing Jewish practice. In 1996, she and her rabbi started offering mindfulness sittings in the conservative synagogue of Rabbi Jonathan Slater. These sittings constituted the genesis of Jewish mindfulness.

Slater and other progressive rabbis of various denominations were then trained by Insight Meditation teachers and started teaching mindfulness within the Jewish world. They constitute the third generation of American mindfulness teachers, but they also represent the first generation of specifically "Jewish mindfulness" teachers.

In 2009, Boorstein hosted at SRMC the first "Jewish mindfulness retreat," which she co-led with another Jewish Buddhist teacher and social activist, Donald Rothberg, together with Reconstructionist rabbis Jeff Roth, Sheila Peltz-Weinberg, and Myriam Plotz for the daily "Torah Yoga" class. This formula was successful beyond their expectations. It drew Jewish Americans from a wide spectrum of generations as well as religious backgrounds, from secular Jews to rabbis.[6]

Jeff Roth, founder of the Awakened Heart Project, has since developed a new practice with his wife Rabbi Johanna Katz. He organizes several retreats a year in America and in Israel with the local facilitation of American Orthodox Rabbi James Jacobson-Maisels. Since 2010, as a teacher at the Jerusalem conservative Yeshiva Pardes and facilitator of a weekly silent meditation, Jacobson-Maisels has also started leading retreats in America. After starting to teach separately in Canada since 2013, Jacobson-Maisels and Roth led their first retreat in England in May 2014. "Jewish mindfulness" has thus expanded in a back-and-forth flow to form a transnational, transatlantic network.

Over the past few years, a second generation of "Jewish mindfulness" teachers has emerged. Thanks to the path opened by their countercultural elders, American Jews were given access to Buddhism in the

Jewish world. They could satisfy their interest in meditation with a more "spiritual" and meaningful Jewish life without having to "go" to Buddhism. It was in this spirit that two Brooklyn-based, twenty-something professional and conservative Jewish women, Alison Laichter and Yael Shy, started the Jewish Meditation Center of Brooklyn (JMC) in 2000. They did so with the expressed desire to sustain their practice on a regular basis and to live "mindfully" as Jews. Shy then founded the Spirituality Project at New York University, where she has invited both guest rabbis and Buddhist speakers.

Laichter and Shy are neither teachers of Buddhism nor meditator rabbis but "simple practitioners" who took their own needs in hand by creating the relevant frame. In this respect, Jewish mindfulness is being built structurally on the "popular religion" prototype. First, it was initiated by the common desire of meditators and rabbis to institutionalize their hybrid practice and to enshrine it within Judaism; second, it has developed spontaneously from the base, from amateur meditators who, in the absence of available structures, started their own grassroots communities. Such a pattern is paradigmatic of today's postmodernity, where it is individuals, rather than Bourdieu's "religious specialists," who have taken on religious creativity (Hervieu-Léger 1999; Roof 1993).

In the absence of any central doctrine or leader, Jewish mindfulness teachers form a cohort of students-teachers-friends, reciprocally teaching each other in a horizontal mode of relationship that radically departs from the hierarchical, vertical teacher-disciple relationship found in Buddhist lineages. Jewish mindfulness therefore exemplifies the contemporary dynamic of new types of religious groups based on "elective fraternities," a mode of religious affiliation that acts by way of "mutual validation" of subjective beliefs between chosen peers (Hervieu-Léger 1999, 181).

Transmission is the sine qua non condition of building a lineage. Jewish mindfulness teachers of the first generation are aware of this and have made efforts in that direction with an eye toward building a sustainable community. This effort extends in two directions: (1) transmission to the youth and (2) creation of a corporation of transmitters, namely, teachers. Hence the JMC and the New York University Spirituality Project have greatly benefited from the support of the existing Jewish mindfulness scene, while Shy and Jacobson-Maisels have begun offering mindfulness retreats near New York for young adults.

But the main element that evidences the institutionalization of Jewish mindfulness as religion rather than individual *bricolages* is the Jewish mindfulness teacher training program initiated in 2010 by Peltz-Weinberg and Roth at the Institute for Jewish Spirituality (IJS). In Weberian typology, this is an example of the routinization of charisma, through the creation of a corporation of "salvation goods" functionaries. With such institutionalization, the holders of the legitimate dogma (orthodoxy) can create an orthopraxy that secures the homogeneity of the practice, thus ensuring the movement's identity and longevity. Let us take a closer look at this orthopraxy.

A Hybrid Practice

Jewish mindfulness follows a pattern that is clearly based on the Vipassana practices from which it has taken inspiration: the core activity is silent meditation, and the teachings focus on "mindfulness" and "lovingkindness."[7] In Jewish mindfulness retreats, everything—the program of silent mindful sitting, silent mindful walking, silent mindful eating, evening "Dharma talks," and interviews with the teachers; the daily schedule (roughly 6 am to 9 pm); the atmosphere created through the use of cushions; and the terminological shibboleths of "mindfulness," "breath," and "awareness"—is modeled on silent Vipassana retreats. But the frame and the aim of the practice are specifically Jewish: the main if not core Buddhist elements (such as the presence of Buddha statues and the practice of bowing) disappear, while central Jewish elements are introduced; the setting often becomes a Jewish center or a synagogue, the teachers are mostly rabbis, and the daily recitation of Jewish prayers (at least the *Kaddish*), as well as the observance of Shabbat or of Jewish holidays, are key components. A daily yoga practice is offered to help participants relax from the constant observation of the mind. The retreats are shorter, the schedule milder, the food more abundant, and prayer and daily yoga allow for a break from meditation (which is precisely why they are forbidden in traditional Vipassana retreats). As participants say, meditating in a Jewish setting is "warmer and more joyful," and in short, more pleasant. Typically, at Jewish retreats participants can expect cake at dessert and Shabbat songs with a guitar, in contrast with the austerity of some Buddhist settings.

Likewise, weekly Jewish mindfulness sittings usually take place in Jewish settings. A meditation intention (or *kavannah*) is often set around the *Parasha* of the week, and an account of each participant's experience, related or not to these themes, will be shared following meditation.

In sum, the practice of meditation in Jewish mindfulness appears much easier, both physically (as evidenced by the flexibility of the posture and of the forms, the shorter length of the sittings, and the alternation with "Torah yoga") and psychologically (as evidenced by the time devoted to instructions, teachings, and sharing and the consequent shortened time of personal silent meditation). The practice of sitting in a circle, facing each other (unlike some Buddhist settings where participants are seated in rows or facing the wall), as well as the "sharings," attest to the importance of notions of community and of discourse in Judaism.

In Buddhist Vipassana, the core principle of compassion doesn't prevent the participant from being "left alone" with the physical and mental pain of sitting. The Jewish interpretation, by contrast, is to extend "gentleness" or "nurturing," even at the stage of "initiatic journey" of meditation: the participants can arrive late, move during the sitting, and even lie down; during student-teachers interactions, encouragement is given and emotions shared. All of these elements induce a feeling of being cared for by the community, which is characteristic of Jewish culture and the mothering role of the community.

Jewish mindfulness is therefore a hybrid practice. It can be seen as the institutionalization of the mixed practices of the so-called Jewish Buddhists. From this institutionalization of religious *bricolages*, we can infer two things: first, that individuals' *bricolages* tend to become systematized; and second, consequently, and in a manner defying dominant conceptions of religious modernity, individual religiosity is not long-lasting. Instead it appears as a transitory phase prior to affiliation. This brings us back to the first "noble truth" of religion offered by Durkheim: no matter how individualistic a society may appear, religion remains a *social* phenomenon.

Jewish mindfulness has thus become a new religious practice—but not a new religion. It hasn't left the mantle of Judaism. On the contrary, the purpose of its founders is to integrate new practices within Judaism in order to enrich it. For this reason, while sharing many features with new religious movements (the use of hybridity, the mode of elective fraternity, and the focus on well-being and self-actualization), Jewish mindfulness cannot be described as a New Religious Movement. Like neo-evangelism, it appears as renewal rather than dissidence. But unlike neo-evangelism, Jewish mindfulness is hybrid. How this is being justified theologically by Jewish mindfulness teachers and rabbis is worth exploring further.

A New Theology and Doctrinal Debates

Jewish mindfulness is a new form of Judaism not only because it has its own teachers and practices, but because it has its own theology. Jewish mindfulness is more than Vipassana with a Jewish twist. What makes Jewish mindfulness specifically Jewish, beyond the cultural translations of the practice, is the introduction of God. This is where it radically departs from Buddhism, even if the theology is itself deeply hybrid and borrows from Buddhist concepts. According to Reconstructionist rabbi Jeff Roth, "Jewish meditation . . . provides the wisdom to understand the nature of mind including those factors of mind that tend to obscure clear seeing. The practice teaches us how to direct our attention into the present moment of experience, which is the only place the Divine Presence can be experienced."[8]

This definition illustrates the appropriation of Buddhist terminology for a new Jewish theology in which God has the last word. Indeed, the aim of Jewish practice is connecting to God. As such, the aim of meditation in Jewish mindfulness is to become closer to God. The well-being and insights obtained by meditation, although sought after as well, are side effects. Merging with the divine gives meaning (a typical postmodern need) to the ritual and devotional practice of Judaism. As renewal founder Reb Zalman argues, this impels individuals to perform the *mitzvoth* (commandments) not because they have to but because they want to (Schachter-Shalomi 1993, 40). This simple shift in intention represents a radically new definition of Judaism.

According to this new theology, all Jewish practices are "mindfulness." Indeed, the function of the *brachot* (blessings) is to help one be mindful of one's actions—but not mindful in an abstract manner, as in Buddhism. In Jewish mindfulness, the aim is to be mindful *of God*, to have the mind "full of God." This is why Jewish mindfulness practitioners identify themselves as mystics, and why their main school of reference in Judaism is Hassidism. Therefore, Jewish mindfulness can be roughly understood as a hybrid offspring of Vipassana Buddhism and Hassidism.

However, some practitioners, especially those in the younger generation, seem hesitant to acknowledge the Buddhist source of their practice. JMC's Laichter, for instance, argues that "Buddhism doesn't have the monopoly on the breath."[9] The question of whether or not to pay tribute to Buddhism in Jewish mindfulness practices is actually currently raising debates in the community. Jay Michaelson, for instance, a Jewish activist and thinker, denounces the absence of "the B word" in Jewish mindfulness discourses.[10]

Could the absence of publications on this topic, in spite of the dynamism of Jewish studies in general, reveal an equal resistance by the academic world to looking into the contemporary hybridity of Judaism? The underlying thesis of the only article written about Buddhism's influence on the revival of Jewish meditation seems to suggest such an interpretation. Comparing Buddhist practices at SRMC with a nearby Jewish renewal center, which the author defines as a "center that presents Jewish mysticism as a form of mindfulness," Cia Sautter flatly denies any appropriation of Buddhism. In spite of her own findings, she contends that Jews "are finding Buddhist mindfulness within their own tradition" (2002). Her depiction of "meditation on Hebrew letters as if they were mandalas, and singing of Hebrew scripture as if it were mantras," echoes exactly, without any critical distance, the new hybrid theology of Jewish mindfulness. In short, her analysis, which is essentially an insider's apologetic approach, fails to offer an accurate depiction of the current transformations within Judaism. It simply does not take into account the sociological dimensions of Buddhism's integration into American culture. Such stances, as well as the new "theological" debates within the Jewish mindfulness community, reveal the claim for "purity" against "hybridity," typical within all religious groups (Droogers 2005). Much more needs to be written on this as well as on the syncretistic processes and modalities within Jewish mindfulness.

CONCLUSION

The case of Jewish mindfulness shows that new religious creations do not necessarily end with the creation of new religions. The desire to return to one's religion may be more powerful. In a way, this desire corresponds to the postmodern ethos of individual healing and universalism. Jewish mindfulness stands as a paradigmatic example of how, in globalized Western societies, hybridity can be utilized to renew tradition. In that respect, the definition of postmodernity might dwell in the apparent paradox of cosmopolitanism as neo-traditionalism.

Drawing many American Jews to meditate in Jewish rather than in Buddhist settings (while also welcoming non-Jews), can Jewish mindfulness compete with Western Buddhism? Jews have always represented a proportionally important segment of Western Buddhism, and applications of Buddhism outside of Buddhism are now proliferating in secular, Christian, and Jewish settings. Is the future of Western Buddhism threatened by such appropriations?

It doesn't seem so. First, Jewish mindfulness remains a quantitatively marginal trend, gathering only a few thousand individuals. Second, many Jewish mindfulness practitioners also take part in the Buddhist world. And, most importantly, perhaps the strongest influence of Buddhism in Western societies may be in its disappearance into social practices: because it matches so well with the contemporary Western ethos (which it has partially informed), Buddhism has become a legitimate expression of contemporary culture. Like water, it has conquered the West by becoming all the forms and colors of its new containers. This reminds us that globalization, often conflated with Westernization (Gillepsie 2011, 99), also occurs through a simultaneous Easternization of the West.

NOTES

1. Hassidism, from *Hessed* ("lovingkindness"), is a mystical and contemplative form of Judaism crafted in eighteenth-century Poland. Persecuted in its time by the orthodoxy, Hassidism is today considered a legitimate form of Judaism.
2. The two others being Japanese Zen and Tibetan Vajrayana.
3. See Insight Meditation Society, "FAQ about IMS," http://www.dharma.org/about-us/faq (retrieved January 27, 2014).
4. Allison Gaudet Yarrow, "Sharon Salzberg on Finding Meditation in Jewish Tradition," *The Jewish Daily Forward* (February 24, 2011), http://blogs.forward.com/the-shmooze/135680/#ixzz1dQYyGIZm.

5. Sharon Salzberg, "What Does It Mean to Be Mindful?" http://www.beliefnet.com/Faiths/Buddhism/2000/12/What-Does-It-Mean-To-Be-Mindful.aspx.
6. From all denominations, at the exclusion of orthodox rabbis.
7. Called *mettā* in the Vipassana movement, it is a meditation consisting of wishing wellness to oneself and others.
8. The Awakened Heart Project for Contemplative Judaism, "What Is Jewish Meditation?" http://www.awakenedheartproject.org.
9. Josh Fleet, "Is the Jew Still in the Lotus?" *Huffington Post* (July 29, 2011), http://www.huffingtonpost.com/2011/07/29/jewish-meditation-movement_n_913445.html.
10. Jay Michaelson, "Judaism, Meditation and the B Word," *The Jewish Daily Forward* (June 10, 2005), http://forward.com/articles/3652/judaism-meditation-and-the-b-word.

SECTION IV

MODERNITY AND MODERNITIES

The question of rhetorical or categorical boundaries was addressed in section 1, with authors both questioning received categories and proposing new theoretical models. In this section, we return to such questions by highlighting a particular conceptual framework used to study Buddhism in the United States and worldwide: modernity. Most often juxtaposed with "tradition," modernity has come to dominate the field and promises new avenues for continued research.

In his contribution, Erik Braun focuses on what may be considered a "traditional" practice and its associated cosmological underpinnings: *jhāna* meditation. By detailing the rise in popularity of jhānic practices and their associated blissful mental states, even and especially by prominent "modernist" teachers, Braun draws our attention to the complexity of this dichotomy, all too easily taken for granted.

David McMahan, whose larger work on Buddhist modernism has been widely applied in the field, calls into question the very category of "modernity" itself and reminds us to be attentive to the specific ways in which modernity is deployed. Whereas earlier generations of scholars presumed modernity to entail progressive cultural and economic development—with modernity seen as essentially synonymous with Westernization—McMahan explores how modernity in China challenges these assumptions by suffusing it with Confucian values as much as Western economic ones. Buddhist modernism, in this case, is properly understood as Chinese Buddhist modernity.

Mitchell and Quli query the utility of the category of "modernism," noting that a religious group labeled "traditional" in one context may be seen as "modernist" in another, as is the case with some Buddhist traditions that are cast as modern in Japan but traditional in the United States. Arguing that what scholars call "modernity" is actually a set of narratives, the authors suggest that Buddhists can choose to appropriate some elements but not others, and these elements are then integrated into existing cultural matrices; this produces multiple Buddhist modernities that blend both "modern" and "traditional" elements. Comparing two contemporary Buddhist groups in the United States leads the authors to question the utility of the label "modernist" itself, which may be seen as part of a larger academic paradigm rooted in ideas of rupture and loss.

TEN

THE UNITED STATES OF *JHĀNA*

Varieties of Modern Buddhism in America

ERIK BRAUN

Since the turn of the millennium, *jhāna* meditation, the cultivation of mental states of deep calm (*samatha*) and concentration (*samādhi*), has surged in popularity in America, both in print and in practice. This is a novel situation. Although the *jhānas* are understood to be profoundly pleasurable—as the monk Ajaan Brahm put it, "better than sex" (Brahm 2006, 1; cf. Spiro 1982, 55)—most meditation teachers in America and in Asia ignored them until recently. This was because they considered such states of rarified consciousness to be inappropriate for regular people. At best, the *jhānas* merely prepared one for the real work of liberation through the separate practice of insight meditation (*vipassanā*); at worst, they created a "*samādhi* junkie" addicted to delusional bliss (Brasington 2007, 6). In the words of a well-known meditation teacher, *jhāna* meditation was viewed as "a kind of meditators' Olympics, a pursuit suited only to extraordinary beings who lived in caves or monasteries, far beyond the ken of 'normal people'" (Gunaratana 2009a, vii).

But this negative attitude notwithstanding, in recent years many books and websites teaching the *jhānas* have appeared, numerous conferences and retreats dedicated to concentration practices have taken place, and popular Buddhist magazines have published articles extolling the *jhānas*' rightful place in Buddhist meditation.[1] A shift has taken place, it seems, toward a sensibility that values the *jhānas*. The teachers Tina Rasmussen and Stephen Snyder liken their cultivation to "Jedi warrior mind training"—a description that suggests the power of the *jhānas* as a force for good.[2] Some teachers even seek to turn the situation on its head, putting these states of mind at the heart of Buddhist meditation. To quote Ajaan Brahm again: "Put bluntly, if it isn't *jhāna* then it isn't true Buddhist meditation!" (Brahm 2006, 127).

This chapter considers what features in American culture and Buddhist teachings have caused the *jhānas* to become popular in recent times. Identifying these features promises to give us a more accurate assessment of the shape and direction of modern Theravada Buddhism.[3] To do this, I quote a variety of voices prominent in the American Theravada Buddhist scene. These sources do not speak as one, but their agreement on key points gives a composite picture of the appeal of the *jhānas*. The picture that develops shows that the growing popularity of jhānic practices dissolves any stable, progressive relationship between forms of Buddhism considered traditional and those seen as modern.

In his examination of the development of Western Buddhism, Martin Baumann has identified a split between modernist forms that stress Buddhism as a rational and scientific system, based in scripture, and traditionalist forms that focus on ritual and devotional acts of merit-making and "hold specific cosmological worldviews" (Baumann 2001, 25). This analytical distinction—similar to those of other scholars examining Asian cultures (cf. Bechert 1994, 257–258; Lopez 2002b, ix)—certainly captures a broad but real difference at present between two Buddhist groups in America, a difference that usually maps onto the "convert" (modernist) versus "immigrant" (traditionalist) divide. But the *jhānas* crosscut these categories. Interest in the *jhānas* has burgeoned among the convert group, those Buddhists or Buddhist sympathizers who are, generally, white and in the middle or upper classes.[4] Such people are often highly secular—reluctant at times even to call themselves Buddhist—and concerned with meditation divorced from ritual practices or belief in rebirth (Fronsdal 1998, 164). In other words, they are exemplars of Buddhist modernism. But, as we shall see later, teachers of the *jhānas* have often included within their presentations of calm and concentration meditation cosmological worldviews that include rebirth and other apparently "traditional" beliefs. Thus, examination of the growing popularity of these practices allow us to reconsider at the end of this chapter what a modern (or even postmodern) American Buddhist can be.

THE *JHĀNAS* IN MEDITATION PRACTICE

Orthodox Theravada Buddhism organizes meditation into two categories of practice, calm meditation (*samathabhāvanā*), which has as a central goal the achievement of states of deep concentration (*samādhi*), and insight meditation (*vipassanābhāvanā*), which aims at a liberative understanding of reality. The relationship between these two practices received perhaps its most authoritative articulation for Theravada Buddhism in the fifth-century compendium on meditation, *Path of Purification* (*Visuddhimagga*). Although the text allows for the possibility of divergences in how a meditator pursues the path to liberation, it assumes as normative the cultivation of morality, then concentration, and then insight.[5] Practices for cultivating concentration are part of *samatha* (calm) meditation, because calm and concentration are understood to be intrinsically connected. This stage of the practice, before one seeks insight, is where the meditator cultivates the *jhānas*.

The *jhānas* arise by focusing the mind on a selected object of meditation. Whether it be the breath (*ānāpāna*), a feeling of lovingkindness (*mettā*), a circle of colored earth (*kasiṇa*), or something else suitable to one's temperament, with effort one becomes immovably fixed on one's object and thus concentrated. A jhānic state comes about through a focus on the meditation object that suppresses the five "hindrances" (*nīvaraṇa*) of sensual desire (*kāmacchanda*), aversion (*byāpāda*), sloth and torpor (*thīna-middha*), restlessness and anxiety (*uddhacca-kukkucca*), and doubt (*vicikicchā*) and promotes the corresponding growth of the five "limbs" of *jhāna*: an initial grasping of an object of attention by the mind (*vitakka*), a sustained hold on that object by the mind (*vicāra*), joy (*pīti*), happiness (*sukha*), and one-pointedness of mind (*ekagattā*). The suppression of the five hindrances and the full flowering of the five limbs puts one in the first *jhāna*, which is the first of eight possible jhānic states.[6] The next three states of *jhāna* are simplifications of the first *jhāna*: the second *jhāna* drops initial grasping and sustained hold, the third drops joy, and the fourth is left with one-pointedness. After these four states, one can travel into four higher realms, called the "formless *jhānas*" (*arūpajhānas*), which are characterized not by a *jhāna* limb (one keeps the one-pointedness of the fourth *jhāna*) but by an object of awareness (Gunaratana 2009a, 107). The meditator drops his or her original object of focus and takes up the particular object of a formless realm, each more subtle than the last. These are infinite space (*ākāsānañcāyatana*), infinite consciousness (*viññānañcāyatana*), nothingness (*ākiñcaññāyatana*), and neither-perception-nor-nonperception (*nevasaññāsaññāyatana*).

As rarified as these states are, they are still only a means to an end, not the end itself. The orthodox view understands that the practice of the *jhānas* comes before insight meditation because it stabilizes the mind and gives it a penetrating focus, but the meditator must then apply that focus in subsequent insight practice. In contrast to calm meditation, insight practice is a close observation of reality, empowered by calm and concentration (and so more than mere "looking" or intellectual reasoning), that confirms, permanently, the Buddhist lessons of no-self (*anatta*), suffering (*dukkha*), and impermanence (*anicca*) (Cousins 1973, 123).

The most commonly taught Theravada-derived method of meditation in America comes from the Burmese monk called the Mahasi Sayadaw (1904–1982). Certainly, there have been a number of other insight meditation techniques that have made an impact in the United States, for instance those of S. N. Goenka, Ruth Denison, and Henepola Gunaratana. But the Mahasi technique still serves as the charter method for insight meditation in America. Other methods are important to consider for this chapter only insofar as they materially change the dominant emphasis—expressed quintessentially through the Mahasi method—on insight practice without prior cultivation of the *jhānas*.[7]

In the system of "first concentration, then insight" outlined here, teachers indebted to Mahasi have put the focus almost entirely on doing *vipassanā* from the get-go.[8] The Mahasi method teaches one to label all sense data as they come in through the six sense-doors of sight, sound, taste, touch, smell, and mind. Eventually, this cataloging of experiences deepens one's moment-by-moment concentration (which is not the same as absorption in the *jhānas*) and allows one to progress through the levels of realization leading to insight. This is called the "pure insight" (*suddhavipassanā*) or the "dry" (*sukkha*) method because it requires no special concentration.[9] From the viewpoint of this practice tradition, one that represents the mainstream in America, cultivating the *jhānas* simply delays the critical insight process.[10]

WHY THE POPULARITY OF THE *JHĀNAS* NOW?

So why have the *jhānas* become so popular in recent times if they have typically been discounted? I suggest a combination of factors—the changing influence of lineages of teaching, the experiences of individual practitioners, a rereading of Theravada Buddhist texts, and cultural context—to explain the growth in interest in the *jhānas*.

While the Mahasi technique is widespread, there is a lineage of teaching *jhāna* meditation within the Thai forest tradition that has started to exert an influence. A number of Thai forest monasteries have been founded since the 1990s in the United States, and various teachers, both Thai- and Western-born and both male and female, have gained prominence. Many are connected to the teacher Ajaan Chah (1918–1992), including Ajaan Brahm, who is perhaps the strongest lobbyist for the *jhānas*. Although he heads a monastery and meditation center in Australia, he has made an impact in America through his book *Mindfulness, Bliss, and Beyond*, as well as his Dhamma talks available through his website (and other sites). Thanissaro Bhikkhu is another influential source for Thai Forest teachings in America. Thanissaro learned *jhāna* meditation as part of his training in Thailand under Ajaan Fuang (1915–1986), and he has stressed the value of the *jhānas* since returning to the United States and becoming abbot of Wat Mettavanaram in southern California in 1993.

Besides teachers who work within a tradition of *jhāna* practice, the exploration of Buddhist texts has led some teachers to promote the *jhānas*. These teachers, in essence, have begun their own lineages of practice. For instance, in her autobiography Ayya Khema describes how she first attained the formless *jhānas* (the *arūpajhānas*) on the basis of her reading:

> It was a full-moon evening and we were getting ready as usual to meditate through the night. As I sat in the meditation hall, I was getting more and more tired and more and more bored. We had already sat there for four hours, had chanted, had heard a talk from Phra Khantipalo, and now it was midnight. *Then I recalled what I had read about meditative absorptions in the Buddha's discourses.* . . . Then it occurred to me that I

> should just once try to realize infinite space, infinite consciousness, the realm of nothingness, and neither perception nor non-perception. And lo and behold, the level of concentration I already had at my disposal was sufficient to allow me to experience these levels of consciousness. (Khema 1997b, 160, italics mine)

Gunaratana, too, states that he learned meditation, including the *jhānas*, not from any teacher but from reading books.[11] Khema and Gunaratana thus used texts not only to confirm prior experience but to produce it, and this has authorized calm and concentration practice.[12] Snyder and Rasmussen also demonstrate the importance of texts. While they did not formulate their method themselves, they follow a highly textualized (and extremely complex) system by the Burmese monk called the Pa-Auk Sayadaw based on the *Visuddhimagga*. It is a typical modernist move to return to originary texts to justify innovative practices. Yet these teachers do not go back just to the original canon. In using commentarial literature as well, they suggest that forms of modern Buddhism can draw on a wider range of sources for inspiration and evolution.

Additionally, even prior to the influence of text or teacher, some sorts of profound yet unexplained experiences of practitioners may have led them to the jhānic inventory of states of concentration. The teacher Leigh Brasington, who studied under Ayya Khema, has argued, for instance, that people can "stumble" into rudimentary *jhānas*.[13] Whatever the actual nature of these states, such experiences can lead practitioners to teachers and texts that espouse the *jhānas*.

Besides acting as charters for experience, texts are also used as authoritative sources to make a case for calm and concentration practice against the view of it as hazardous or unnecessary. Many *jhāna* teachers argue, in fact, that *jhāna* practices are not only presented as acceptable within the Buddhist texts but actually as preferable if not outright required. To make this point, a number of teachers quote the Buddha from verse 327 of the *Dhammapada*:

> There's no *jhāna* for one with no insight,
> no insight for one with no *jhāna*.
> As for him with both *jhāna* and insight,
> he is near enlightenment.[14]

Thanissaro Bhikkhu makes this clear in his own words as well: "When they depict the Buddha telling his disciples to go meditate, they never quote him as saying 'go do vipassana,' but always 'go do jhana.'"[15] Other teachers make much the same point: Snyder and Rasmussen, responding to the question of whether it is necessary to cultivate the *jhānas*, say, "For us, the answer lies in the practice of the Buddha himself. If he is our role model, should we not follow the path that he not only taught but personally practiced throughout his life, even at the moment of death?" (Snyder and Rasmussen 2009, 129). Ayya Khema says, writing around 1996, "In Asia too, as well as in the United States and in Australia, only my students and two other teachers even speak of the absorptions at all. But these absorptions are the real meditation" (Khema 1997b, 199). And this chapter began with Ajaan Brahm's statement that *jhāna* is what Buddhist meditation is all about.

It could seem that such arguments for *jhāna* cultivation push enlightenment farther away, since one must now strive for rarified and difficult-to-achieve states of consciousness, instead of simply turning to insight practice using regular consciousness as the starting point. But these teachers argue that, in fact, cultivating the *jhānas* may be the missing component that would allow for speedier enlightenment. Gunaratana and Brahm, for instance, both mention the fact that at the end of the *Satipaṭṭhāna Sutta* (MN 10; also see DN 22), the Buddha mentions that a person who follows properly the four foundations of mindfulness (body, feelings, mind, and mental contents) will attain enlightenment in as little as seven days. In recognition of the fact that this is not a schedule to which many successfully adhere, Brahm says, "Many Buddhists, monastic and lay, have completed many meditation retreats lasting longer than seven days and remain unenlightened. Please do not blame the Buddha!" (Brahm 2006, 104). He explains that what has been missing from a proper observance of the foundations of mindfulness is the purified and focused mind that emerges from *jhāna* practice. This argument elevates the status of the *jhānas* by presenting them as vital to reach enlightenment (cf. Catherine 2008, xii; Gunaratana 2009b, 65).

To recapitulate the reasons for the appeal of the *jhānas* so far, we can see that personal experience can drive interest, the influence of authoritative lineages and teachers, and a desire to adhere more closely to what is perceived as the much more pronounced valuation of the *jhānas* in the canonical texts than previously acknowledged. And we have, too, a sense that the *jhānas* are practically useful in order to "turbo-charge"—to use Brasington's expression (Brasington 2007, 6)—progress toward enlightenment, even in as little as seven days. And, if difficult, this adds a sense of status. These are all, I think, important reasons for the rise in the prominence of the *jhānas*, but would they be enough to fuel a sustained interest? To convince publishers to release so many books, to fill *jhāna* retreats? As important as they are, I think we also need to look beyond these reasons, which emerge largely from the top-down vantage point of individual teachers and practitioners embedded within the Theravada tradition, to what makes these arguments for the *jhānas* resonate within the American cultural context.

Recall that Ayya Khema said part of her motivation for seeking the formless absorptions was, quite simply, boredom. This touches upon another, and I think key, reason for the growing popularity of the *jhānas*: the more overt pursuit of this-worldly happiness. Of course, dry insight meditation offers happiness as its ultimate goal as well, but the direct cultivation of states of bliss are not part of the process. Indeed, to "bliss out" is something of a pejorative in *vipassanā* circles, implying that one is wallowing self-indulgently in ephemeral states rather than focusing on the goal of self-knowledge. Nyanaponika, who in his influential *The Heart of Buddhist Meditation* advocates the Mahasi method, says, "In taking up this practice, one should not expect 'mystical experiences' or cheap emotional satisfaction" (Nyanaponika 1996, 88).

But with the emphasis on the *jhānas* comes an emphasis on feeling good. Given the previous passages, it is perhaps no surprise that the most blatant proponent of the inherent good in the bliss of the *jhānas* is Ajaan Brahm: "Do not fear delight in meditation. Happiness in meditation is important! Moreover, you deserve to bliss out. Blissing out on the breath is an essential part of the path" (Brahm 2006, 132). This is an argument that one pursues bliss for its own sake. After all, the Buddha is said to have sanctioned their enjoyment, and the teachers do stress the immediate benefits of such pleasures. Brahm quotes the Buddha thinking, "Why am I afraid of the pleasure which has nothing to do with the five senses nor with unwholesome things? I will not be afraid of that pleasure [of *jhāna*]!" (Brahm 2006, 130).[16] Ayya Khema even hazarded the guess in a public talk that the reason so many Western monastics eventually disrobe is that they do not have the pleasure of the *jhānas* to offset the rigors of renunciation. Gunaratana notes the incredible joy and peace in daily life (Gunaratana 2009a, 19); the lay teacher Christina Feldman says the *jhānas* are good in and of themselves (Feldman 2004, 73); and Shaila Catherine states that "jhanas are states of deep rest, healing rejuvenation, and profound comfort" (Catherine 2008, xii). In the many comments made about the wholesomeness of the *jhānas*, what comes to the fore is an emphasis on a positive and healthful *experience*. This is how Snyder and Rasmussen describe the effect of the *jhānas*: "After *jhāna* has ended, there remains a deeply felt peace. In our experience, the purified personal sense of consciousness merges into unobstructed, impersonal, universal consciousness" (Snyder and Rasmussen 2009, 72). Snyder and Rasmussen do not suggest that this is the end goal of Buddhist practice, but their book ends with such states. The overall "sell" of the *jhānas* by all these teachers is such that, at the very least, the impetus to practice is not predicated only on something past the jhānic experience. While it may be true the *jhānas* hasten enlightenment as the Buddha promised, the *jhānas* are presented as complete in themselves and very powerful.

This appeal to transcendent states is a powerful draw, because it taps into an emphasis on religion as, fundamentally, about an individual's affective experience.[17] Influenced by Friedrich Schleiermacher, William James, Rudolph Otto, and others, Westerners frequently assume a personal, powerful experience of some sort as the heart and soul of religion. Thanks to the influence of Romanticism, many believe such an experience culminates in feelings of unity and interconnection beyond the individual ego in something like the "universal consciousness" mentioned by Snyder and Rasmussen.[18]

Thanissaro Bhikkhu, although an advocate for *jhāna* practice, resists an assumption that meditation, whether dry insight or *jhāna*, is intrinsically defined by a sense of universal oneness. In his article "The Roots of Buddhist Romanticism," he argues that the discipline of psychology has helped to carry into Buddhism currents of Romanticism that present personal integration within an interconnected flux of reality as the overall objective of self-cultivation. Meditation in such a view becomes a therapeutic process, a matter of healthy self-adjustment through a sense of oneness amid daily life rather than the pursuit of world transcendence.[19] Thanissaro points out how much this assumption diverges from the stated goals of the Buddhist texts, and his trenchant critique calls our attention to cultural factors in America that create an elective affinity with the *jhānas*, even as they reorient their overall purpose. But, while accepting the importance of the Romantic strain in American

Buddhism, such an affinity suggests that we can understand the appeal of the *jhānas* more fully if we look beyond the influence of Romanticism to the nature of the American religious sensibility.

Catherine Albanese has identified three strands in American religious life: the evangelical, the communal, and the metaphysical. The metaphysical strand of religious life is relevant here, for it is the American form of religiosity that emphasizes the mind and a belief in the mind's "magical" ability to affect the material world (Albanese 2007, 6–7). This strand has four qualities: a preoccupation with the mind and its powers, a predisposition toward microcosmic-macrocosmic correspondences, thinking in terms of movement and energy, and—to quote Albanese—a "yearning for salvation understood as solace, comfort, therapy, and healing" (Albanese 2007, 15). These qualities resonate with the ways in which the *jhānas* are presented. Jhānic meditation obviously concerns the mind, yet it also trades upon a correspondence between mental and cosmological states (think of the immaterial sphere of infinite consciousness), states that have literal correspondences to realms of being in traditional Theravada cosmology. Such realms are seen as in flux, too, driven on by karmic energy. And as we have noted, many teachers stress the *jhānas* as a powerful means to well-being.

One aspect of the cultivation of the *jhānas* that is relatively neglected in Western discussions of the practice is morality (*sīla*). Its fairly cursory treatment throws into sharper relief the emphasis on experience, pleasure, and healing. For instance, morality usually receives only brief treatment at the start of books on the *jhānas*, and the authors present it as a preliminary requirement rather than an end goal. Yet for most Theravada Buddhists in the world, moral practice—whether donating to monks and nuns, building religious edifices, following the precepts, or visiting sacred sites—is the cornerstone of the religious life. Carrithers reported, for instance, that even Sri Lankan forest monks famous for their meditative prowess absolutely rejected his suggestion that meditation was more important than practices of morality (Carrithers 1983, 20). The authors and teachers I have mentioned certainly do not reject moral practices. In fact, they all teach that proper concentration emerges only out of a moral life. Still, their principle ways of teaching the *jhānas*—through books and articles focused almost exclusively on technique and through retreats outside of the traditional moral milieu of the monastery—means that moral practices receive relatively little attention.

The fairly loose connection between practice and a moral system also feeds into the appeal of the *jhānas* as religious experiences that cross sectarian lines. An open-ended, even diffuse approach to morality attracts practitioners who identify with another religious tradition, have an aversion to any teaching of exclusivity, or who view Buddhism as a pragmatic, therapeutic tool of mind that can be freed of any cultural baggage. And teachers of the *jhānas* find support for the argument that the *jhānas* are not exclusively Buddhist in the Buddhist texts themselves. Many note that the Buddha learned concentrative techniques from two teachers (Āḷāra Kālāma and Uddaka Rāmaputta) prior to his enlightenment. Furthermore, they point out that the Buddha-to-be spontaneously fell into the first *jhāna* as a child (mentioned by the Buddha in MN 36). From this they extrapolate to the idea that the *jhānas* are non-Buddhist, universal experiences. Snyder and Rasmussen say, "The story of the *jhānas* is a long one, so ancient that it predates written history and even Buddhism itself" (Snyder and Rasmussen 2009, 2). The report on the 2001 conference on the *jhānas*, organized by Leigh Brasington, noted that a retreat center manager observed that the *jhānas* were "familiar territory" to many religious practitioners.[20] In her autobiography, Ayya Khema relates the *jhānas* specifically to the Christian tradition: "Especially Teresa [of Ávila]'s instructions to her nuns in her book *The Interior Castle* made a particular impression on me, for there she describes the meditative absorptions that I teach also—only in her own personal way and connected with visions shaped by Christianity" (Khema 1997b, 193).

A sense of the *jhānas* as an objective experience outside of a particular belief system may account for the interest in relating these states to research on the mind, too. Brasington, for instance, mentions in an interview that research suggests (and he has participated in this research, even meditating inside an fMRI machine) that each jhānic state can be clearly differentiated on brain scans.[21] Brahm, too, mentions scientific studies of the brain at a number of points in his book. References to such research frames meditative experiences as objective events that lie outside any particular religious system.[22]

For insight-focused teachers, the fact that the *jhānas* are not intrinsically Buddhist is a reason to relegate them to minimal preparatory exercises or not to teach them at all. The opposite is true for *jhāna* advocates. Both groups agree broadly on the *jhānas*' relationship to insight practices, yet they value the cultivation of these two aspects of meditation differently.[23] Ajaan Brahm diverges from my other sources—and so far as I know from most meditation teachers in Theravada traditions—in arguing that the *jhānas* are, in fact, a specific discovery of the Buddha and not part of a general mystical heritage (Brahm 2006, 127–130). Interestingly, Brahm's view is in accord with some recent scholarship in Buddhist studies, which has argued that the *jhānas* are the original core of Buddhist meditation (cf. Bronkhorst 1986; Vetter 1988). But whatever the original status of the *jhānas*, works that have contributed to the recent positive attention paid to these concentrative states tend to stress their objective accessibility. This aspect of their presentation underscores their fit within American culture's stress on individual experience and the healing powers of the mind.

By connecting the *jhānas* to currents in American religiosity, I do not mean to suggest that the *jhānas* are only popular here in the United States, for they are present in Asia and elsewhere. And we have seen that teachers can find ample textual legitimation in the canonical and paracanonical sources for their celebration of the *jhānas* as acceptable pleasures. But the fit between jhānic states and a strong strand in American religious history toward personal experience that "means healing and therapy" and an ecumenical outlook can help to explain their appeal here (Albanese 2007, 15). This is particularly true for so-called convert Buddhists or sympathizers, who are likely to be indebted to the metaphysical strain of the American religious sensibility to a much greater degree than those with stronger roots in longstanding Asian forms of Theravada Buddhism.

IMPLICATIONS OF THE RISE OF *JHĀNA* PRACTICE FOR MODERN BUDDHISM

The reasons for the popularity of the *jhānas*—personal experience, lineages of practice, teacher charisma, textual demands, and American cultural influence—complicate our understanding of the trajectories of Buddhism's development in a globalizing age, for their rise calls our attention to how a form of Buddhism can change in ways that make it appear to go back as much as forward in terms of processes of modernization. The possibility of such seemingly retrograde, nonlinear movement undercuts the assumption of any enduring pattern of development among Buddhist groups.

Typically modernist features (particularly a focus on individual experience, a lack of ritual or elaborate moral injunctions, and a sense of ecumenical connections across religions) drive much of the appeal of concentrative practices. Yet the presentations of the *jhānas* by modern teachers often contain many apparently traditional elements. For instance, many of the teachers of *jhānas* advocate a literal understanding of karma and cosmology. Ajaan Brahm in his book discusses his own and his students' recollections of past lives gained through *jhāna* meditation. Snyder and Rasmussen have also recounted in interviews how turning to insight after the *jhānas* can enable a meditator to see his or her future lives leading up to enlightenment.[24] Gunaratana discusses how jhānic accomplishment leads to an awareness of rebirth.[25] And Ayya Khema mentions how she invites celestial beings to meditate and that "some of them are happy and willing to listen to the Dhamma and meditate with us."[26] To be sure, some teachers, such as Catherine and Brasington, present the *jhānas* with very little reference to karma, rebirth, or other realms of existence. Nevertheless, and accepting that a part of the *jhānas*' appeal is their purported accessibility across religious boundaries, their practice has demanded more fealty, not less, to Buddhist sources. This fealty brings in train, implicitly if not explicitly, intricate correspondences to cosmological realms and teachings of rebirth that are not easily extricable from the logic of jhānic cultivation.

Such developments among white "convert" Buddhists and sympathizers remind us that forms of Buddhism do not follow a single or simple process of modernization or rationalization but are, in fact, distinctive cultural formulations that can become—at least from the perspective we have now—*more* traditional in certain ways. This is not to say that *jhāna* practitioners in America are actually becoming more traditional. It is important to remember that the label "traditional" is not a neutral term but a way to separate beliefs or practices seen as somehow poised for the future (and so "modern") from those judged to be aligned with (and ultimately consigned to) the past. Thus, it is only from a perspective that has set the parameters for modern Buddhism in a certain way that the *jhānas* appear traditional. In fact, as the reasons we have explored for the *jhānas*' popularity show, the cosmological elements that frequently crop up in discussions of them do not signal a retreat from modernity but the development of a new variety of modern Buddhism.

The *jhānas*' rise in America points to the fact that changes in forms of Buddhism will depend in part on the specific contexts in which they are engaged. So, in a sense this is an argument for a particular Buddhism within the borders of America. Certainly, some of the reasons for the success of the *jhānas*, especially their "metaphysical" features, are rooted in American culture. But, at the same time, we should remember that as much as the demands of contemporary culture drive religious change, such demands only make sense and are articulated in particular ways that depend on continuities of belief and practice across borders in a globalized context. This complex situation points to the power of a past shaped both by sources within and sources beyond the borders of American culture. This is not a conception of the past as some static tradition but rather, to use an economic term, as a "path dependency," the culmination of prior choices and emphases that determines a range of potential innovations (Kaviraj 2005, 516).

It is in light of this situation that we can return to the issue mentioned at the start of this chapter about what counts as modern Buddhism in America. The practice of the *jhānas* among modernist Buddhists destabilizes a clear trajectory for Buddhist development. Martin Baumann has argued that a new period of Buddhist history is emerging from modernist Buddhism, one that is postmodern or "global." A defining characteristic of this period is the fact that many Western practitioners are secularizing and psychologizing Buddhist teachings to such an extent that they may jettison Buddhism altogether (Baumann 2001, 32). In doing so, these folks would be the vanguard of a movement of post-Buddhist practitioners. Baumann's description of this trend strikes me as accurate. But the whole story of Buddhism's development, even among modernist "convert" meditators, is unlikely to follow such a linear periodization (if it ever has). The growing popularity of *jhāna* meditation suggests that radical secularization is only one of a number of possibilities, for the *jhānas* tend to promote a vision of practice that actually demands a greater commitment to Buddhist teachings and modes of practice.[27] As I have noted, calm and concentration meditation calls up Buddhist cosmologies, and teachers often frame such meditation in karmic terms rooted in a deep engagement with Buddhist texts of all sorts. These facts suggest that the growth of the *jhānas*, while clearly a modern development, might inspire a sort of return to tradition, too.

NOTES

1. In 2001, Leigh Brasington organized the first conference in America specifically on the *jhānas. Tricycle: The Buddhist Review* had a special section on the *jhānas* in its Winter 2004 issue, and *Buddhadharma: The Practitioner's Quarterly* had an article on the *jhānas* in its Winter 2009 issue. Thanissaro Bhikkhu has published a number of works—both on the Internet and in print—that include the teaching of the *jhānas*. Finally, a number of books have been published that deal specifically with cultivating the *jhānas*, such as Ayya Khema's *When the Iron Eagle Flies* (1991), Ajaan Brahm's *Mindfulness, Bliss, and Beyond* (2006), Shaila Catherine's *Focused and Fearless* (2008), Richard Shankman's *The Experience of Samadhi* (2008), Gunaratana's *Beyond Mindfulness in Plain English* (2009a), and Stephen Snyder and Tina Rasmussen's *Practicing the Jhānas* (2009).
2. Snyder and Rasmussen got this term from a participant in a *jhāna* retreat. This interview is available at "The Jedi Mind Training of Concentration," http://www.buddhistgeeks.com/2010/02/bg-160-the-jedi-mind-training-of-concentration (retrieved February 27, 2010).
3. I follow here Wendy Cadge's definition of Theravada Buddhism: "Rather than viewing Theravada Buddhism as a coherent system, I imagine it and all religions as collections of teachings, institutions, people, and practices that are gathered in various combinations by people who want to understand or practice the tradition" (Cadge 2005, 11). For the history of the use of the term "Theravada," which has a relatively recent provenance, see Skilling (2009).
4. They are often called "convert" Buddhists, since they typically come to Buddhism by choice in adulthood, as opposed to "immigrant" or "cradle" Buddhists born to Buddhism. This is not to say that all convert Buddhists are white or well off, or that cradle Buddhists are not interested in meditation. The use of these categories here serves the heuristic purpose of describing a broad demographic distinction at present, but these terms have received much critical reflection and critique as enduring divisions (see Fronsdal 1998, 178; Numrich 2003; Seager 2002, 116ff.; and Tweed 2002, 22).

5. Buddhaghosa contrasts the procedures in regard to doing both practices or only insight in the chapter on the purification of view (*diṭṭhivisuddhiniddesa*) (see Ñāṇamoli 1999, 605–616).
6. Division into eight is standard, though canonical and postcanonical sources have fourfold, fivefold, and ninefold classification schemes as well (Griffiths 1981, 620n3).
7. Jack Kornfield, Joseph Goldstein, and Sharon Salzberg were among the first American "reverse messengers" (to use Wendy Cadge's expression) who brought Theravada meditation to America in the 1970s. Together they founded the Insight Meditation Society in Barre, Massachusetts, which has served as the home base and training center for many subsequent teachers of meditation (Fronsdal 1998, 165–166).
8. There is, however, an awareness of the *jhānas* among Mahasi-style teachers. In fact, they understand that a certain form of jhānic awareness will arise from their method. But this sort of *jhāna*, termed *vipassanā jhāna*, comes after progress in insight and does not have the absorptive qualities of initial *jhāna* practice (see Pandita 1993).
9. For the justification of the Mahasi method based merely on "momentary concentration" (*khaṇikasamādhi*), see Cousins (1996).
10. As many of the revivalists of *jhāna* I will discuss in a moment point out, the canonical texts often stress the importance of the *jhānas*. It is too technical an issue to explore here exactly how Mahasi teachers justify skipping the *jhānas*—in fact, most American teachers seem unaware of any need for justification or do not care—but the Mahasi Sayadaw and his Burmese disciples have provided a sophisticated argument, rooted in textual analysis, for doing so (see Cousins 1996).
11. "Bhante Gunaratana (16) How he learned meditation," http://www.veoh.com/watch/v744926AtNTcz8f.
12. For a discussion of this phenomenon of reading descriptions of experience where perhaps there was only scholastic analysis, see Sharf (1995a and 1998). For a qualification of Sharf's view that Buddhism had no category of experience before influence from the West, see Gyatso (1999).
13. http://www.youtube.com/stephnashmeditation0#p/c/8D7C8C5B06209E4B (retrieved February 26, 2010). See also Brasington (2007, 4).
14. Natthi jhānaṃ apaññassa, paññā natthi ajhāyato; Yamhi jhānañca

paññā ca, sa ve nibbānasantike (http://www.tipitaka.org/romn, retrieved February 22, 2010). For quotes of these verses, see, for example, Brahm (2006, 172) and Gunaratana (2009a, 14).

15. Thanissaro Bhikkhu, "One Tool among Many: The Place of Vipassana in Buddhist Practice," http://www.accesstoinsight.org/lib/authors/thanissaro/onetool.html (retrieved February 26, 2010).
16. Brahm (2006, 130). The bracketed words are in the original. The Buddha also talks about the good of indulging in the pleasure of *jhānas* in DN 29, the *Pāsādika Sutta.*
17. Robert Sharf has pointed out the centrality of the category of experience, both for academics and believers: "Many lay adherents feel that the only *authentic* form of worship or scriptural study is one that leads to a personal experience of its 'inner truth'" (Sharf 1998, 94).
18. Sharf (1995a). See Carrithers (1983, 26–46) for an analysis of the strong influence of German Romanticism on the German-born monk Nyanatiloka.
19. Thanissaro Bhikkhu, "The Roots of Buddhist Romanticism," http://www.purifymind.com/BuddhistRomanticism.htm (retrieved February 27, 2010).
20. Lloyd Burton, "Gathering Fruit and Planting Seeds: The First Western Conference on Jhana Practice in Theravada Buddhism," http://www.leighb.com/jhanarptleb.htm (retrieved February 28, 2010).
21. "Brain Study on Jhanas—Leigh Brasington with Stephanie Nash," http://www.youtube.com/stephnashmeditation0#p/c/8D7C8C5B06209E4B/4/5rMj4_CrFpU (retrieved February 28, 2010).
22. There are many sources on this topic. See Lopez (2008).
23. *Jhāna*-friendly teachers have tended toward an argument that the *jhānas* and insight practices form one singular path. See, for instance, Gunaratana (2009a, vii). See also Richard Shankman's interview with Jack Kornfield (Shankman 2008, 107–116). This brings up the apparent longstanding tension in Theravada Buddhism between ascetic and absorptive means of liberation versus those that are more cognitive. Griffiths (1981) articulates this tension clearly.
24. "The Jedi Mind Training of Concentration," http://www.buddhistgeeks.com/2010/02/bg-160-the-jedi-mind-training-of-concentration (retrieved February 27, 2010).
25. For example, describing stream-entry, he says, "Knowing that there

is birth before and after death, fear arises" (Gunaratana 2009a, 185).

26. Brahm (2006, 185–188); the interview in which Snyder and Rasmussen discuss seeing future lives is available at http://personallifemedia.com/podcasts/236-buddhist-geeks/episodes/81591-jedi-mind-training (retrieved February 27, 2010); Ayya Khema (1997a, 9).
27. Brasington, for instance, requires students who come to his *jhāna* retreats to have completed at least two seven-day retreats. And his *jhāna* retreats last two weeks to a month.

ELEVEN

BUDDHISM AND MULTIPLE MODERNITIES

DAVID L. MCMAHAN

Scholars in recent decades have paid increasing attention to the ways in which Buddhist individuals, groups, and institutions have responded to, adapted to, and engaged with modernity. Most of these studies, including my own, have relied on largely Western conceptions and manifestations of modernity. Such studies have yielded and elaborated the concepts of Protestant Buddhism, modern Buddhism, and Buddhist modernism to refer to Buddhisms that have been significantly shaped by their engagement with the discourses, institutions, and practices of Western modernity. Studies of the early development of this phenomenon have shown how deeply Buddhists, especially in the late nineteenth and early twentieth centuries, adopted the discourses of Western modernity and translated the Dharma into modernist vocabularies effectively creating a new genre of Buddhist literature, new idioms of Buddhist practice, and new kinds of Buddhist institutions. I suggest that, especially when addressing contemporary forms of Buddhism and their engagement with modernity, there is increasingly a need to expand our conceptions of modernity itself, and that the recent paradigm of multiple modernities put forth by Shmuel Eisenstadt, Charles Taylor, and others is promising in this regard (see Eisenstadt 2002; Gaonkar 2001; Taylor 2001).

The "classical" sociological theories of modernity offered by Marx, Weber, Durkheim, and their successors all saw modernity as entailing progressive economic growth, industrialization, rationalization, urbanization, standardization, structural differentiation, and secularization.

According to these theorists, modernity inevitably fosters a naturalistic outlook and tends to erode religious life, metaphysical thinking, and supernaturalism. In Weber's famous formulation, it contributes to secularization and disenchantment of the world, replacing a world alive with magic and spiritual meaning with a mechanized worldview, its natural rhythms replaced by the routines of factories and capitalist bureaucracies. At the same time, it erodes social and family structure, fragmenting local communities with the demands of mobility. Social theorists of the twentieth century assumed that modernity characterized by these features would inevitably spread from its origins in Europe throughout the world in a uniform and predictable manner, inexorably replacing local cultures with homogeneous modern systems of social organization and economies and with a rationalized, disenchanted, secularized worldview.

Empirical research and theoretical developments in recent decades cast doubt on this picture of a singular, uniform modernity. Many studies suggest that as the forces of Western modernity infuse themselves into a wide variety of cultural contexts, they are not simply passively adopted, nor are aspects of culture affected by Western modernity merely displaced by it. Rather, different communities, nations, and religious groups selectively adopt and adapt elements of Western modernity, combining them in unique ways with local concepts and practices. True, many indigenous cultures face threats to their very existence from the seemingly inexorable forces of now globalizing modernity. However, many very modern and modernizing societies do not, in fact, resemble Western Europe or the United States in morals, media, government, and attitudes toward science; rather, they have taken up these features of modernity in unique ways determined by their own preexisting social formations. And in contrast to the predictions of the decline of religion, many societies are experiencing religious revivals and attempting to engage religion directly with modernist ideas and practices or using religion to resist elements of Western modernity.

There are, in effect, multiple modernities: ways of being modern that creatively blend elements of indigenous cultures with the globalizing forces of modernity. European and American versions of modernity, though they enjoy historical precedence, turn out to be just that: particular versions among others. Various Asian cultures today employ indigenous cultural resources as tools for asserting their own unique forms of modernity; thus, some sociologists today resort to terms like

"Asian modernity" or "Chinese modernity." They have analyzed, for example, how Confucian values are implicit in East Asian practices of capitalism or how Southeast Asian countries have become economically modernized without widespread secularization taking place as it has in Western Europe. Examples of unique configurations of phenomena commonly associated with the "modern" proliferate, as well, in the Islamic world and the global South. Modernity and Westernization, in short, are not identical.

This thesis seems clearly relevant to Buddhist studies and the issue of Buddhist modernism. I would suggest that, while in the early phases of the Buddhist engagement with modernity—the late nineteenth and early twentieth centuries—reformist Buddhists vigorously attempted to translate Buddhism into the discourses of Western modernity and were willing to jettison large swaths of Buddhist thought, practice, and culture in order to modernize in Western terms, more recently there are more complex intertwinings of Buddhism and modernity that require a more pluralistic conception of modernity.

The early phases of Buddhist modernism relied heavily on conformity to Western modernity. Early modernists liberally translated Buddhist thought into the languages of scientific rationalism, Romanticism, transcendentalism, Protestant Christianity, and (a bit later) Western psychology. These discourses set the terms by which Buddhism would become a serious option for Westerners, as well as for many Asians educated in European systems. Even when Buddhists resisted Western colonialism and political and ideological hegemony, they often did so by adopting many of the West's categories and concepts, using them to express—and thereby transform—aspects of Buddhism. Advocates emphasized Buddhism's rationality and compatibility with science, often in contrast to Christianity. And yet they also offered critiques of narrow scientism by means of vocabulary borrowed from Romanticism and transcendentalism, with their critiques of mechanistic views of the cosmos, their celebration of nature, their organismic cosmology, and their insistence on the importance of interior exploration of the depths of the psyche.[1]

In this way, Buddhist modernism took up what might be considered the fundamental dynamic tension in the West between the rationalist and Romantic, infusing itself into this tension and attempting to resolve it, carrying forward the rational, scientific enterprise while at the same time tempering it with interior exploration and an emphasis on creativity. Thus one might conclude that it was unfolding according to a Weberian logic with a twist, fostering the rational while offering new ways toward the reenchantment of the world. Since it took up this tension between two Western discourses, defined itself by them, Buddhist modernism might well have been interpreted in this early phase as confirming monocultural theories of modernity that predicted the large-scale transformation of societies on the model of modern European culture.

If we look at Buddhism across the globe today, however, such theories seem problematic. There are, in fact, elements of Western modernity that have embedded themselves firmly in at least the Buddhism of the elites around the world, but even these elements lend themselves to a wide variety of inflections based on combinations of social, cultural, and political factors unique to different communities. In recent decades the transformation of various Buddhisms has accelerated, as formerly isolated forms have gone global, while global influences flow into virtually every local Buddhist culture, creating unique creoles and hybrids. This interfusion proceeds at an ever more rapid pace occasioned by migration, media, state influences, and political contingencies. With this increasing hybridity comes more diversity, more creative blendings of Asian and Western, and, though Western elements remain, there is less of a feeling of obligation to articulate Buddhism wholly on the West's terms and capitulate to all of the axioms of Western modernity.

The modernizing of Buddhism has not produced the uniformity that early modernizers might have imagined. When we think of contemporary iterations of Buddhist modernism, we tend to think of direct descendants of these early modernist reform movements, that is, a network of transnational, trans-sectarian, cosmopolitan Buddhisms that are global, deterritorialized, largely demythologized, articulated in the vocabularies of modernity, often meditation centered, and catering mostly to the educated middle class around the world. Consider, however, the existence of counter-cosmopolitan movements, such as the rather ethnocentric nationalist versions of Buddhism in Sri Lanka based on (re)creating a Sinhala Buddhist nation. This Buddhism fiercely criticizes globalization and international influence as corrupting, emphasizes "tradition" (which, of course, is a modern reinvention of tradition constructed as an antithesis to these forces), and, although it rhetorically resists globalization and international influences, it depends on them, especially on its technology: messages are distributed through television and the Internet. It also relies heavily on modernist interpretations of Buddhism as scientific and eschews "superstition" and many popular practices. The threat of colonialism in this movement has been replaced by the perceived threat of various "others": NGOs, human rights organizations, greedy businessmen, Christian missionaries, among others (Berkwitz 2008).

Moreover, not all intertwinings of modernity and Buddhism involve the negation of classical cosmology, "superstition," and the "supernatural," as was predicted by the classical equation of modernization with secularization. Consider, for example, the lucrative religious talisman trade in Thailand, in which various sacred objects thought to confer protection—amulets, buddha images, votive tablets—are blessed by monks and sold to the faithful. Although the practice of icon reverence is an ancient one in most Buddhist cultures, this particular form in Thailand is inseparable from the modern commercial forces of globalized capitalism. The trade in sacred material objects has immense commercial significance, according to some reports generating commerce comparable to that of real estate (Swearer 2003, 16). Stanley Tambiah (1987) argues that the flourishing (though not the origin) of this cult of amulets is a response to the rapid destabilization of Thai society by modern economic and political forces, which have produced great uncertainty in many lives and fostered an *increased* tendency to rely on the supernatural. The popularity of amulets, therefore, represents a kind of return to not-so-modern practice fueled by some of the distinctive forces of modernity.

Even contemporary articulations of Buddhism that rely on the staples of Buddhist modernism take on divergent significance in different cultures. I would like to offer a more elaborated example of how one of these staples is articulated and deployed differently in different communities in ways that suggest distinctive modernities. The theme is the compatibility of Buddhism and science. I don't intend to evaluate this claim[2] but, rather, to examine briefly how three different intersecting communities understand and employ it in different ways, thus illustrating how a single modernist theme can be refracted in varying hues in different cultural and political contexts. These different contexts are: first, the American and European educated class; second, the Tibetan community in exile; and third, the People's Republic of China.

The attempt to establish a correlation between Buddhism and science began in the nineteenth century. Early translators of Pali texts, notably Eugène Burnouf and Thomas and Caroline Rhys Davids, saw the "core" of Buddhism as a rational, psychological, and ethical philosophy, with the more "religious" elements being secondary cultural accretions (Burnouf 2010; T. Rhys Davids 1882; C. Rhys Davids 1912). Buddhist leaders and reformers in Asia appropriated this interpretation as well, both in attempts to revitalize Buddhism in their own countries and to represent it to the West. Buddhist representatives to the World's Parliament of Religions in 1893, for example, presented a Buddhism shorn of ritual, mythical cosmology, and supernatural agents. Both Anagārika Dharmapāla, of Ceylon, and Sōen Shaku, of Japan, highlighted and reinterpreted Buddhist doctrines of karma and the arising of things through causes and conditions in ways that appeared to render them compatible with modern evolutionary theory, scientific causality, and Western conceptions of natural law (Dharmapāla 1965; Sōen 1993). The perception of Buddhism as a religion that might circumvent the problems that Christianity faced in the age of Darwin, positivism, and widespread questioning of faith was compelling to many liberal North Americans and Europeans. Indeed German American author and publisher Paul Carus was so enthused by the idea of the compatibility of Buddhism and science that he published a number of books insisting on Buddhism as the quintessential exemplar of the "Religion of Science" that would grow and flourish in the new era. Buddhism, he claimed, "is a religion which knows of no supernatural revelation, and proclaims doctrines that require no other argument than the 'come and see.'" It is, he insisted, "a religion which recognizes no other revelation except the truth that can be proved by science" (1897, 114). The early Buddhist sympathizer C. T. Strauss likewise claimed that "genuine Buddhism is the reverse of mystical, rejects miracles, is founded on reality, and refuses to speculate about the absolute and other so-called first causes" (1922, 105). Moreover, he said, it deems prayers, rituals, and ceremonies as "not only useless but a hindrance to spiritual advancement" (53–54). On this interpretation, the Dharma of the Buddha was utterly distinct from the rituals, celebrations, image veneration, and attempts to control spirits common in the popular Buddhism that Westerners often found in lands they colonized.[3]

By the mid-twentieth century, the rhetorical alliance of science and Buddhism had shifted somewhat from the notion of Buddhism as broadly compatible with modern science to the idea that it was itself a kind of science. The German-born Theravada monk Nyanaponika Thera (born Siegmund Feniger, 1901–1994), in 1954, wrote of Buddhist meditation as a "science of mind" and presented the method of "bare attention" as essentially the same as that of the scientist: "unprejudiced receptivity" to things, reduction of the subjective element in judgment, and "deferring judgment until a careful examination of the facts has been made." This, he claimed, is the "genuine spirit of the research worker" (Nyanaponika 1996, 42). Henceforth, the characterization of Buddhist meditation as an "internal science" has become quite common among Buddhists in both Asia and the West. B. Alan Wallace, for example, insists that Buddhism offers methods for discerning empirical truths about the mind and the world and that these discoveries are subject to a kind of "peer review" among expert meditators (Wallace 2003).

The attempt to ally Buddhism and science is more vigorous and sophisticated now than ever and is currently the province of neuroscientists in some of the most prestigious universities in the United States. These researchers have been employing the most advanced brain-imaging technology and using as their subjects experienced meditators, some of whom have spent years perfecting their vocation. The subjects are hooked up to hundreds of electrodes or placed into functional magnetic resonance imagery (fMRI) machines so that scientists can attempt to observe what their brains are doing in various kinds of meditation. This research has yielded results suggesting various cognitive and health benefits of meditation and thus has garnered tremendous media coverage. It has increased the visibility and cultural cachet of Tibetan Buddhism, the members of which, in part due to the Dalai Lama's interest in the science of meditation, tend to be the most frequent collaborators.[4]

This kind of research occupies a particular place in the cultural milieu of the United States and the "West" more generally. It implicitly offers a secularized, deinstitutionalized view of meditation as something available to anyone, Buddhist and non-Buddhist—a kind of spiritual technology that can work independently of any institutional, dogmatic, authoritative, or religious affiliation. This is quite different from how meditation has usually been understood in Asian Buddhism, where, until the rise of twentieth-century lay-meditation movements, it has largely been the province of specialist monastics. In the new reenvisioning of meditation, this ostensibly central feature of Buddhism is seen as the most detachable from the institutional, cosmological, doctrinal features, not to mention those "superstitious" practices that most scientific researchers and consumers of such research see as having nothing to do with science (or, for that matter, Buddhism itself).

In the United States, the way such a polarity between "scientific" meditation and "superstitious" religious practice plays out is to make available Buddhist techniques to an educated and often relatively secularized segment of the public interested in health, self-cultivation, psychological therapy, and "spirituality" but usually decidedly uninterested in doing merit-making rituals, praying to deities, prostrating before images, and participating in the institutional dimensions of Buddhism. It also embodies a Protestant suspicion of clergy, authority, and religious institutions and sees meditation techniques as means to foster happiness, health, and creativity without the dogmas, rituals, and other "trappings" of religion. There are institutional implications to this characterization as well. Meditation must be presented as a secular therapy that can be studied and employed according to rigorous scientific protocol in order to receive funding, especially government funding, in public universities. The Buddhism that emerges in this context is modern in distinctively Western ways that treat science as the dominant discourse and yet offer Buddhism as a more humane "internal science."

The desire for such a science is deeply rooted in the Western discourses of modernity. The tension between Enlightenment conceptions of the world as a giant mechanism and the idealist and Romantic visions of the world as a spirit-infused organism have shaped an enduring ambivalence in the West about science. During the rise of Buddhist modernism in the Victorian age, the emergence of positivism and a general enthusiasm about empirical science and its potential to improve the lot of humankind was countered by the emergence of "occult science," Theosophy, and other spiritualist movements. These groups rebelled against the mechanistic and disenchanting tendencies of positivism while still attempting to embody a more expansive scientific approach that allowed for spirits and other planes of existence. Not coincidentally, these groups were pivotal in introducing Buddhism to the West. The unfolding of the twentieth century provided ample reasons for disillusionment with modern science, as the technologies of warfare and environmental destruction showed that scientific advancement, while undoubtedly improving humankind's lot in many ways, could also spell its demise. Countless machines have eased human burdens, but others have enabled destruction on an unprecedented scale. Biological research has led to vaccines that have saved millions of lives but also portends frightening changes in the very structure of biological life itself, including human life. Thus the desire for an alternative science, free of nihilism, hubris, and destructive potential, is deeply embedded in the modern West, as is the dream of ancient wisdom from afar coming to rescue the West from its modern anomie, disenchantment, and self-destructiveness.

This secularization of meditation has also had significant effects not just on Buddhism but on various aspects of Western culture. It has become disembedded from the Buddhist tradition and rearticulated as a technique of self-investigation, awareness, personal satisfaction, and ethical reflection, taking on a life of its own in some cases altogether outside of Buddhist communities. Having attained the aura of a scientific—or at least scientifically testable—technique, psychologists and medical professionals have converted meditation into a therapeutic tool for addressing a wide variety of problems. It is now used for stress reduction, pain management, lowering blood pressure, and increasing focus among Buddhists and non-Buddhists alike, including people who don't even know they are doing something derived from Buddhism. Meditation and mindfulness are often presented as a "spiritual" rather than religious technique; something one can do as a Buddhist but also as a Christian, Jew, or agnostic. Moreover, this is not just a matter of Westerners appropriating a slice of Buddhism to their own ends. Many Asian Buddhists present meditation as separable from "Buddhism as a religion" and extol its scientifically proven benefits to both Buddhists and non-Buddhists.[5]

Let us now look at the stakes of such scientific experimentation and the publicity it garners from the perspective of the Tibetan diaspora community. Among Tibetans interested in studying meditation and Buddhism in scientific terms, there is surely a combination of motives. I take it as a given that scientific curiosity for its own sake and the genuine desire to share practices believed to be conducive to human flourishing and well-being, and perhaps investigating ways of refining these techniques, are factors in the enthusiasm the Dalai Lama and others have for these studies. No doubt Donald Lopez (2008) is correct in asserting that the Tibetan community also has a nationalistic stake here, as did Buddhists in colonized Ceylon over a century ago. Tibet as a nation within China is essentially helpless in securing its own autonomy. By promoting Buddhism as something akin to a benign, humanistic, and scientific enterprise, Tibetan Buddhism gains recognition and prestige among elites in countries that could bring pressure to bear on China to grant greater autonomy to Tibet. The deemphasizing of the nonscientific elements of Tibetan Buddhism and its reconstruction as a kind of scientific religion help this effort in that they tap into both the prestige of and the ambivalence toward science in Western culture, offering the hope that there can be a more humane science that produces enlightened beings rather than just increased technology, bombs, and environmental destruction.

Beyond this, the engagement of Tibetan Buddhists with scientific discourse is also one part of how Tibetans in exile refashion their tradition in the midst of their unique and rather abrupt confrontation with the divergent forces of modernity. Tibetan Buddhism did not follow the longer path of engagement with modernity begun in the nineteenth century in, for example, Ceylon and Japan but was thrust into the modern world through its colonization by China and the subsequent exile of hundreds of thousands of Tibetans. Thus, Tibetan Buddhist modernism indeed looks different than some of the rather radically demythologized versions inaugurated in the Victorian era. Tibetans are essentially negotiating new ways of being Buddhist and modern and blending the two in ways sometimes different from their Buddhist predecessors in other countries. Among some of the Tibetan diaspora in the West, such blendings take on a particular shape that tends to avoid presenting Tibetan Buddhism as a rich, polytheistic tradition full of rituals to honor and appease unseen beings, which much of the tradition on the ground, in fact, is. Rather, it tends to be presented as a "science of mind" or a spiritual technology. Deities are interpreted symbolically and translated into psychological archetypes or abstract "energies" that adepts can manipulate through advanced techniques of meditation, visualization, and concentration. Thus, Tibetans come to be seen in the West as, in Robert Thurman's words, "the quintessential scientists of nonmaterialist civilization" (1994, 110) who possess "sophisticated methods of software analysis and modification [that] can help with the individual's inner reprogramming" (1991, 64).

Thus, the bifurcation of the "rational" and "scientific" from what many in the West would consider "superstitious" serves a particular purpose here, too, one that overlaps with, but is not identical to, that of Westerners interested in distinguishing the "spiritual" and "scientific" from the "religious" and "superstitious." For many Tibetans themselves, however, the engagement of Buddhism with science has in no way led them to embrace a secularized version of Buddhism like that often embraced by Western sympathizers. Most monasteries still follow the traditional curriculum developed over many centuries, perform rituals to honor and appease deities, and perform divinations to help determine the course of future plans. The discourse of Buddhism and science is in many respects peripheral to the lives of most Tibetan Buddhists, though it has potential to make greater and greater inroads as it continues to gain recognition and shape what people in the West understand by—and expect from—Buddhism.

Meanwhile, in the People's Republic of China (PRC), the modernist, scientific, secularized representation of Buddhism is deployed in yet another way, one that explicitly attempts to foil the interests of Tibetan independence while attempting to control the current revival of Buddhism in China. Let me illustrate this by way of an article from the government-controlled Xinhua News Agency, published March 30, 2009,[6] that reports on a conference in the Eastern Chinese city of Wuxi called the Second World Buddhist Forum that, according to the article, brought together over 1,700 Buddhist monks with scientists and business leaders. The main thrust of the article is not the talks given at the conference but rather a characterization of Buddhism that insists on its harmony with science and technology and its discouraging of "superstition." It says:

> It is acknowledged by both Buddhists and experts of social sciences that Buddha is a human being, but not a god, and everybody's destiny is in his own hand [*sic*], not in Buddha's.
>
> It is also a consensus that Buddhism does not worship superstition, or the enemy of science. On the contrary, it opposes superstition and stresses "cause and effect." In addition, Buddhism . . . supported science and technological development all along.
>
> "In my view, Buddhism is a religion of atheism and it is very rational," says a professor from the Institute for Science, Technology and Society at Tsinghua University.

The article also emphasizes that "Buddhism has never fought against science in [its] history" and notes that a number of Chinese monks themselves have been astronomers, mathematicians, and mechanical engineers. Modern monks, it also asserts, "enjoy the conveniences brought by science and technology—communicating [with] 'this world' via cell phones and promoting their doctrines via computers and [the] Internet." Buddhism is a form of knowledge, not a religion, insists a former president of the University of Science and Technology of China, and those who see Buddhism as "burning incense and praying" are straying from "its real spirit." This rational, scientific Buddhism is then explicitly connected with the nation. In building its "harmonious society," says the author of the article, China has been "rallying all positive forces" and "seeking wisdom and inspiration from its profound traditional culture."

Insofar as this is an article from a government-run news agency, we can assume that this is a kind of prescriptive map indicating the ways in which the current revival of Buddhism in China will be permitted to proceed. Tibetan Buddhism is explicitly absent in this description of rational, scientific Buddhism as part of "traditional Chinese culture" and "nation." In contrast to the representation of implicitly "Chinese" Buddhism as rational and scientific, representations in the news agency's paper, Internet site, and television channels portray Tibetans and other ethnic minorities in a very different light. The PRC is currently carrying out development projects in rural areas at a frenetic pace. The government hopes that tourism dollars will be one of the main sources of revenue for bringing roads, sanitation, natural gas, clean water, and television to these areas. Part of the campaign to lure tourists involves reversing the fear and suspicion of the dominant culture toward minorities, transforming it into the lure of the mysterious, sensual, and exotic charm of the primitive. It is a move that borrows liberally from Western orientalism, through which European representations exoticized "the East," depicting it as the irrational, primitive, feminine, sensual, mysterious Other to Western modernity, with its rationalism, masculinity, technology, and progress. This East/West picture from the nineteenth century has now been transposed onto Han and minority cultures in China, including that of Tibet. Billboards across rural freeways, pamphlets at tourist sites, and hotel magazines featuring local color all display attractive minority (nearly always) women dressed in their beautiful and ornate ceremonial garb, wild with colorful embroidery, silver ornaments, and headdresses. A hotel magazine describes various minority cultures as "mysterious" and "exotic." This packaging of ethnic minority culture is pervasive in southwestern and Tibetan areas.

And in contrast to the countless articles in the American press on Tibetan Buddhists as scientific explorers in fMRI machines, articles and documentaries on Tibet from Xinhua exclude Tibetan Buddhists from the rational and national Buddhism of the Han Chinese. Articles and news shows tend to focus on traditional Tibetan crafts, "folk art," restored monasteries that have been transformed into museums, and the alleged Tibetan enthusiasm for the new technologies and higher standard of living. A special on China Central TV 9, the English-language channel, captures it well. It features an array of "traditional Tibetan folk music," one act of which presents a group of singers in embellished versions of traditional Tibetan costumes. On the giant stage are huge pillars that seem to fuse Roman columns with Tibetan prayer wheels. Behind is an immense screen with a slow-moving succession of photos emblematic of Tibet—snow-peaked mountains, a yak in an open field, a sunbaked smiling farmer, and the Potala Palace (now safely transmuted from home of a god-king to tourist attraction). The singers intone Tibetan melodies to the lavish accompaniment of Western orchestral music. It resembles American musical theater with a Tibet theme. In between acts, the attractive young hostess of the show introduces the next example of "traditional Tibetan folk music," a Tibetan pop group called Snow Lotus, with lithe young women in skimpy, midriff-baring versions of Tibetan dress, singing and shaking their hips to the chords of synthesizers and electronic drums. Lyrics, which flow in translation across the bottom of the screen, are uniformly banal: we are a simple, happy, strong people; the snowy mountains are all around; the beautiful flowers bloom; the sheep and yaks are in the pasture.

Clearly a picture of primitive tradition versus rationalistic modernity is being constructed here in relation to specific state interests. Chinese Buddhism, part of the great intellectual and scientific heritage of China, is the rational cultural resource in harmony with technology, development, atheism, and communism. Tibetan Buddhism and other minority religions are the exotic others within—the mysterious East within the East—displayed as cultural entertainment in order to promote development by, first, demonstrating the need to bring progress to backward peoples, and second, to bring the tourist dollars that are required for this development to the area. Their folkways, religions, and "superstitions" are translated from backward, threatening practices into charming bits of packaged exotica, not to mention erotica—the feminized, primitive other in opposition to the masculine rationality of the official self.

My point here is not to criticize the PRC government (though it richly deserves critique on this point) but to show how this rhetorical polarity of modern, rational, and scientific versus primitive, superstitious, and traditional fundamental to Buddhist modernism (indeed to modernity in general) has been deployed differently in different cultural and nationalistic contexts, suggesting the existence of different configurations of the modern within different communities. In the Chinese case, there is a single, overarching, and official modernity, and to the extent that Buddhism contributes and conforms to this configuration, it is welcome to help constitute it. Likewise scientists studying Buddhist meditators in university laboratories help constitute different understandings of Buddhist modernity, as well as what is essential and peripheral in Buddhism. And among the Tibetan diaspora struggling to gain global support for autonomy, the vision of scientific Buddhism presents a particular face to Western supporters and is also a point of negotiation within Tibetan Buddhism itself as it works out its own ways of combining modernity with received practice and belief. These three examples show the way a single theme perhaps central to the very concept of modernity is deployed in different configurations in order to help constitute different senses of what the modern is and how it relates to state, society, and individual. In this sense, they suggest not just differing interests but actually different versions of Buddhist modernity.

NOTES

1. For a more thoroughgoing analysis of the history of these developments, especially in the West, see McMahan (2008).
2. For diametrically opposed evaluations of this discourse, see Lopez (2008) and Wallace (2007).
3. For extended discussions of the development of this early Buddhist modernism, see Almond (1988), Lopez (2008), McMahan (2004, 2008), and Tweed (1992).

4. For an overview of this research see Lutz, Dunne, and Davidson (2007).
5. This should in no way be taken to imply that this secularized approach to Buddhist meditation exhausts the ways that it is understood and practiced in the United States. Even among distinctively modernist forms of Buddhism, there are in fact a number of different ways in which meditation is rhetorically and experimentally linked to science. The aforementioned should be understood as one general tendency.
6. See http://news.xinhuanet.com/english/2009-03/30/content_11096669.htm.

TWELVE

BUDDHIST MODERNISM AS NARRATIVE

A Comparative Study of Jodo Shinshu and Zen

NATALIE E. F. QULI AND SCOTT A. MITCHELL

In this chapter, we argue that use of the category "Buddhist modernism" obscures the diversity of Buddhist traditions, which appropriate various modernist narratives selectively and produce significantly different modernities. To highlight the plurality of Buddhist modernities, we favor Taylor's cultural model—rather than the more Weberian acultural model—of modernity. By comparing American convert Zen to the Buddhist Churches of America (usually characterized as "modernist" and "traditional," respectively, in the literature), we demonstrate that both groups display characteristics associated with "modernism" and "tradition," though in different ways. We note that "Buddhist modernism" is a shorthand term for a rather substantial set of narratives (on science, democracy, nature, etc.) rather than an objective, easily delineated category; the term lacks a concise definition (Obadia 2006; see also Blackburn 2010, 212) and has come to include so many hallmarks that virtually no contemporary group can escape being labeled as such. Furthermore, that the same group in two different cultural contexts (for example, Japan and the United States) can be described as modernist in one setting but traditional in another reveals the non-objective nature of the term "Buddhist modernism" and suggests its usage is closely associated with judgments of authenticity and questions of pollution. That American convert Zen groups, which in many ways strictly adhere to perceived Japanese traditions, are frequently labeled "modernist" in the literature suggests that the term is being used inappropriately to mean simply "non-Asian," revealing the Western/Asian bifurcation often underlying the modernist/traditional dichotomy. We suggest redefining "modernism" as *a set of narratives*, which, when selectively appropriated and embedded in a larger set of narratives, produces a variety of configurations of "modern" and traditional," yielding multiple Buddhist modernities.

OVERVIEW OF CURRENT USAGE

One of the dominant theoretical paradigms used to analyze contemporary manifestations of Buddhism has been "Buddhist modernism." This term has come to stand in for a rather lengthy list of qualities (described in more detail later) that are said to differentiate "modern" Buddhisms from "traditional" forms. "Buddhist modernism," coined by Bechert in his multivolume work *Buddhismus, Staat und Gesellschaft in den Ländern des Theravada-Buddhismus* (1966–1973), is used by him and others to describe changes in Buddhism resulting from the Asian Buddhist encounter with modernity and Westernization. He argues that

> Buddhist modernism is characterized by the emphasis laid on rationalist elements in Buddhist teachings, by the belief that the teachings of Buddhism and those of modern science are not only in conformity but identical, by the tacit elimination of the traditional cosmology, and by a reinterpretation of the objective of the Buddhist religion in terms of social reform and the building of a better world. (Bechert 1973, 91)

He further argues that the "resurgence" of Buddhism in terms of reformism in Asia occurred in tandem with the early spread of Buddhism in the West (Bechert 1984, 275), making Buddhist modernism a global phenomenon. Gombrich and Obeyesekere (1988) argue for a similar set of changes in Buddhism in Sri Lanka, which they prefer to call "Protestant Buddhism."[1]

Lopez expands his analysis beyond South and Southeast Asia to include Buddhist groups throughout the world, particularly in the West, beyond the nineteenth century. Arguing that Buddhist modernism now enjoys widespread acceptance throughout Asia and the West (Lopez 2002a, ix–x), Lopez suggests it is an autonomous "sect" or "school" of Buddhism with its own lineage, scriptures, and saints

(Lopez 2002a; Lopez 2006, 249n3; see also Huber 2008, 420; McMahan 2008, 8).

While Lopez (2002a) provides a sampling of Asian and Western Buddhist (or perhaps "Buddhish") authors as representative of the "canon" of this new "sect," McMahan (2008) concentrates more carefully on Western manifestations, explaining that because it represents a response to modernity, Buddhist modernism inevitably reacts to issues of "individualism, egalitarianism, liberalism, democratic ideals, and the impulse to social reform" (McMahan 2008, 13). However, McMahan stresses that neither modernity nor Buddhist modernity are homogeneous; there are a variety of responses representing a multiplicity of adaptations (McMahan 2008, 14; see also chap. 11 in this volume).

The characteristics said to represent Buddhist modernism in the burgeoning literature on the topic comprise a lengthy laundry list of items, all of which derive from the basic issue of modernity and its attendant rationalization and democratization of religion. The list of qualities describing Buddhist modernism—all variations on basic themes of rationalism, textualism, experience, and democracy—includes an emphasis on reason and rationality, with the corollary that Buddhism is a philosophy and not a religion; the rejection of ritual; the symbolic reinterpretation of cosmology; psychologization of the teachings; articulations of the compatibility of science and Buddhism; a refocusing on doctrine and text over "superstitious" practices such as relic veneration or Buddha-name recitation; laicization and democratization; a focus on meditation with an optimistic view of nirvana, especially as manifesting in the historically unprecedented practice of meditation among the laity; an ecumenical attitude toward other Buddhist sects and a universalization of Buddhism; increased status of women; social engagement and a "this-worldly" emphasis; a return to the "original" teachings of the Buddha (especially as reconstructed through texts, in particular the Pali canon); and the rejection of the cultural accretions that have appended over the centuries (Baumann 2000; Bechert 1984; Levine and Gellner 2005, 11; Lopez 2002a; McMahan 2008; Quli 2008, 2009).

CULTURAL AND ACULTURAL MODELS OF MODERNITY

Charles Taylor (2001) has described two models of modernity employed by social scientists—that is, two ways of understanding narratives regarding the perceived differences between contemporary and past societies: cultural and acultural models, the former incorporating newer ideas regarding multiple modernities popular in anthropology, and the latter largely represented by secularization theory as articulated in classical sociology.[2] Taylor identifies the acultural model as the dominant theory of modernity in use over the last two centuries or so (Taylor 2001, 174). This model, often narrated with a tone of nostalgia (see Taylor 2001, 175; cf. Rosaldo 1989, esp. chap. 3), frames modernity as a kind of universal development in which traditional (i.e., nonrational) societies are gradually replaced by modern ones, thus stressing rupture and the loss of tradition (Obadia 2006; see also Payne, the afterword in this volume). When viewed either as an intellectual development (the replacement of superstition with rationality and science) or a social development (institutionalization and the construction of Weberian rationalized bureaucracies), traditional beliefs and old ways of understanding are seen as being lost (or perhaps conquered) through the implementation of (a universal) "reason" or science (Taylor 2001, 191), which gives rise to more efficient institutions and the disenchantment of the world.[3]

Because the acultural theory posits that "modernity" is a universal and value-neutral (or culture-free) process, all societies will eventually modernize and thereby become the same (Taylor 2001, 181). It is the process of "coming to see" the Truth, that is, a scientific, "rational," Enlightenment version of reality (Taylor 2001). As a "culture-neutral operation," one can insert any society for the variable on the left side of the equation, and, after applying the force of modernity, one will end up with the same answer on the right side of the equation: a society of individuals free of superstition who base their decisions on instrumental rationality (Taylor 2001).

The cultural model of modernity rejects the idea of modernity as a value-neutral operation. It takes seriously the diversity of cultures both past and present, "each of which has a language and a set of practices that define specific understandings of personhood, social relations, states of mind/soul, goods and bads, virtues and vices, and the like" (Taylor 2001, 172). Any beliefs we might have—"rational" or otherwise—are held within and related to a larger set of cultural models about how the world works, the nature of human relationships, and so on. This cultural matrix Taylor identifies as being in some sense unformulable and prereflexive (Taylor 2001, 186). Those tropes that scholars identify as reflective of "modernity" (science, ideas about the individual, bureaucracies, etc.) are always contextualized within existing cultural patterns.

Hefner argues that "secularization theory has oversimplified modernity and its nonmodern 'other.' Rather than recognizing that modernity might be multiple, [secularization theory] offered an idealized model of the West as the prototype for modernization in all societies" (Hefner 1998, 86). But there is no one version of modernity; narratives are always contextualized in larger worldviews. Rather than recognize this messy plurality, acultural models, like those that have for some time dominated Buddhist studies, are forced to use "modernity" with increasing vagueness to account for all the diversity we see when there should be none, resulting in the long list of attributes now used to describe Buddhist modernism. As Obadia notes (2006), part of the ability of the term "modernity" to describe societies is its ambiguous, plastic nature. This masks the truth that modernity is neither a singular, fixed operation, nor is it a singular, fixed narrative.

The claim to a universal modernity is undercut by the heterogeneity underlying it (T. Mitchell 2000b, viii). There are too many articulations of the modern, too many various origins of the modernity narrative to support a single, identifiable definition of the term "modernity" or the condition of the "modern." Even if we meticulously detail the "modern" elements originating in "the Protestant Reformation, the scientific revolution, the European Enlightenment, Romanticism, and their successors" (McMahan 2008, 9), each of these strands are peopled by individuals with multiple understandings of reason, freedom, and so on, producing contested discourses. Perhaps more importantly, these strands of European Enlightenment, Romanticism, and so on, have their own sources from the past. "Each new parent can reveal another parent, another logic. The identity claimed by the modern is contaminated. It issues from too many sources and depends upon, even as it refuses to recognize, forebears and forces that escape its control" (T. Mitchell 2000c, 13). What we have are multiple tropes on science, instrumental reason, freedom, individualism, rationality, and so on, representing "multiple and competing narratives" of Buddhist modernism (McMahan 2008, 9).

Seen in this way, "Buddhist modernism" is a *set* of similar narratives rather than a singular one. These narratives or ways of understanding can be, like other kinds of culture, transmitted across cultures. This transmission may be a forced one, as in the implementation of British notions of the separation of church and state in Sri Lanka (disestablishment). Or the narratives may be appropriated willingly, for example in King Mongkut's reforms in Thailand. But because ideas of the modern are brought into conversation with underlying (and often invisible) cultural assumptions about the nature of human action, morality, community, and so on, modernities differ from one another.

Theories of multiple modernities (e.g., Eisenstadt et al. 2002; Gaonkar et al. 2001), when they allow for a cultural rather than an acultural definition of modernity, are better situated to account for the diversities we see in the contemporary world. In particular, they problematize the notion that non-Western countries modernize by becoming more Western. Only *some* modernist narratives are selectively appropriated (Eisenstadt 2002, 14), and these narratives are situated in relation to existing cultural norms. This results in the creation of new forms that, while perhaps resembling Western modernities in some ways, are distinctly their own. As Inda and Rosaldo (2008, 28) remark on this process of globalizing cultural forms, "The peoples of the periphery do not simply or necessarily absorb the ideologies, values, and life-style positions putatively embedded in the cultural goods they consume. More often than not they actually customize these imported forms, interpreting them according to local conditions of reception." Specific actors may make use of modernist narratives in different ways as they pursue diverse visions of what makes a society "modern" (Eisenstadt 2002, 2), creating not just a single nationally or culturally bounded version of modernity but diverse versions within nations or cultures. As Hefner reminds us (1998, 87), even in the "West," modernity is envisioned dissimilarly by different religious traditions.

The idea of multiple modernities also helps to account for the fact that "modern" religious traditions are not only dissimilar from other modern traditions but exhibit "traditional" characteristics as well. Timothy Mitchell notes:

> How does one make sense of these "non-modern" elements coexisting and reconfirmed in the face of capitalist modernity? A conventional account . . . would treat the non-modern as no more than residuals, fragments of a past that cannot be relinquished only because [the] transition to modernity is incomplete, or has happened so rapidly that different phases have

> been telescoped together and therefore overlap rather than succeed one another. This is the inevitable analysis of modernizing approaches, which must gather all the different histories of colonialism into a singular narrative of the coming of modernity. They can deal with the non-modern only as the absence of modernity, only as forms that lack the discipline, rationality, and abstraction of the modern order of things—and therefore, since they are defined by what they are not, as essentially similar to non-modern forms everywhere else. It is not sufficient . . . to explain these forms as "the invention of tradition" or through the idea of the "modernity of tradition." These invocations of the restored, contrived, or resistant powers of a tradition accept the notion that there is a universal narrative of modernity, against which local variations can be measured. The alternative would be to acknowledge that modernity "is constituted by tensions that relate to each other asymptomatically," so that there cannot be "any one unitary history of its becoming." (2000a, xvi; quoting Chakrabarty 1994, 81)

By recognizing that articulations of "Buddhist modernism" are voiced within traditions[4] with historical continuity, the rupture narrative is replaced by one that is able to account for the continuity and resilience of traditions as well as their creativity. Such traditions—such as the Buddhism of, for example, Anagārika Dharmapāla and his followers—show considerable connection to the past (e.g., veneration of relics) even while expressing more modernist ideas (the compatibility of science and Buddhism). Individual Buddhist temples may be seen to hold both "modernist" and "traditional" positions in the services they offer (for example, traditional merit-making alongside lay meditation; see McLellan 2008), and individuals at a temple may likewise hold a variety of modernist and traditional positions, for example, in the way that they interpret Buddhist cosmology (Cadge 2005, 90). Narratives of modernity have been appropriated by individuals, groups, and institutions in a variety of creative ways and integrated into the already-existing cultures underlying them, producing unique forms with their own logics and histories.

The ability of religious traditions to integrate new cultural forms (such as those identified with "modernity") points toward an understanding of religions not as fixed or static, having an ageless core of beliefs, practices, and so forth, but as inherently hybrid or syncretic (Queen 1999, xviii; Stewart and Shaw 1994, 5; Tweed 2002, 18). Such a perspective on religious change enables us to address both continuity and discontinuity without becoming embroiled in issues of authenticity, which haunt the writings of many authors with their thick tone of nostalgia and loss (see Quli 2009).

Beyer, for example, sees religious traditions as discourses, suggesting that while contemporary religions may incorporate new elements, this does not make them purely "invented traditions" (cf. Hobsbawm and Ranger 1983). Rather, we are witnessing the "partial dissolution of received patterns of communication and their recombination with new elements to create a new form that bears strong resemblance to old ones. . . . [Because] all communication exhibits this combination of old and new [it] thereby obviates the question of which is more 'authentic'" (Beyer 2006, 11). Tweed, too, has been helpful in visualizing the mutability of tradition by articulating water metaphors to describe its essencelessness. Basing his model on Buddhist notions of non-self (*anatta*) and impermanence (*anicca*) (Tweed 2006, 55; see also chap. 1 in this volume), he imagines a religious tradition as a river, the content of which is always in movement. A deluge may flood the banks, creating offshoots that join nearby streams. A stream may dry up, or it may be fed by multiple sources. Looking at religious traditions with this lens, the question of whether someone like Dharmapāla is a "real" Buddhist is less about orthodoxy as determined by a set of doctrinal assumptions or "traditional" practices and more about placing him within one of the many streams that have flowed out of that big Buddhist river; in the case of Buddhist modernities, these are streams that are also fed by Western Romanticism and other traditions. This perspective also curtails the trend toward the deconstruction of traditions, epitomized by the view that all contemporary traditions are merely "invented" (an extension of the rupture paradigm),[5] which Stewart and Shaw contend has "invented another kind of intellectual imperialism" via anthropological hegemony (1994, 23).

TRADITIONAL AND MODERNIST TRAITS IN CONVERT ZEN AND THE BUDDHIST CHURCHES OF AMERICA

The limitations of the modernist/traditionalist dichotomy are made evident in a closer examination of specific American Buddhist communities. For the sake of brevity, in what follows we examine two aspects of this dichotomy within two specific American Buddhist traditions: American Shin Buddhism in its largest incarnation of the Buddhist Churches of America in comparison with the more nebulous manifestations of "convert" Zen founded by mid-twentieth-century Japanese missionaries such as Taizan Mazumi and Shunryu Suzuki, among others. Specifically, we explore the issues of (a) laicization or the displacement of traditional hierarchical authority structures with typically Western democratic or egalitarian forms and (b) the rejection of superstition and traditional Buddhist cosmology, which often carries with it an explicit rejection of ritual. What makes the American Shin and convert Zen cases particularly pertinent here is that these communities have been largely and uncritically assigned to the traditionalist and modernist categories, respectively. Baumann (2001) frames the traditionalist and modernist forms of global Buddhism as "Weberian ideal types" and claims that traditional forms of Buddhism are alive and well within "ethnic" (i.e., Asian immigrant and Asian American) communities. These communities' predilection for rituals and gaining merit and a preoccupation with Buddhism's rich cosmology are in sharp contrast to the meditation-centric and textually grounded character of "convert" modernist Buddhists. Thus, by merely replacing "ethnic" and "convert" with "traditional" and "modern," Baumann replicates the racialized features of the "two Buddhisms" debate well critiqued by Hickey in chap. 3 in this volume, revealing in the process his identification of modernity with the West and tradition with Asia. Moreover, as is shown later, this divide makes less and less sense in the face of ethnographic fieldwork within these communities.[6]

Laicization, Democratization

Articulated in a variety of ways, the rejection of monastic hierarchies and an embrace of more democratic institutional structures coupled with lay-centric practice is one of the hallmarks of what has been called modern Buddhism. The case of the Jodo Shinshu sect of Japanese Pure Land thus presents us with our first major stumbling block. In the early thirteenth century, former Tendai monk Shinran Shōnin left the monastic establishment and became a disciple of Hōnen, a Pure Land teacher who had been proselytizing to the laity in Kyoto. Quickly running afoul of the local authorities, both Hōnen and Shinran were stripped of their monastic rankings and exiled from the capital. Shinran embraced this turn of events, referring to himself as "neither monk nor lay" for the remainder of his career while spreading Pure Land teachings among the laity in the Kanto region. The community that grew up around his teachings was from its very inception "lay centric," rejecting a celibate monastic clergy (Dobbins 1989). As one would expect, over the centuries a priestly class has developed; however, we must be attentive to the fact that this priestly class has never been a celibate monastic one as we would expect to find in other forms of "traditional" Buddhism. Moreover, during the Meiji reforms of the late nineteenth century, this model of "neither monk nor lay" was grafted onto virtually all forms of Japanese Buddhism as part of the government's forced modernization of Japanese cultural institutions that effectively laicized Buddhism across the country. Thus, if we take laicization to be a hallmark of the modern, how do we account for a Buddhist tradition that has been laicized for more than seven hundred years?[7]

Because we are here concerned with more contemporary matters, let us for the moment not dwell on the long and complex history surrounding the modernization of Japanese Buddhism and instead turn to the American case. Shin Buddhism in the United States is dominated by the Buddhist Churches of America, which was established in the late nineteenth century, thus representing the oldest Buddhist institution in the United States. In many ways, the community is very much a "traditional" form of Japanese Buddhism. And despite Shinran's thirteenth-century laicization, there remains a rigid hierarchy in place that seems to defy democratization. Each of the BCA's sixty-one temples and churches are assigned a minister by the bishop (*sōchō*). Each minister is qualified to be a minister only insofar as he or (less likely) she has undergone a codified training and ordination procedure that includes several years of study and culminates in a complex and centuries-old ritual held at the denomination's head temple, the Honganji, located in Kyoto. This hierarchy and connection to Japan seem to fall in line with a traditional model of Japanese Buddhism that is at odds with the more egalitarian spirit of "convert" Buddhist groups in the United States.

Nevertheless, while there is a deep connection between the Buddhist Churches of America and the Honganji establishment, it would be naive to assume that the BCA is nothing more than a transplanted Japanese form of Buddhism in a new locale beholden to a rigid Japanese hierarchy. Rather, the BCA negotiates its place within American culture in multiple ways, and upon closer inspection both the connection to Japan and hierarchical structure are easily circumscribed in a typically modern American and democratic fashion. To begin, at the local level, each BCA-affiliate church is administered by a board of directors as one would expect to find in any American religious organization.[8] While each church has a minister, the minister is understood to be an employee of the church, hired by the board. This is in sharp contrast to the Japanese system, which has long had a patrilineal system of leadership wherein temples are run by ministers who pass them on to their eldest sons. The American employer-employee relationship between the board and the minister is perhaps in starkest relief when a Japanese minister comes to the United States with the expectation that he will have sole authority over his new assignment only to discover that his authority is at the pleasure of the board. Furthermore, whereas American ministers are, on paper, "assigned" to their churches by the bishop, this is not really the case. Decisions regarding ministerial assignments are often made "behind the scenes" in conversation with multiple parties and lay leaders and groups. Finally, on a day-to-day basis, whereas any given minister is the de facto spiritual head of the community, it is the lay leadership who takes the lead in running the church, from setting the ritual and liturgical calendar to running the Dharma schools that educate young Buddhists. American Shin Buddhist ministers rarely take the lead in Dharma school education, a task that most often falls to laywomen in the community. Thus, while there is a connection to Japan and a type of hierarchy in place within American Shin Buddhism suggesting a type of traditionalism, the community embraces lay-centric and democratic organizational structures that are a hallmark of modernist narratives.

When compared with the case of American convert Zen, something of the opposite seems to be true. The various "Zen centers" that have proliferated across the United States since the late 1960s and 1970s are assumed to be as modernist as the BCA is traditionalist. This typecasting is rather straightforward to the extent that American Zen practice is focused almost exclusively on seated meditation, a form of practice heretofore restricted not just to monastics but to specific classes of monastics. Thus, without even examining American Zen's social engagement, the role of Zen women, or any other markers of so-called "modernity," the fact that within the Zen center laypeople act like monks is enough to convince most that the community is thoroughly modern. Moreover, one of the successes of the Zen center model may be its rejection of centralized institutional power structures. That is, once a student has received Dharma transmission (i.e., been "certified" in some sense by his or her teacher or *rōshi*), the student will feel empowered to go off and start her own Zen center, host meditation retreats or trainings, attract students, and go on to become a *rōshi* herself without necessarily traveling to Japan to engage in traditional and rigorous ordination rituals.

Just as one can peel back the layer of traditionalism in the BCA case to discover modernism, here one can pull back the layer of modernity to discover traditionalism. Whereas the process of Dharma transmission seems unregulated and even antiauthoritarian, it remains nevertheless grounded on an extremely traditionalist understanding of Zen, that is, the authority of lineage. Zen is rooted in the belief that there has been a direct, mind-to-mind transmission of the Dharma, "outside the scriptures," in an unbroken lineage dating back to Śākyamuni Buddha himself, when he famously and silently held out a flower before his disciples—and only Mahākāśyapa smiled, knowingly. The assumption that one can be a Zen Buddhist teacher only after receiving this Dharma transmission is very much akin to Weber's "authority of the eternal yesterday," a traditional form of authority or domination, a notion that runs counter to the idea that American convert Zen rejects traditionalism in all its forms. Furthermore, the level of power traditional authority figures have within the tradition is perhaps most acutely felt when teachers abuse this power. Arguably, the only way that one can abuse power is if she or he has power to abuse in the first place, and the history of American convert Zen is, regrettably, rife with examples of Zen teachers doing just that. Without dwelling on the abuses of power by such teachers as Richard Baker and Maezumi Rōshi or the more recent case of Shimano Roshi, it is arguable that the broader American Zen community invests within its leaders a significant amount of authority and power despite its more democratic and egalitarian tendencies. Finally, it would be naive to think that the American convert Zen scene is driven by free-wheeling anti-establishment types with neither a concern for organized structures nor the authority of traditional Japanese institutions. The opposite is true and evident in such organizations as the Soto Zen Buddhist Association, which provides resources and training for the American Zen community and the Soto Zen Text Project that cooperates with the traditional Sotoshu Shumucho hierarchy in Japan to translate and standardize Zen Buddhist liturgical and canonical texts. Thus, while the tradition cultivates a particular rhetoric of iconoclasm and a democratic ethos, traditional authority figures and structures are easy to locate within the community, once again bespeaking the complex ways in which Buddhists both embrace and reject various modernist narratives.

Superstition and Ritual

The second hallmark of modernity under consideration here is the rejection of traditional Buddhist cosmology and superstitious ritualized practices, both of which run counter to "modern" (Western) scientific, psychological, or rational knowledge. In this regard, American convert Zen fits well within the modernist category, employing as it does a rhetoric grounded on the efficacy of seated meditation practices. *Zazen* in convert Zen communities is framed almost exclusively as a primarily psychological experience stripped of both its cosmological and ritual aspects. As Sharf (1995a) has noted, this primacy of experience runs counter to the ways that meditation has been thoroughly ritualized in premodern forms of Buddhism. Despite this rhetoric that foregrounds meditation practice while either deemphasizing or denigrating ritual, ritual is nevertheless easy to locate within any given Zen center. In addition to formal meditation practice, most Zen centers will enact several traditional Sotoshu rituals replete with the chanting of sutras and mantras as well as ritualized prostrations before altars, ritual behavior that is based on traditional Japanese cultural practices and grounded in nonscientific cosmologies or merit-making behavior endemic to Buddhism at large. Even when recast as somehow "modern," generalized ritual behavior pervades most Zen centers: one is expected to enter the *zendo* or Buddha hall on the right foot while one's hands are clasped in *shashu* and held just above the navel; silence is maintained throughout a session; members bow before altars, before their meditation cushions, and reflexively bow to one another. This behavior is most often dismissed as merely "etiquette," and it is rhetorically recast as "practice," as an "opportunity for mindfulness." However, it is precisely this type of repetitive behavior that is subsequently given symbolic meaning that lies at the heart of ritualized practice.[9]

Apart from this type of generalized ritual behavior, specific ritual practices are easy to locate in convert Zen. As Wilson has noted in *Mourning the Unborn Dead* (2009), a post-pregnancy loss ritual known as *mizuko kuyō* (literally, "water baby ceremony") has become widely popular in American Zen communities. This ritual originated in Japan as a response to women who had lost children either through miscarriage, still birth, or abortion and were concerned about their unborn child's future rebirth. Japanese versions of this ritual typically employ devotion to Jizō, the Japanese incarnation of the Bodhisattva Kṣitigarbha. Thus, the ritual relies on a host of traditional Mahayana concepts and cosmologies that run counter to the "rational" or antisuperstitious nature of "modern" Buddhism. Wilson's research discloses that the American version of *mizuko kuyō* departs dramatically from the Japanese version. Whereas in Japan the ritual is conducted in a rather private manner between a priest and a single family, the American version includes multiple families coming together in a style not unlike a group therapy session modeled more on Western psychotherapy than Eastern esotericism. However, let us not be fooled by this obviously modernist construction. During the American "water baby ceremony," participants ritually sew bibs that will then be placed on small statues of Jizō, and Wilson notes that the rhetoric surrounding the ritual speaks very much to notions of prayer and a sense among the participants that they are getting in touch with some inner spiritual part of themselves. This is not to suggest that convert Zen ritualists are deluding themselves and undermining their rational tendencies while embracing a superstitious mythos. Rather, it merely raises a question: Where do we draw the line between "rational" or modernist thinking and "superstitious" ritualistic behavior? At what point does a ritual cease to be little more than a reflection of superstitious appeal to some traditional cosmology and become a rational attempt to engender psychological healing?

The American Shin case is somewhat more problematic. Pure Land Buddhism is based on longstanding Mahayana Buddhist cosmologies that posit the existence of multiple world systems to which one can travel either through meditative practices or through death-bed rituals and attain a favorable rebirth. In the soteriology of Jodo Shinshu, the karmic mechanism of this rebirth, however, is not located in the individual ego-self but rather in the external workings of the Buddha of Infinite Light. This reliance on an externalized and powerful Buddha, superficially similar to Christian notions of grace, coupled with complex otherworldly depictions of paradisiacal pure Buddha fields, superficially similar to Christian notions of heaven, have given Jodo Shinshu the reputation of being a superstitious and antirational form of Buddhism, that is, very much not modern.

However, once again we can find hints of the modern in early Shin Buddhist history. As Shinran was spreading Pure Land teachings outside the capital, a debate emerged within the early community regarding the efficacy of performing rituals to the local *kami* or spirits endemic to Shinto practice. Shinran and his immediate successors generally denounced such practices using normative Pure Land doctrine; if there is nothing one's limited ego self can do to affect one's rebirth in the Pure Land, believing that self-centered, egoistic local spirits would care at all about one's awakening is just illogical. Now, this is not to suggest that Shinran and his early followers' conversation about whether or not they should engage in local spirit cults is similar in any way to contemporary debates regarding traditional superstitions versus modern science. Rather, it is merely to point out that this early rejection of Shinto ritualism within Shin Buddhism set a precedent that has stuck with the tradition much in the same way that the lay-centric spirit has stuck as a result of Shinran's rejection of his monastic status. As a consequence of this historical rejection of ritual, in contemporary Japan Shin Buddhism is widely regarded as the least superstitious brand of Buddhism, the one most rational and consonant with the modern world. In contrast, Zen and esoteric forms of Buddhism are generally considered to be less modern and more superstitious, exactly the opposite as in the United States. What accounts for this reversal of roles?

The answer can be found in ritual. Because Jodo Shinshu has long rejected self-powered practices and embraced a rhetoric that suggests that rituals are more or less pointless, despite the fact that the tradition engages in a wide variety of ritual behavior, Shin Buddhists have cultivated an anti-ritualistic mythos and rhetoric. In contrast, other forms of Buddhism have long embraced ritual as being extremely efficacious not only in affecting one's awakening but in affecting all manner of changes in the phenomenal world. Once in the modern period, this embrace of ritual has worked against Japanese Buddhist institutions as they came under attack for being anathema to modern (Western) scientific understandings of the world. Since the Meiji period, Buddhist institutions have been widely regarded as little more than "funeral Buddhism," more concerned with charging the laity for complex funeral rites whose stated intent is to help the dead achieve favorable rebirth (a decidedly traditional aim) while unscrupulously taking money from the common masses. For example, as Wilson (2009, 21–22) has noted, because Shin Buddhism rejects self-powered practices, Japanese Shin Buddhism generally does not engage in *mizuko kuyō* rituals, thus saving the community from the critique of being traditionalist.

This is not to suggest that American scholars have gotten it wrong, that Zen is traditional whereas Shin is modern. We merely point out that what is "modern" on this side of the Pacific turns out to be "traditional" on the other. Any attempt to employ "modern" as an objective qualifier is undermined by the subjective and culturally conditioned way in which "modern" is used within different Buddhist communities and for different ends. Clearly, one way to employ the traditional/modern dichotomy is in a polemic argument either for or against a particular practice. Contemporary Japanese critics of "funeral Buddhism" may employ a rhetoric that rejects traditionalism in order to champion a type of secular modernism. What is modern then is very much at the whim of one's particular location and is more often than not a reflection of polemical arguments whose true intent is to define which Buddhists are more or less authentic.

CONCLUSIONS

We share with Obadia the view that the category of "modernity" represents a type of *discourse* (a narrative) that is deeply colored by the cultural patterns and subjectivities of the storyteller. This is as true about scholars using the term as it is about the people scholars seek to describe and understand. In this sense, modernity "est un récit, un narrative selon la terminologie anglo-saxonne, un «texte» culturel, pour emprunter l'expression à Clifford Geertz, un «mythe», pour les plus enclins à y voir soit de la pure fiction imaginative, soit de la pensée religieuse en acte—un mythe au sens anthropologique du terme" (Obadia 2006).[10] Rather than a neutral descriptive term, "modernity" is a narrative category used by scholars, not infrequently as part of a larger project involving a theoretical paradigm based on ideas of rupture and discontinuity.

Obadia (2006) has noted the presence of a rhetoric of "crisis" in much of the literature concerned with Buddhist modernism. This literature is by and large not a neutral assessment of continuities and discontinuities in Buddhist traditions. More often than not, it becomes a veiled judgment of authenticity, usually made through arguments concerning pollution due to cultural mixing (Quli 2009; see also Stewart and Shaw 1994). Spencer notes that the idea of "tradition," rather than an innocent category of analysis, is "a central weapon in arguments about what Buddhism is and what it should try to be in the contemporary world" (Spencer 1990, 130; quoted in Samuels 2007, 120). Given (1) that traditions inevitably change over time, (2) that we lack a clear and concise definition of "tradition," and (3) that the list of possible indications of Buddhist modernism is so lengthy, one wonders: Exactly how much innovation makes something, to use the word Gombrich and Obeyesekere employ to describe certain orientations in Sri Lankan Buddhism, a "pseudo-tradition" (1988, 242)? Exactly how much integration of modernist narratives makes a group representative of Buddhist modernism rather than "traditional" Buddhism?

For the preceding reasons, we do not find "Buddhist modernism" (in the singular) a useful analytic tool for understanding Buddhist traditions in the United States. Rather than providing a neutral assessment of continuities and discontinuities in Buddhist traditions, the singular, acultural concept of Buddhist modernism essentializes traditions by denying their ongoing transformation throughout history, characterizing the modern as a radical rupture from the past and ignoring not only the fluid and contested nature of culture and traditions but the continuity of adaptations with forms from the past. This Buddhist modernism paradigm does not provide succinct definitions that would draw a defining boundary between "modernity" and "tradition," instead preferring an ambiguous definition of "Buddhist modernism" and using "tradition" as a mere placeholder or "empty" term (AlSayyad 2004; Blackburn 2010, 211). "Buddhist modernism" is so all-encompassing in its ambiguity that no contemporary group can escape being characterized as having some trait associated with it, making it useless in terms of offering a category to differentiate between groups. The applications of the theory often conflate modernity with the West and tradition with the East (and with this distinction comes much baggage from orientalism), which is especially problematic in terms of

Asian American Buddhist groups (who are, by definition, a mixture of West and East). It is a not-so-veiled judgment of authenticity but with no valid argument pointing to how much cultural mixing is permissible before "spoiling" a pure and authentic tradition. It is a dualism that does not capture the richness and messiness of lived religion. And finally, in its application by Western academics, it displays the "salvage" paradigm that anthropologist Renato Rosaldo has described as a symptom of "imperialist nostalgia," the colonial agent's longing for pre-Western traditional culture that she herself destroyed (Rosaldo 1989; see also Quli 2009, 4). For all of these reasons, we favor a cultural model of modernities that recognizes the presence of multiple modernist narratives and subnarratives, which are appropriated selectively by individuals and groups to meet their religious needs. In this respect, we see both contemporary Jodo Shinshu and Zen as appropriating various narratives associated with Buddhist modernism while simultaneously cultivating more traditionalist narratives, producing groups that could be called either "modernist" or "traditionalist," depending on one's vantage point and political purpose.

NOTES

Parts of this chapter are adapted from Quli (2010).

1. For critiques of the Protestant Buddhism paradigm, see Blackburn (2010) and Harris (2006).
2. This is an important distinction to make in Buddhist studies, where the dominant paradigm of "Buddhist modernism" currently en vogue is largely indebted to a sociological, acultural, Weberian model of modernity and its assumption of a universal march toward a monolithic rationality. The notion of a "this-worldly" development as part of Buddhist modernism, for example, reveals the strong Weberian influence underlying dominant uses of the term in Buddhist studies. For more on Weber's importance in Theravada studies in particular, see Choompolpaisal (2008).
3. This is the classic secularization theory as proposed by Max Weber. Secularization theory has been challenged not only on theoretical grounds but based on evidence in Western societies such as the United States, where religion continues to be a major component of people's lives—despite the premonition of the destruction of

religion in "modern" societies. For more on the state of secularization theory in contemporary sociology, see Christiano, Swatos, and Kivisto (2008).

4. We use the term "tradition" here to refer simply to cultural forms with some recognized historic continuity, though all traditions are by nature in conversation with the present and are necessarily in some sense "modern." For more on the difficulty in decisively distinguishing "traditional" from "modern," see AlSayyad (2004).
5. On "invented" traditions, see Hobsbawm and Ranger (1983) and, to a lesser extent, Kemper (1984).
6. What follows is based on fieldwork conducted between 2004 and 2010 within several BCA and Zen communities. See S. Mitchell (2006, 2008, and 2010).
7. It is worth mentioning that in Sri Lanka, too, there was a premodernist tradition of lay clergy/temple owners called *gaṇinnānses* (see Blackburn 2003, 132–134, 139; and Malalgoda 1976, 54, 57–58, 59, 65), drawing our attention to the danger of using laicization as an indicator of modernist influence.
8. For a discussion of how immigrant groups are impacted by US laws pertaining to the incorporation of religious institutions, see Cadge (2008); cf. Ama (2010).
9. For a fuller discussion of how ritualized practice is enacted within North American Zen communities, see Preston (1988).
10. Modernity "is a story, a narrative in Anglo-Saxon terminology, a cultural 'text' to borrow an expression from Clifford Geertz, a 'myth,' best seen as either pure imaginative fiction, or religious thought in action—a myth in the anthropological sense of the term." Quli's translation.

AFTERWORD

Buddhism beyond Borders: Beyond the Rhetorics of Rupture

RICHARD K. PAYNE

INTRODUCTION

The complexity and variety of themes running through the essays comprising this collection reflect the complexity and variety of both Buddhism in the United States in the early twenty-first century and the complexity and variety of perspectives required to study it. It would be misleadingly artificial, therefore, to summarize the collection in such a fashion as to suggest a single, unified, coherent research program. Instead, we seek to highlight important aspects of its contributions that reveal the collection as a nexus of several different theoretical issues. To adequately accomplish this it is necessary that the scope of the field of study within which the collection is framed be radically expanded. These themes are ones not only relevant to Buddhist studies' unloved stepchild, Buddhism in the West, but to the entirety of Buddhist history. In other words, instead of segmenting off contemporary expressions of Buddhism as somehow distinctly different from (which usually implicitly signifies lesser than) the major areas of specialization in Buddhist studies, this essay proposes that Buddhism in the West is better understood as part of a continuity of ongoing adaptations and transgressions—adaptations to new environments and transgressions against expectations. To accomplish this end, it is necessary to critique a pervasive trope—the rhetoric of rupture. Despite its frequent use as a historical device, rupture is a fundamentally religious formulation by which a sharp separation of the past from the future is drawn at the boundary of the prophet, at the boundary of the millennial realignment, at the boundary of whatever serves the rhetorical ends of an author. Like all good rhetorics, the rhetoric of rupture not only serves to pre-structure thought, but it is so deeply rooted in our literary culture as to flow from an author's fingers almost entirely unthinkingly and to pass before a reader's eyes almost entirely unnoticed.

THE RHETORICS OF RUPTURE

The foundations of much of present-day discourse on religion, both academic and popular, are built upon a variety of rhetorics of rupture. Simply as an introductory example, let us consider Hans Kippenberg's claim that "the global disembedding of all traditions was accompanied by a global reflection on modernization" (Kippenberg 2002, 192).[1] This might be read as a simple pair of equations: "modern = disembedded" and "traditional = embedded." While the pairing of these two rhetorical ruptures might appear to be descriptive, in this simplified form it instead imposes an interpretive or even polemical distinction—one that may come to be widely accepted because it resonates with certain values and preconceptions. The resonances of these pairings play both on Romantic idealizations of the primitive and on antimodernist nostalgia. Given the widespread presumption of such idealizations and nostalgia, it becomes easy to construct a rhetoric of rupture along the lines of traditional versus modern in which religion is "embedded" in premodern societies and "disembedded" in modern ones.

However, the notion of "embedded" religion, employed to highlight those post-Enlightenment conceptions according to which "all cultures everywhere had a well-defined, autonomous sphere of life called religion" (Nongbri 2008, 442), cannot be uncritically employed in considering societies other than those formed by Enlightenment solutions to the Wars of Religion—that is, denaturalizing certain configurations of social praxis as "religion," thus forming a category autonomous from politics, economics, and so on.[2] The apparent mirroring conception, however, that premodern traditions are—or were—in some sense "naturally" embedded in their societies, is problematic.[3] For this reason it is important not to allow Kippenberg's "all religions" to be obscured by the rhetorical power of the twin pairings of modern and traditional, and disembedded and embedded. As universal, his claim makes no distinction between modern Western Christianity—whose history may perhaps be meaningfully sorted along the divide of the Enlightenment in which the isolation of "religion" as one of many realms located within the social order grows out of quasi-theological reflections originating from within the tradition itself (Gillespie 2008)—and Buddhism as well as other "Asian religions" in which the distinction was imposed by colonialism (Oberoi 1994; cf. Pennington 2005). In other words, the two pairs of categories cannot simply be aligned with one another.[4] As with the other rhetorics of rupture we are examining, each needs to be employed critically.

In this collection Erik Braun's discussion of *jhāna* meditation demonstrates the necessity for critical use of such categories as "modern" and "traditionalist." The introduction of such "un-modern" concepts as the cosmological system involved in explicating the *jhānas* and belief in rebirth make the understanding of "convert" Buddhism much more complex than the purportedly explanatory tropes of modernization and secularization. This is not meditation simply as stress reduction or some other secularized representation but instead arguably a religious tradition. Certainly in terms of the three criteria for a religion employed by Mira Niculescu (chap. 9 in this volume), that is, lineage, practice, and theology—though in the case of Buddhism the term "theology" is problematic (Payne 2011)—the movement associated with *jhāna* meditation comprises a religious tradition within the broader framework of Buddhism.

If we consider the notion of disembedding alone, it would seem to cover (at least) two distinct kinds of events. One is the general disembedding of "religion" in the process of the concept's modern creation, that is, the ideological disembedding concomitant with modernism. The other would be the effects of colonialism, and both economic and cultural imperialism. There have indeed been violent and involuntary dislocations and disruptions, such as the incarceration of Americans of Japanese descent during World War II discussed by Michihiro Ama (chap. 4 in this volume) and both the conquest of Tibet by China and the intersectarian disputes discussed by Jeannine Chandler (chap. 5 in this volume). However, the entire history of religion[5] seems to be at least equally marked by virtually constant voluntary dislocation and disruption,—and the ability of premodern religions to move in this fashion indicates that they are not as "embedded" as the rhetoric of traditional versus modern might lead one to believe. Is there really a significant difference between the movement of Chinese Buddhists to San Francisco from the mid-nineteenth century through the third quarter of the twentieth and the movement of Buddhists between China, Korea, and Japan from the sixth century to the late Kamakura era (1185–1333)? Or, more specifically, is the situation of a present-day Tibetan lama, moving either from his "home in exile" in South India to the Buryat Republic (Bernstein 2013a, 2013b) or from Kathmandu to Los Angeles (Moran 2004, 1) significantly different from that of the Chinese Vinaya master Jianzhen (Ganjin 鑑眞, 688–763), who introduced ordination procedures in Nara era Japan (710–794)? And if significantly different, such differences need to be explicitly theorized rather than simply presumed.

In other words, the dynamics of Buddhism in motion considered in this volume should not be seen as unique either to the modern era or in the Western cultural zone. Much of what is evident here is characteristic of the entire history of Buddhism and can be viewed more productively against that much broader backdrop. Within the academy, rather than being seen as simply the most recent phases in a long history of movement and adaptation, the study of "Buddhism in the West" remains ghettoized by intellectual preferences for the ancient and exotic, by the modern/premodern[6] and embedded/disembedded dichotomies, by greater attention to the stable forms of Buddhism found in centers than to the instability and ambiguities of the margins, and by a bibliocentric and philosophical focus on the great, authoritative doctrinal classics rather than on lived religion and practice.

RELOCATING THIS COLLECTION

The editors introduce this collection of essays by referencing the 1994 Numata lecture series Buddhism in America: An Expanding Frontier. There is another academic event that provides a broader context for this collection. In January of 1993, Jan Nattier together with the late John McRae organized a research conference entitled Buddhism across Boundaries.[7] The focus of that conference was the movement of Buddhism through Central Asia, and it marks a shift away from looking at Buddhism as a series of monolithic set pieces usually identified either by reference to modern nation-states, such as Chinese Buddhism, Indian

Buddhism, Tibetan Buddhism, and so on, or by reference to sectarian lineages, such as Zen, Theravada, Gelug, Pure Land, and so on. Either knowingly or, as seems to be the case most commonly, unknowingly, geopolitical categorizations deploy a generalized characterization, such as "Chinese Buddhism," across a highly diverse and complex history, such as the varieties of Buddhisms that have existed in and moved through the geographic, linguistic, and cultural territories now known as China. In a similar fashion, lineal organizations tend to privilege one form as normative for the entirety of the tradition. For example, the Pure Land teachings of Hōnen and Shinran are often taken as normative for the entire tradition of Pure Land Buddhism either because other forms are not as easily accessible or for reasons of sectarian historiography.[8] Such generalizations will unavoidably privilege some form of Buddhism—either the best-known (sometimes simply a historical accident[9]) or the one considered most "typical"—over other kinds, frequently unknowingly replicating in the Western episteme some sectarian agonistic historiography.[10] The shift evidenced by Buddhism across Boundaries went beyond the obvious alternative formula, "Buddhism in . . . ," to consider movement and change—what has been called "an ethnography of processes and interconnections" (Moran 2004, 4, citing Malkki 1995)—as the primary alternative to thinking about Buddhism in static terms.[11]

IN PROCESS: TALKING ABOUT MOVEMENT

Terminology is always important. In addition to "crossing and dwelling," the terms introduced by Thomas Tweed (chap. 1 in this volume, and 2006), the pairing "local and translocal" also provides a way of thinking about the phenomena in ways that help avoid the connotative dangers of other categorizations based on either generalizations or generalities. Despite all of the literature that attempts to categorize Buddhism by general categories, such as nation-state, ethnicity, generation, historical period, or sectarian lineage, all Buddhism is local.[12] And when we consider its movement, it is some specific local form that is being moved and relocated to another specific locale. In other words, not only is all Buddhism local, but all movement is translocal.[13]

Together with "crossing and dwelling" and "local and translocal," Lewis Lancaster has employed another pair of concepts that address the same issues from another perspective. These are fixed and portable sanctity (Lancaster 2012, 226). Fixed sanctity identifies that kind of sanctity that has a specific geographic location. If sanctity exists in some particular location, such as Fujisan, or Putuo shan, or Diablo Canyon, or Jerusalem, or Bodhgaya, then it is fixed.[14] If, however, sanctity is located in an object that can be moved, such as relics, icons, holy persons, texts, or teachings, or that can be ritually instantiated in different locations, such as by means of foundation rituals, then it is portable. These are not hermetically sealed categories, however, as there are ambiguous cases. For example, there are miniature replicas of the Shikoku pilgrimage in many locations; though the Shikoku pilgrimage is fixed in the sense that it is the specific eighty-eight locations on the island, clearly its sanctity has been relocated to its miniaturized replicas.[15]

These three pairs of concepts all attempt to provide language for describing related dimensions in which stability and movement are evident in religion. Dwelling and crossing emphasize two dimensions of human experience; local and translocal focus on institutional forms and their emplacement, displacement, and re-emplacement; and fixed and portable attend to the character of that which is considered sacred.

WHOSE DEFAULT IS IT, ANYWAY?

Because the dynamics considered in this collection cannot be determined to be unique to the modern era or to Western culture, I think it is most useful to redirect thinking about this collection away from such categories as "American Buddhism," or "Buddhism in America," or "Buddhism in the West." These categories, with their limited utility, already constitute a well-worn path, one that is found in the standard geopolitical categories that structure the field of Buddhist studies by default. Since these geopolitical categories are almost entirely untheorized, they function like folk taxonomies. As William E. Arnal and Russell T. McCutcheon note, "there are times when the analytic utility of widely used folk taxonomies (i.e., conceptual systems that members of social groups use to delimit and thereby manage their environment and, in so doing, determine their place within it) can be so diminished as to make their continued use part of the problem to be analyzed rather than being among the tools needed to begin an examination of other things" (2013, 2).

After four decades of study employing the category of "American Buddhism," or "Buddhism in America,"[16] the inadequacy of the category—evidenced by the definitional issues discussed by Shannon Hickey in chapter 3 in this collection—reveals not only the problems inherent within it but points to the problematic character of its well-established analogues: Chinese Buddhism, Japanese Buddhism, Thai Buddhism, and the like. While these categories seem coherent, much of their apparent coherence results either from uncritical acceptance of them as received tradition, such as in the form of academic specializations, or from the appeal they have for nationalistic or ethnic pride. Perhaps the problems with the default geopolitical categories can be made evident by suggesting that if those categories were valid, then taken cumulatively, one would know about Buddhism per se. In other words, the corollary to the default categorization is that

> Buddhism = Indian Buddhism + Chinese Buddhism + Tibetan Buddhism + Thai Buddhism + Lankan Buddhism + Japanese Buddhism + Newar Buddhism + . . . + X Buddhism

If expressed that baldly the idea seems preposterous, then that evaluation should be read back into the system of categorization itself.[17]

The theoretical problems made manifest, either explicitly or implicitly, by the contributors to this collection reveal that the category "American Buddhism" (and its correlates) is stressed to the point of failure. Because the attempt to replicate the received rubrics, that is, the geopolitical categories employed by default, in the form of "American Buddhism" fails, then the failings of those rubrics—previously concealed by geographic, cultural, linguistic, or temporal distance, and supported by the interests of imperialism, whether political, economic, intellectual, or religious—are made evident.[18] Concern about the inadequacies of geopolitical divisions as default categories is in fact not new, much less "postmodern." In his 1928 "Address to the International Congress of Historical Sciences," Marc Bloch states that "it is high time to set about breaking down the outmoded topographical compartments within which we seek to confine social realities, for they are not large enough to hold the material we try to cram into them" (cited in Skaff 2012, 3).

A LITTLE MORE LOCAL

As discussed earlier, one of the problems with the very category "American Buddhism" is its dependence on the default organization of the field of Buddhist studies into geopolitical monoliths. Jeff Wilson's contribution to this collection proposes one solution to this problem, regional studies. Wilson proposes five modes of analysis based on regions, which can contribute much more finely nuanced investigations into the dynamics of Buddhism in motion. These are in terms of distribution by region, cultural determinants of regions on Buddhism, cultural influences of Buddhism on regions, regional segmentation of lineages, and the influences of differing built environments (Wilson, chap. 2 in this volume). Regional analyses can provide generalizations over a smaller scope and, therefore, help with the kind of demographic questions that Wilson highlights. Wisely, Wilson notes that regions themselves are not fixed but are rather contingent upon the questions motivating inquiry (Wilson 2012, 36; and Wilson, chap. 2 in this volume). We may wish to add a note of caution, however. Although regionalism is purely descriptive in nature, it may easily come to be treated as explanatory. This would be the case were causal agency mistakenly attributed to a region as such. The attribution of agency to a region—something that can only have agency in a metaphoric sense—would thereby unfortunately elide the events, actions, and decisions by historical agents that actually explain the divergences he notes.

OLD DHARMA? NEW BOTTLES?

The significance of Buddhism in contemporary social discourse is made evident by the role it plays in literary and artistic criticism. In addition to providing us entrée into the areas at the margins where artistic creation, Buddhist practice, and neo-Romantic spirituality mingle, Richard Hughes Seager's and Kimberly Beek's essays disclose how well integrated into Western cultural discourse Buddhism has become: it is now an acceptable interpretive category. These two essays point to the changes in Buddhist studies that have taken place in the less than two decades that separate the 1993 Buddhism across Boundaries conference and the 2010 Buddhism without Borders conference. The inclusion of works on Buddhism and the arts reflects a more general redefinition of the field from texts and doctrines to practices and expressions. The work done on epigraphy and archeology, on material culture and art historical studies, have all enriched our understanding of the history of Buddhism.

Like most religious art prior to the modern Romantic cult of the artist as an individual creative genius, and aesthetic sensibility as a mark of the viewer's refined spiritual sensitivity, Buddhist art and artists largely adhered to specific stylistic constraints. Rhetorically, this creates a rupture between *traditional* artists, frequently conceived of as "anonymous" in placing their own identity behind the devotional function of their work, and *modern* creative artists who use art as a matter of self-expression.[19] As Seager highlights in the central thesis of his essay, "A useful distinction can be made between those Americans who use Dharma images for religious practice in community and those who use them as vehicles for artistic self-expression. For the first group, Buddhist images are markers of religious identity. In the second, they signify creativity and individuality expressed in the production of art" (Seager, chap. 7 in this volume). This reinforces a modernizing rhetoric distinguishing the collective, conservative, and uncreative role of art in religion from the individual, liberative, and creative role of art as self-expression. Seager describes the "Dharma images" used in practice as "markers of religious identity"—a characterization that if taken in isolation might locate them simply as commodities acquired as expressions of personal identity, providing their owners with a certain social cachet. As Seager himself goes on to discuss, however, such images serve important liturgical functions for many Buddhists. One may consider in this regard adherents of Soka Gakkai, whom Seager has himself studied in quite some depth (Seager 2006). Certainly possessing a Soka Gakkai *gohonzon* marks an individual in such a fashion that a particular religious identity can be read by others. For the adherent who chants before it daily, it is far more than simply an expression of his or her religious identity but rather a manifest presence of the power of the Lotus Sutra.

We find in both Seager and Beek that literary and artistic works are interrogated in quest of influences from or expressions of Buddhism, and indeed at times such influences and expressions are read onto such works. Whether in exegesis or eisegesis, discussions of the boundaries—What is Buddhist art? What is Buddhist literature? What demonstrates the influence of Buddhism? What constitutes an expression of Buddhism?[20]—reveal the relocating of Buddhism into the modern conception of the creative artist. In relation to premodern cultures, or in this case actually pre-Romantic cultures, this is effectively a dislocating of the praxis of Buddhist art. This is, of course, not to say that there was not any change or development or that individual talent and skill may have been the motivating force for such change. But it reflects the contextual difference between the gallery and museum on the one side and the temple and altar on the other.

Ron Grimes (1992) has discussed the effects of displacing sacred objects into a museum context, noting that the ritual basis for their significance in a temple or church is lost. Viewed as art, they are no longer the potent objects of ritual action. Consideration of provenance, influence, style, execution, among other factors, displaces efficacy, turning the object from part of a ritually potent ensemble[21] into an object to be examined. The distinction between temple and altar on the one hand and studio and museum on the other parallels Beek's strategy for treating "Buddhist fiction" as a unique genre.

This genre is identified, tentatively, by Beek as "an emerging genre of fiction, written in English [that] has major Buddhist themes, Buddhist characters, or Buddhist-influenced plot structures. . . . But the defining characteristic of Buddhist fiction is a storyline that hinges on or is structured by distinctly Buddhist experience" (Beek, chap. 8 in this volume). Before proceeding, we should note that she does not indicate what constitutes a "distinctly Buddhist experience."[22]

She also tells us that Buddhist fiction is "not the Buddhist story we're used to—not *jātakas* or *avadāna* stories, nor Chinese or Japanese miracle tales." Citing Kate Wheeler, Beek introduces the notion of "reading stories for their own sake" and notes that the difference between such stories and doctrinal expositions is perhaps "because fiction is a confrontation with life as it is, just like the Dharma" (Beek, chap. 8 in this volume). Here we again see not only rhetorics of rupture between modern, Romantic (art for art's sake) and traditional (religious texts as didactic[23]), and between the Western ("in English") and other cultural zones but also the anti-intellectual strain of Romanticism with its elevation of "experience" ("life as it is") over reflection. The claim equating fiction and the Dharma as both being "confrontation with life as it is," is suggestive of the anti-intellectual strain that pervades much of Buddhist modernism. More broadly, however, an attitude found increasingly among Buddhist scholars is that lived religion is the proper object of study, and that it is to be found almost any place other than in the classic doctrinal texts. The study of such texts as the Perfection of Wisdom literature, or Dōgen's *Treasury of the True Dharma Eye*, or Tsongkhapa's *Great Treatise on the Stages of the Path to Enlightenment*, or Buddhaghosa's *Path of Purification*, has been an important part of the Buddhist tradition throughout its history (Blackburn 2001; McDaniel 2008; Nance 2012). Although perhaps understandable as a corrective to the longstanding privileging of doctrinal studies in Buddhist studies, Beek has demonstrated the study of Buddhist fiction is more than adequately valuable enough to stand on its own as an equal partner in the study of Buddhist literature more broadly defined.

Beek's discussion of the contexts for the creation of "Buddhist fiction" could also perhaps benefit from considering the contextual elephant in all the rooms of religious studies: economics. Buddhist fiction does not simply come into being but comes into being as a commodity within consumer capitalism. It is not simply authors and readers, or other "literati," who create the genre but publishers who promote the genre to a market. In other words, a genre does not simply emerge but exists dialectically—works are identified as members of the genre, and such identification then serves to create additional works that fit within that genre. That dialectic is itself, however, propelled by the ceaseless demands of consumer capitalism for new products to offer into the marketplace.

RATIONALITY AND SUPERSTITION

In his essay here David McMahan points out that the rhetoric of rupture between spiritual and religious is grounded on earlier oppositions between science and superstition and between rational and irrational. While these topics have been discussed at length in the field, McMahan's articulation constellates the relative valorizations with new clarity.[24] The rhetorical alignment of spiritual, scientific, and rational helps us to understand such developments as the present fascination with the scientific study of meditation. Modernizing developments in the religious culture of the United States and Europe during the late nineteenth and early twentieth century sought to unify science and "religion" under the rubric of "mind science."[25] (At that time the same semiotic opposition as now expressed by the pairing of spiritual and religious was represented under an opposition between religious and churched.) Thus, building on the cultural resources of mind science, the contemporary interplay between Buddhism and science—especially now the neurosciences—can be seen as another attempt by religion to colonize science.[26]

OCCULTISM: THE IGNORED DYNAMIC

The background to the current Buddhism and science discourse discussed by McMahan also opens the topic of occultism as a significant, though often seemingly actively ignored, factor in the dynamics of Buddhist history. Erik Braun draws attention to the American cultural religious stream labeled "metaphysical" by Catherine Albanese. Although this strain does link to the therapeutic enculturation of Buddhism, it also links to the interest in extraordinary power/s. This interest hardly differs at all from the appeal of the occult in the United States. As Quli and Mitchell note in this volume, the modernist image of Buddhism as rational and scientific hardly captures a uniform set of attitudes, or their expression in a uniform rejection of traditional practices. That image is more one constructed for propaganda purposes by late nineteenth-century apologists.

Similar propaganda is found in biographies of Buddhist missionaries to China, which include some stories that "may have been told by the master himself, as edifying or self-advertising accounts about miracles performed or witnessed, contacts with superhuman beings and acts of clairvoyance. Some miracle stories unmistakably bear the stamp of traditional Buddhist lore, and they no doubt contributed to the image of the foreign monk as a great magician in popular imagination" (Zürcher 2012, 15).[27] Not only does the American metaphysical religious culture encompass an acceptance of magical beliefs, but much of the way in which Buddhism is promoted, that is, as a meditative technique for attaining happiness, health, and indeed in some cases wealth, relies on similarly magical conceptions.

NEW MEDIA

Although the media involved appear radically different, in the transmission and establishment of Buddhism in both ancient China and the contemporary West, the availability of new media played an important role. Erik Zürcher notes that Buddhism entered China at a time when paper, "that cheap and mass-produced writing material . . . was taking the place of the more bulky and expensive writing-strips made of wood or bamboo" (Zürcher 2012, 12). In this case the oasis towns "mainly in Kucha, Qarašahr, and Khotan" (Sander 2012, 37) in Central Asia—an area often ignored in light of nationalist pretensions ossified in the geopolitical categorization of Buddhism (Sen 2013)—played a pivotal role in the interconnected (and not economically insignificant) projects of producing paper, copying Buddhist texts, and translating them into Chinese. "The copying and writing down of those sacred texts formerly known by heart goes hand-in-hand with their translation into local languages" (Sander 2012, 37).

The effects of electronic media on Buddhism and Buddhist studies has been addressed by several authors (Hubbard 1995). Helen Baroni's study of Aitken Rōshi's maintenance of a "Distant Membership" demonstrates that even a communications medium as longstanding as the postal service has played a role in the way Buddhism has been disseminated to new regions within the United States. One question that may be worth pursuing is the extent to which such long-distance media as the postal service and the Internet work against the grain of regionalization (Wilson chap. 2 in this volume and 2012) by "smoothing over" regional differences.

CONTEXT OF CONVERSION

The struggle with conceptualizing Buddhism includes not only the geopolitical categories but is reflected in the ways in which Buddhism in the Euro-American West has been categorized. Hickey (chap. 3 in this volume) considers the issues of white privilege lying hidden beneath various schemas that have attempted to provide an orienting framework for considering the processes of acculturation. Intersecting with Hickey's focus on white privilege is the tendency for convert Buddhists to garner more attention than natal ones (Payne 2005). There are a variety of reasons that this would be the case, including, as Hickey notes the fact, that "white Buddhists have gained disproportionate public attention from white scholars and journalists, who have focused on people like themselves in terms of race, class, and education." Sunya

Pratt, discussed by Michihiro Ama in chapter 4 in this collection, is a specific instance in which it would seem that this kind of journalistic attention was paid to a white convert. Ama's essay also provides an important window on the role of women in the early establishment of Buddhism in the United States.

I believe an important, if subtle, additional factor is the religious culture within which these discussions have taken place. Conversion per se is a religiously charged topic for Christian thought, one that introduces the emotionally and morally significant concepts of "belonging" and "loyalty." In this framework, conversion implies denying that one belongs to one religion and has chosen to belong to another. Such an act further implies disloyalty to the one while declaring loyalty to another. Thus, in the context of Christian religious culture, conversion is an ethically valorized act. Although this kind of language is not employed in the discussions of two Buddhisms or three, it certainly is employed in the "dual-belonging" discourse (Cornille 2002; Drew 2011). The perspective of Christian religious culture within which discussions of dual-belonging are taking place—discussions that are perhaps invisible to most people actually engaged in some form of dual-belonging—gives a strong, though covert, negative valence to the category of convert Buddhists.

FROM LINES TO NETWORKS: DECENTERING GLOBALIZATION

One of the common representations of Buddhist history is linear, that is, following a trajectory from geographic West to geographic East (as distinct from cultural East to cultural West), beginning in India, spreading both north and east into Tibet, China, Korea, and Japan, and south and east into Sri Lanka, Burma, Thailand, Cambodia, and Indonesia.[28] It is not uncommon to see this kind of linear historiography continue to inform representations of the movement of Buddhism from Asia to the West—the United States and Europe. Conceptualizing history as a linear trajectory is not unique to Western culture. The specialist in the Buddhisms of Japan will, for example, be familiar with what is known as the "three countries" (*sankoku*, 三国) model of Buddhist history, the three countries in this case being India, China, and Japan.

Three aspects of such historiographic structures are important to note: first, what is erased; second, the conflation of history and progress; and third, what is ignored.

What is erased. In the classic three countries model, for example, the importance of Korea in the history of Buddhism in Japan is placed under erasure. China carried much greater cultural authority for Japan, and the rhetorical politics of sectarian identity formation pushed to link the Buddhisms of Japan with those of China, ignoring the actual historical role of Korea (Lewin 1994). Whether such ignoring is intentional or not does not change the effects of erasure.

The conflation of history and progress. Implicit in this model is a conflation of history and progress, that is, the last term of the trajectory is not uncommonly interpreted (either explicitly or implicitly) as in some way better than what has gone before. Although referred to in Western philosophy of history as "Whig historiography," it is also found in other societies as well. These interpretations of history as a progressive improvement seem often to dominate the discourse in the United States, given the emphasis on progress in its popular and official cultures. The alternative, that is, rhetorics of decline seem to serve more delimited functions, as for example in claims to authority by a return to the original and pure teachings of the founder. Under an interpretive rhetoric of progress, no matter how shallow and distorted contemporary understandings of Buddhist thought and practice may be, they are implicitly assumed to be superior to previous understandings.

What is ignored. When theorized, it becomes clear that linear histories ignore the multidirectionality of history. A perhaps familiar example is the way that Pure Land history is often written as if it stops in China with the Tang, that is, once Hōnen and Shinran became active in Japan. A lineal historiography thereby ignores the fact that Pure Land thought and practice continued in China into the Song and beyond (Mochizuki, forthcoming). Matthew Kapstein's *Buddhism between Tibet and China* (2009) specifically works against the grain of lineal historiography and seeks to expose what has been ignored by the sectarian emphasis on India as the legitimizing source of Tibetan Buddhism. Again, this distortion by ignoring is not somehow uniquely Western in origins but is also found in other societies as well. In other words, these characteristics of linear historiography seem to reflect not a cultural phenomenon but rather a "natural" human tendency to understand the world from one's own location, not even in any sense "egotistical" but simply existentially egocentric.

In the case of our studies here, on the movements of Buddhism across sociocultural boundaries, it is important, therefore, to not simply displace a Euro-American-centered understanding of globalization with some other—an act of "recentering"[29] as it were—but to decenter the discourse and to conceptualize the movements of Buddhism as simultaneously multidirectional. One example of such multidirectionality is Yogi Chen, who was born in China but eventually brought a version of Tibetan tantric Buddhism learned among the Tibetan expatriate community in India, and filtered through Chinese cultural categories, to the immigrant Chinese communities of the greater San Francisco Bay Area (Payne 2010).

Not only are there web-like interactions between different regions and lineages, but the ideological development of modern Buddhism—as distinct from Buddhist modernism—also demonstrates a web-like structure. For example, Braun (chap. 10 in this volume) questions the linear periodization of Buddhism as leading from a religious conception of Buddhism to a secular and psychological conception, or even to a post-Buddhist abandonment of Buddhist identity altogether. The "growing popularity of *jhāna* meditation" with the traditional cosmology that it brings with it demonstrates that any linear representation evades the complexities of actual history. (This topic has also been addressed by Quli 2008 and by McMahan, chap. 11 in this volume.)

PREMATURE CLOSURES: RHETORICS OF RUPTURE AND THE COMPLEXITIES OF ACTUAL HISTORY

Rhetorics of rupture declare a dramatic difference from one time or place to another. Thus, the category of "modern," which plays such an important role in the formation of the topic of this collection, is itself established by declarations of dramatic differences between the preceding and the present. Similarly, the category "American" or "the West" also effectively constitute declarations of dramatic difference—the attitude known as "American exceptionalism" is not limited to the political realm, but extends into the religious as well. From the colonial era we have John Winthrop's 1630 sermon, "City upon a Hill," in which he declares what will become American exceptionalism: "that wee shall be as a Citty upon a Hill, the eies of all people are uppon us."[30] American exceptionalism underlies the expression of American Buddhist exceptionalism. Expectations that American Buddhism should be somehow unique, and both distinct from and superior to other kinds, lends credence to the quest for an authentic or genuine American Buddhism—despite the role claims of authenticity and genuineness play in strategies for power or simply the ultimately incoherent nature of such a quest.

Such ruptures, however attractive for narrative historiography, tend toward prematurely closing off consideration of the complexities of history. This is the by now familiar problem with historical periodization, particularly when linked to the sharp delineations of dynastic changes. Thus, we have the Buddhism of the Tang dynasty or of the Kamakura era. Yet, the practices, traditions, institutions, and people that made up Buddhism in the preceding and succeeding periods were largely continuous across the temporal boundaries marked by these periodizations. Acts of suppression, such as that which took place in the ninth century in China, or in the nineteenth century in Japan, do make for sharp changes but rarely correspond to other periodizations.

Geopolitical categorizations also form rhetorics of rupture. Thai Buddhism is distinct from Korean Buddhism is distinct from Japanese Buddhism is distinct from American Buddhism and so on. Yet, the history of Buddhism in East Asia is highly interactive, stretching across these geopolitical boundaries. Indeed, there are very few forms of Buddhism that are actively nationalistic so as to self-define with a nation. Nichiren, who sought to establish the identity of Japan with his version of a Lotus Sutra cult, is relatively rare in the history of Buddhism. Contemporary violence against Muslims being instigated by Buddhist monks in Myanmar may be seen as another such identification of Buddhism and the state. But the notion that a nation-state forms a coherent category for Buddhism presumes similarities within the category—where they do not necessarily exist—and at the same time presumes differences between such categories. Such imposed similarities and differences serve to obscure more than they reveal. This then is the problem with analyses based on rhetorics of rupture. Unless the ruptures actually correspond to a significant change of some kind, they serve rhetorical ends by introducing difference or change where similarity or continuity may be of more explanatory significance.

NOTES

1. Kippenberg is here drawing on the work of Anthony Giddens (1990). I would note that "traditions" as used by Kippenberg in his referencing Giddens is not code for religion but rather refers to "all human practices."
2. See also Nongbri (2013). For a more complex explanation, see Zagorin (2003).
3. Another issue is the dichotomous relation that some might read as implicit in the pairing of "modern" and "tradition." Such a reading needs to be problematized. Not only is "tradition" used simply as a synonym for "religion," but often it is also used to suggest a positive evaluation, that is, "authentic."
4. There seems to be a regular pattern of cognition that can be called the "semiotic convergence of oppositions." This occurs when one term of each of two oppositions appears to be very similar to one another. Because of this, it is assumed that the other terms of each of the two oppositions are also similar to each other, when in fact they may be distinct. An example is the relation between spiritual and religious, on the one hand, and experience and doctrine on the other. Because spiritual is commonly considered to be experiential in nature, religion is automatically aligned with experiences presumed opposite, doctrinal.
5. The term is being used here as a scholarly category, that is, what Jonathan Z. Smith has called "redescription" (2004, 28–32).
6. Or, traditionalist/modernist. For example, the inadequately nuanced formulation proposed by Martin Baumann, who treats these two "Weberian ideal types" (2001, 4) as referring to historical periods: "Traditional or historical Buddhism started with the reign of Aśoka and lasted until the beginning of revival or reformist Buddhism in the mid- to late nineteenth century" (3). Also relevant to the consideration of Buddhism as it has come to be represented in the West is the problematic equation he makes between the Pali canon and early Buddhism.
7. Held at the Hsi Lai Temple in Hacienda Heights, California; selected papers were published first in 1999 in a very hard to locate version and then more recently (March 2012) as part of the Sino-Platonic Papers series, a visionary approach to publishing very important works of scholarship created and guided by Victor H. Mair.

8. For an example, see Fujita (1996, 6), where he asserts that the three sutras identified by Hōnen "are the primary sources for the study of Pure Land Buddhism." Such "primacy" appears to have been determined *a priori*, solely on the basis of a sectarian historiography rather than upon an actual examination of the full range of possible texts that could be considered (see Payne 2007).
9. For example, Zen remains one of the most widely recognized—and commercialized (see the blog "Zensanity," http://zensanity.net)—forms of Buddhism, despite its demographically minor position in Japan. (The claim that its prominence in the literature simply reflects it importance in the religious culture of Japan, despite its demographically minor role, is simply a matter of sectarian polemics, now in the mouths of Western scholars attempting to justify their own interests and specializations. Because of such claims of its central role in the religious culture of Japan, and limited knowledge to the contrary, Zen is seen even in places where it is not—"Zen" gardens—while other strains of Buddhism remain unrecognized, such as the formative role of Tendai and esoteric Buddhism on Zen.) The status of being so visible is a consequence of the highly successful efforts of D. T. Suzuki, who worked to promote it to Western audiences, while at the same time Shin ministers were working to serve the immigrant communities. As a consequence Shin still remains little known outside those communities, a situation which, however, is gradually changing.
10. Consider the ongoing awkwardness of the Theravada/Hinayana terminology in Western scholarship, which results from the adoption of Mahayana categories. Footnoting his use of the term "Hinayana," Robert Thurman explains that he is using it "here to designate the teachings aiming at self-liberation from suffering by separate individuals, philosophically divided into eighteen schools during the centuries after Śākyamuni's death. . . . Lest any reader be offended by any presumed derogatory tone implied in the term, let me make clear that I mean 'individual' (not 'inferior') by 'Hīna-' and 'universal' (not 'superior') by 'Mahā-' of Mahāyāna" (Thurman 2004, 37n1). Although Thurman has gone on to use this philologically justified stipulative definition consistently, as for example in rendering the title of the *Mahāyānasūtrālaṃkāra* as *The Universal Vehicle Discourse Literature* (Thurman 2004), in the boo itself he ambivalently uses Hinayana as both an attitude and as a historical stage that was surpassed with the rise of the Mahayana.

As careful and as well informed as Thurman has been in creating this stipulative definition, the problems of its status as a Mahayana polemic remain.

11. This trend is evidenced in the present collection by Thomas Tweed's essay as well as his other recent work (2006, 2011). This shift is also evident in Miyazaki and Williams (2001).
12. There is a valid alternative to the local-translocal conceptualization, and that is true (i.e., statistical) generalizations. Any statement that is about general characteristics not informed by a statistical analysis is simply a generality. Generalities are almost always distortions resulting from preconceptions, impressionistic or anecdotal evidence, insufficient evidence, or other forms of bias. Segal (2006, 157) is wrong to assert that "theories are generalizations." Theories are explanations and as such can be tested, such tests sometimes producing generalizations based on the methodology employed. Segal equates theories with the identification of similarities. This essay seeks to identify similarities, but only to reject what may be called the "rupture" thesis, as discussed by Quli and Mitchell (chap. 12 in this volume).
13. The "trans-" in translocal and translocative might easily be read as short for "transcending" the local. This reading would, however, simply redeploy the metaphysics of essence and instantiation or manifestation in different terminology. This metaphysics is so deeply embedded in our ordinary thought and language that it is easy to slip into talking in terms of "Buddhism and its various manifestations," such as Mahayana Buddhism, Theravada Buddhism, Nikaya Buddhism, and so on. The familiarity of the Aristotelian definitional strategy of genus and species naturalizes thinking about a general category and the defining characteristics of each entity that category encompasses.
14. The Protestant roots of American culture—which emphasize the transcendent and which in turn make for portable sanctity, in contrast to the immanent, which makes for fixed sanctity—is evident in the vexed legal nature of claims regarding land sacred to Native Americans; see Wenger (2009, 252–264).
15. Such replicas feature eighty-eight stations, each of which has been made potent by the presence of soil from each of the corresponding temples along the pilgrimage route. The replica thereby stands both as a record of some individual's own pilgrimage during which

he or she collected soil from each temple and also as a means for others to participate in the pilgrimage—partake of the sanctity of the pilgrimage—as well. I have visited one such miniature replica in Japan and two in Hawaii and have heard of a fourth in California.

16. Taking Emma McCloy Layman's pioneering *Buddhism in America* (1976) as the actual starting point defining the field of study.
17. A useful analogy would be to consider how problematic an equivalent category, such as "French Christianity," would be.
18. The author is aware of the lovely irony implicit in the fact that these categories structure our academic specializations, such as is included in his own title: Yehan Numata Professor of Japanese Buddhist Studies. Perhaps this acknowledgment of the irony involved will ward off vapid accusations of hypocrisy.
19. Hans Belting has argued that the category of "fine art" was created in the period of the Counter-Reformation, following on the Protestant critique of religious images. This (rough) division between pre- and post-Reformation attitudes reflects a shift from a religious conception of image to an aesthetic conception of refined appreciation, one that allowed collectors to appreciate religious art in an individual or privatized setting, while not countenancing it in a Protestant church. This distinction, however, does not correspond to categories outside Europe. In China, for example, painters were generally valorized as individual, named creative artists, while sculptors were not (Pat Berger, personal communication, March 26, 2014). See Barber (1995, 5), where Belting's theory is summarized as following from "the belief that sixteenth-century Europe saw a rupture in the perception of the work of art. Before this period the work of art should be thought of as an image and above all should be perceived in terms of its cult function. After this period, the work of art, no longer the image, should be considered in terms of its framing by an aesthetic discourse of the Renaissance and Reformation."
20. These considerations also participate in the same processes of category making that constrains conceptualizing Buddhism either along the contours of geopolitical divisions or along the contours of historical eras. At the risk of repeating myself, such categories need to be made relevant to an inquiry on the basis of theory, not just what question is being asked—for it is quite possible for questions

to be asked simply because that is the kind of question that has been asked so frequently in the past—but why is that question being asked? If geopolitical divisions or historical eras are relevant to the why question, then they require definition in order to demonstrate that relevance. If they are not, then employing them risks unknowingly eliminating possibly significant options for research.

21. See for example Bogel (2009) for an extended consideration of the ritual function of Buddhist art.
22. To express the problem more succinctly: if Buddhist fiction is defined in terms of a distinctly Buddhist experience, and we don't know what a distinctly Buddhist experience is, then we can't determine what Buddhist fiction is.
23. The rhetorical rupture between didactic and creative, and the alignment of those categories with traditional and modern, obscures the nature and role of the "Buddhist stories" that Beek denies are in the same genre as Buddhist fiction. Perhaps it is only because Aśvaghoṣa's poetry and drama has not been treated in the same fashion that someone like Shakespeare has that his creativity is not evident. His works were also influential in the spread of Buddhism across Central Asia (see Salomon 2012). One is reminded in this regard of the claims made that the first novel is Cervantes's *Don Quixote* (1605 and 1616), claims apparently based on European exceptionalism but contested by Murasaki Shikibu's *The Tale of the Shining Prince* (early eleventh century).
24. Classic instances that remain important as framing the discussion include Malinowski (1948—and many later reprints) and Tambiah (1990).
25. For a treatment of one form of this, see Slatter (1999).
26. Earlier attempts to colonize environmental sciences, being largely based simply on relatively superficial similarities between Buddhist doctrine and the imagery employed in environmental science, came to a dead end. The similarity was not strong enough to motivate the scientific undertakings. Having developed from the 1990s on, the field of religion and science has actively promoted venues designed to validate scientists for publicly expressing their religious views—no matter how theologically ill-informed and philosophically unsophisticated. A similar banality and arrogance inhabits the Buddhism and psychology/neuroscience discourse, propagating simplistic caricatures of Buddhism and being given credence by

the pervasive influence of American anti-intellectualism on Buddhist modernism. After more than two decades, it has now become acceptable for neuroscientists to take religious claims, including those based in Buddhism, as hypotheses to be tested.

27. Also, "Such masters often were believed to possess supernatural powers and secret knowledge" (Zürcher 2012, 18).
28. Indeed, there is a now noticeably dated distinction made between "northern Buddhism" and "southern Buddhism."
29. See, for example, Iwabuchi (2002).
30. https://www.mtholyoke.edu/acad/intrel/winthrop.htm, retrieved October 8, 2013.

WORKS CITED

Adams, Sheridan, Mushim Ikeda-Nash, Jeff Kitzes, Margarita Loinaz, Choyin Rangdrol, Jessica Tan, and Larry Yang, eds. 2000. *Making the Invisible Visible: Healing Racism in Our Buddhist Communities.* Self-published.

Adderson, Caroline. 2003. *Sitting Practice: A Novel.* Toronto, ON: Thomas-Allen Publishers.

Ahlstrom, Sydney E. 1962. *The American Encounter with World Religions.* Beloit, WI: Beloit College.

Aitken, Robert. 1974. "The Zen Buddhist Path of Self-Realization." In *What Is Meditation?*, ed. John White, 129–137. New York: Anchor Books.

Albanese, Catherine. 2007. *A Republic of Mind and Spirit: A Cultural History of American Metaphysical Religion.* New Haven and London: Yale University Press.

Almond, Philip C. 1988. *The British Discovery of Buddhism.* Cambridge: Cambridge University Press.

AlSayyad, Nezar. 2004. "The End of Tradition, or the Tradition of Endings?" In *The End of Tradition?*, ed. Nezar AlSayyad, 1–28. New York: Routledge.

Ama, Michihiro. 2010. "The Legal Dimensions of the Formation of Shin Buddhist Temples in Los Angeles." In *Issei Buddhism in the Americas*, ed. Duncan Ryûken Williams and Tomoe Moriya, 65–81. Champaign: University of Illinois Press.

———. 2012. *Immigrants to the Pure Land: The Modernization, Acculturation, and Globalization of Shin Buddhism.* Honolulu: University of Hawaii Press.

Ames, Diane P., ed. 1994. *The Wider Shin Buddhist Fellowship Newsletter.* Berkeley: Wider Shin Buddhist Fellowship.

Anderson, Benedict. 1983. *Imagined Communities: Reflections on the Origin and Spread of Nationalism.* London: Verso.

Anderson, Carol S. 2004. "*Anitya* [Impermanence]." In *Encyclopedia of Buddhism*, ed. Robert E. Buswell Jr., 1:23–24. 2 vols. New York: Thompson-Gale.

Appadurai, Arjun. 1996. *Modernity at Large: Cultural Dimensions of Globalization.* Minneapolis: University of Minnesota Press.

Armitage, David. 2007. "The Elephant and the Whale: Empires of Land and Sea." *Journal for Maritime Research* (July): 1–13.

Arnal, William E., and Russell T. McCutcheon. 2013. *The Sacred Is the Profane: The Political Nature of "Religion."* Oxford and New York: Oxford University Press.

Ba, Jin. 1931. *Jia.* Chengdu: Sichuan renmin chubanshe.

Baas, Jacquelyn. 2005. *Smile of the Buddha: Eastern Influences in Western Art from Monet to the Present.* Berkeley: University of California Press.

Baas, Jacquelyn, and Mary Jane Jacob, eds. 2004. *Buddha Mind in Contemporary Art.* Berkeley: University of California Press.

Bailey, Alison. 2004. "Privilege: Expanding on Marilyn Frye's 'Oppression.'" In *Oppression, Privilege, and Resistance: Theoretical Perspectives on Racism, Sexism, and Heterosexism*, ed. Lisa Heldke and Peg O'Connor, 301–316. New York: McGraw-Hill.

Baird, Robert. 1844. *Religion in America. Or, An Account of the Origin, Progress, Relations to the State, and Present Condition of the Evangelical Churches in the United States. With Notices of Unevangelical Denomination.* New York: Harper.

Barber, Charles. 1995. "From Image into Art: Art after Byzantine Iconoclasm." *Gesta* 34 (1): 5–10.

Barnett, Robert. 2001. "'Violated Specialness': Western Political Representations of Tibet." In *Imagining Tibet: Perceptions, Projections, and Fantasies*, ed. Thierry Dodin and Heinz Räther, 296–316. Boston, MA: Wisdom Publications.

Baroni, Helen J. 2012. *Love, Rōshi: Robert Baker Aitken and His Distant Correspondents.* Albany: State University of New York Press.

Bastide, Roger. 1967. *Les Amériques Noires.* Paris: Payot.

Batchelor, Stephen. 1998. "Letting Daylight into Magic: The Life and Times of Dorje Shugden." *Tricycle: The Buddhist Review* 7 (3): 60–66.

Bauman, Zygmunt. 1998. "Post-Modern Religion?" In *Religion,*

Modernity and Post-Modernity, ed. Paul Heelas, David Martin, and Paul Morris, 55–78. Oxford: Blackwell.

Baumann, Martin. 1993. *Deutsche Buddhisten: Geschichte und Gemeinshaften*. Marburg: Diagonal-Verlag.

———. 1994. "The Transplantation of Buddhism to Germany: Processive Modes and Strategies of Adaptation." *Method and Theory in the Study of Religion* 6 (1): 35–61.

———. 1997. "The Dharma Has Come West: A Survey of Recent Studies and Sources." *Journal of Buddhist Ethics* 4: 194–211.

———. 2001. "Global Buddhism: Developmental Periods, Regional Histories, and a New Analytical Perspective." *Journal of Global Buddhism* 2: 1–43.

———. 2002. "Protective Amulets and Awareness Techniques, or How to Make Sense of Buddhism in the West." In *Westward Dharma: Buddhism beyond Asia,* ed. Charles S. Prebish and Martin Baumann, 51–65. Berkeley: University of California Press.

Bechert, Heinz. 1966–1973. *Buddhismus, Staat und Gesellschaft in den Ländern des Theravada-Buddhismus*. 3 vols. Wiesbaden: O. Harrassowitz.

———. 1984. "Buddhist Revival in East and West." In *The World of Buddhism*, ed. Heinz Bechert and Richard Gombrich, 273–285. London: Thames and Hudson.

———. 1994. "Buddhistic Modernism." In *Buddhism in the Year 2000*, 251–260. Bangkok: The Dhammakaya Foundation.

Berkwitz, Stephen. 2008. "Resisting the Global in Buddhist Nationalism: Venerable Soma's Discourse of Decline and Reform." *Journal of Asian Studies* 67 (1): 73–106.

Bernstein, Anya. 2013a. "Indigenous Cosmopolitans: Mobility, Authority and Cultural Politics in Buryat Buddhism." Paper presented as part of the panel "Buddhism and Inter-Asian History" at the Association of Asian Studies meeting, San Diego.

———. 2013b. *Religious Bodies Politic: Rituals of Sovereignty in Buryat Buddhism*. Chicago and London: University of Chicago Press.

Blackburn, Anne. 2001. *Buddhist Learning and Textual Practice in Eighteenth-Century Lankan Monastic Culture*. Princeton: Princeton University Press.

———. 2003. "Localizing Lineage: Importing Higher Ordination in Theravadin South and Southeast Asia." In *Constituting Communities: Theravada Buddhism and the Religious Cultures of South and*

Southeast Asia, ed. John Holt, Jonathan Walters, and Jacob Kinnard, 131–149. Albany: State University of New York Press.

———. 2010. *Locations of Buddhism: Colonialism and Modernity in Sri Lanka*. Chicago: University of Chicago Press.

Bogel, Cynthea. 2009. *With a Single Glance: Buddhist Icon and Early Mikkyō Vision*. Seattle and London: University of Washington Press.

Boorstein, Sylvia. 1997. *That's Funny, You Don't Look Buddhist: On Being a Faithful Jew and a Passionate Buddhist*. San Francisco: Harper.

Boyce, Barry, ed., 2006. "Diversity and Divisions in America [*sic*] Buddhism." *Buddhadharma* (Fall): 48–57.

Brahm, Ajaan. 2006. *Mindfulness, Bliss, and Beyond: A Meditator's Handbook*. Boston: Wisdom Publications.

Brasington, Leigh. 2007. "Sharpening Mañjuśrī's Sword: An Interview with Leigh Brasington." *Insight Journal* 28: 4–8.

Bronkhorst, Johannes. 1986. *The Two Traditions of Meditation in Ancient India*. Stuttgart: Franz Steiner Verlag.

Buddhist Churches of America. 1969. *Newsletter* 7 (6).

———. 1974. *Buddhist Churches of America: Seventy-Five Year History, 1899–1974*. 2 vols. Chicago: Nobart.

Burdett, John. 2003. *Bangkok 8*. New York: Random House.

Burnouf, Eugène. 2001. *Introduction to the History of Indian Buddhism*. Chicago: University of Chicago Press.

Cadge, Wendy. 2001. "Tensions in American Buddhism." *Religion and Ethics Newsweekly* 445 (July 6). http://www.pbs.org/wnet/religionandethics/week445/buddhism.html.

———. 2005. *Heartwood: The First Generation of Theravada Buddhism in America*. Chicago: University of Chicago Press.

———. 2008. "De Facto Congregationalism and the Religious Organization of Post-1965 Immigrants to the United States: A Revised Approach." *Journal of the American Academy of Religion* 76 (2): 344–377.

Carrithers, Michael. 1983. *The Forest Monks of Sri Lanka: An Anthropological and Historical Study*. Delhi: Oxford University Press.

Carroll, Bret. 2000. *The Routledge Atlas of Religion in America*. New York and London: Routledge.

Carus, Paul. 1894. *The Gospel of Buddha*. Chicago: Open Court Publishing.

———. 1897. *Buddhism and Its Christian Critics*. Chicago: Open Court Publishing.

Cao, Lan. 1997. *Monkey Bridge*. New York: Viking.

Catherine, Shaila. 2008. *Focused and Fearless: A Meditator's Guide to States of Deep Joy, Calm, and Clarity*. Boston: Wisdom Publications.

Chadwick, David. 1999. *Crooked Cucumber: The Life and Zen Teaching of Shunryu Suzuki*. New York: Broadway Books.

Chakrabarty, Dipesh. 1994. "The Difference-Deferral of a Colonial Modernity: Public Debates on Domesticity in British Bengal." In *Subaltern Studies 8*, ed. David Arnold and David Hardiman, 50–88. Delhi: Oxford University Press.

Chandler, Jeannine. 2009. "Hunting the Guru: Lineage, Culture and Conflict in the Development of Tibetan Buddhism in America." PhD diss. University at Albany, State University of New York.

Chandler, Stuart. 2004. *Establishing a Pure Land on Earth: The Foguang Buddhist Perspective on Modernization and Globalization*. Honolulu: University of Hawaii Press.

Chen, Carolyn. 2008. *Getting Saved in America: Taiwanese Immigration and Religious Experience*. Princeton: Princeton University Press.

Chisolm, Lawrence. 1963. *Fenollosa: The Far East and American Culture*. New Haven: Yale University Press.

Choompolpaisal, Phibul. 2008. "Constrictive Constructs: Unravelling the Influence of Weber's Sociology on Theravada Studies since the 1960s." *Contemporary Buddhism* 9 (1): 7–51.

Chow, Rey. 2008. "Translator, Traitor; Translator, Mourner (or, Dreaming of Intercultural Equivalence)." *New Literary History* 39 (3): 565–580.

Christiano, Kevin J., William H. Swatos, and Peter Kivisto. 2008. "The 'Religion' of Secularization and the History of Religions." In *Sociology of Religion: Contemporary Developments*, 55–84. Lanham, MD: Rowman & Littlefield.

Clark, John. 2007. *Guardian of the Sea: Jizo in Hawai'i*. Honolulu: University of Hawaii Press.

Clarke, J. J. 1997. *Oriental Enlightenment: The Encounter between Asian and Western Thought*. London and New York: Routledge.

Clasquin, Michel, and J. S. Krüger, eds. 2000. *Buddhism and Africa*. Pretoria: Unisa.

Coff, Pascaline. 1991. "The Inner Journey: Reflections on the

Awakening of Mind and Heart in Buddhism and Christianity." *Buddhist-Christian Studies* 11: 173–195.
Cohen, Myron L. 1988. "Souls and Salvation: Conflicting Themes in Chinese Popular Religion." In *Death Ritual in Late Imperial and Modern China*, ed. James L. Watson and Evelyn S. Rawski, 180–202. Berkeley: University of California Press.
Coleman, James William. 2001. *The New Buddhism: The Western Transformation of an Ancient Tradition*. Oxford and New York: Oxford University Press.
Conze, Edward. 1951. *Buddhism: Its Essence and Development*. New York: Philosophical Library.
Cornille, Catherine, ed. 2002. *Many Mansions? Multiple Religious Belonging and Christian Identity*. Eugene, OR: Wipf & Stock.
Cousins, Lance S. 1973. "Buddhist Jhana: Its Nature and Attainment According to the Pali Sources." *Religion* 3: 115–131.
———. 1996. "The Origin of Insight Meditation." *The Buddhist Forum* 4: 35–58.
Cuevas, Bryan J. 2004. "Intermediate States." In *Encyclopedia of Buddhism*, ed. Robert E. Buswell Jr., 1:377–380. 2 vols. New York: Macmillan Reference USA.
———. 2007. "The Death and Return of Lady Wangzin: Visions of the Afterlife in Tibetan Buddhist Popular Literature." In *The Buddhist Dead: Practices, Discourses, Representations*, ed. Bryan J. Cuevas and Jacqueline I. Stone, 297–325. Honolulu: University of Hawaii Press.
Dalby, Liza. 2009. *Hidden Buddhas: A Novel of Karma and Chaos*. Berkeley: Stonebridge Press.
Devitt, Amy J. 1993. "Generalizing about Genre: New Conceptions of an Old Concept." *College Composition and Communication* 44 (4): 573–586.
———. 2004. *Writing Genres*. Carbondale: Southern Illinois University Press.
Dharmapāla, Anagārika. 1965. *Return to Righteousness: A Collection of Speeches, Essays and Letters of the Anagārika Dharmapāla*. Ceylon: Government Press.
Dobbins, James C. 1989. *Jōdo Shinshū: Shin Buddhism in Medieval Japan*. Bloomington: Indiana University Press.
Donovan, Anne. 2004. *Buddha Da*. New York: Carroll & Graf Publishers.

Dörrie, Doris. 2001. *Where Do We Go from Here?* Trans. by John Brownjohn. London: Bloomsbury Publishing.

Douglas, Mary. 1970. *Natural Symbols: Explorations in Cosmology.* New York: Pantheon Books.

Drew, Rose. 2011. *Buddhist and Christian? An Exploration of Dual Belonging.* London and New York: Routledge.

Dreyfus, Georges. 2005. "From Protective Deities to International Stardom: An Analysis of the Fourteenth Dalai Lama's Stance toward Modernity and Buddhism." In *The Dalai Lamas: A Visual History*, ed. Martin Brauen, 172–179. Chicago: Serindia Publications.

Droogers, André. 2005. "Syncretism and Fundamentalism: A Comparison." *Social Compass* 25 (4): 463–471.

Einstein, Mara. 2008. *Brands of Faith: Marketing Religion in a Commercial Age.* New York: Routledge.

Eisenstadt, S. N., ed. 2002. *Multiple Modernities.* New Brunswick, NJ: Transaction Publishers.

Ellwood, Robert. 1979. *Alternative Altars: Unconventional and Eastern Spirituality in America.* Chicago: University of Chicago Press.

Ellwood, Robert, and Harry Partin. 1988. *Religious and Spiritual Groups in Modern America.* Englewood Cliffs, NJ: Prentice Hall.

Feldman, Christina. 2004. "Opening the Gates of Consciousness." *Tricycle: The Buddhist Review* 14 (2): 73.

Fields, Rick. 1986. *How the Swans Came to the Lake: A Narrative History of Buddhism in America.* Boston: Shambhala.

———. 1994. "Confessions of a White Buddhist." *Tricycle: The Buddhist Review* 4 (1): 54–56.

———. 1998. "Divided Dharma: White Buddhists, Ethnic Buddhists, and Racism." In *The Faces of Buddhism in America*, ed. Charles S. Prebish and Kenneth K. Tanaka, 196–206. Berkeley: University of California Press.

Finucane, Juliana. 2006. Review, *Buddha Mind in Contemporary Art. Journal of Media and Religion* 5 (2): 135–138.

Foye, Addie. 1994. "Buddhists in America: A Short, Biased View." *Tricycle: The Buddhist Review* 4 (1): 57.

Fronsdal, Gil. 1998. "Insight Meditation in the United States: Life, Liberty, and the Pursuit of Happiness." In *The Faces of Buddhism in America*, ed. Charles S. Prebish and Kenneth K. Tanaka, 163–180. Berkeley: University of California Press.

Fujita, Kotatsu. 1996. "Pure Land Buddhism in India," trans. Taitetsu

Unno. In *The Pure Land Tradition: History and Development*, ed. James Foard, Michael Solomon, and Richard K. Payne, 1–42. Berkeley: Berkeley Buddhist Studies Series.

Gaonkar, Dilip Parameshwar, ed. 2001. *Alternative Modernities*. Durham and London: Duke University Press.

Gaustad, Edwin. 1962. *Historical Atlas of Religion in America*. New York and Evanston: Harper and Row.

Gaustad, Edwin, and Philip Barlow. 2001. *New Historical Atlas of Religion in America*. New York: Oxford University Press.

Gez, Yonatan. 2011. "The Phenomenon of Jewish Buddhisms in Light of the History of Jewish Suffering." *Nova Religio: The Journal of Alternative and Emergent Religions* 15 (1): 44–68.

Giddens, Anthony. 1990. *The Consequences of Modernity*. Stanford: Stanford University Press.

Gillespie, Marie. 2011. "The Role of Media in Religious Transnationalism." In *Religion, Media and Culture: A Reader*, ed. Gordon Lynch and Jolyon Mitchell with Anna Strhan, 98–110. New York: Routledge.

Gillespie, Michael Allen. 2008. *The Theological Origins of Modernity*. Chicago and London: University of Chicago Press.

Goddard, Dwight. 1938. *A Buddhist Bible*. Boston: Beacon Press.

Gombrich, Richard, and Gananath Obeyesekere. 1988. *Buddhism Transformed: Religious Change in Sri Lanka*. Princeton: Princeton University Press.

Gottowik, Volker. 2010. "Transnational, Translocal, Transcultural: Some Remarks on the Relations between Hindu-Balinese and Ethnic Chinese in Bali." *Sojourn: Journal of Social Issues in Southeast Asia* 25 (2): 178–212.

Gregory, Peter N. 2001. "Describing the Elephant: Buddhism in America." *Religion and American Culture* 11 (2): 233–263.

Griffiths, Paul J. 1981. "Concentration or Insight: The Problematic of Theravada Buddhist Meditation Theory." *Journal of the American Academy of Religion* 49: 605–624.

Grimes, Ronald. 1992. "Sacred Objects in Museum Spaces." *Studies in Religion* 21 (4): 419–430.

Gunaratana, Henepola. 2009a. *Beyond Mindfulness in Plain English*. Boston: Wisdom Publications.

———. 2009b. "The Taste of Liberation." *Buddhadharma: A Practitioner's Quarterly* 8 (2): 60–67.

Gyatso, Janet. 1998. *Apparitions of the Self: The Secret Autobiographies of a Tibetan Visionary.* Princeton: Princeton University Press.

———. 1999. "Healing Burns with Fire: The Facilitations of Experience in Tibetan Buddhism." *Journal of the American Academy of Religion* 67 (1): 113–147.

Hall, Stuart. 1992. "The Question of Cultural Identity." In *Modernity and Its Futures*, ed. Stuart Hall, David Held, and Tony McGrew, 273–326. Cambridge: Polity.

———. 1993. "Culture, Community, Nation." *Cultural Studies* 7 (3): 349–363.

Hallisey, Charles, and Anne Hansen. 1996. "Narrative, Sub-Ethics, and the Moral Life: Some Evidence from Theravāda Buddhism." *Journal of Religious Ethics* 24 (2): 305–327.

Hannerz, Ulf. 1990. "Cosmopolitans and Locals in World Culture." In *Global Culture: Nationalism, Globalization, Modernity*, ed. Mike Featherstone, 237–253. London: Sage.

Harris, Elizabeth. 2006. *Theravāda Buddhism and the British Encounter: Religious, Missionary, and Colonial Experience in Nineteenth Century in Sri Lanka.* New York: Routledge.

Harvey, David. 1990. *The Condition of Postmodernity.* Cambridge and Oxford: Blackwell.

Hay, William H. 1956. "Paul Carus: A Case Study of Philosophy on the Frontier." *Journal of the History of Ideas* 17: 498–510.

Hefner, Robert W. 1998. "Multiple Modernities: Christianity, Islam, and Hinduism in a Globalizing Age." *Annual Review of Anthropology* 27: 83–104.

Heisig, James W. 2002. *Philosophers of Nothingness: An Essay on the Kyoto School.* Nanzan Library of Asian Religion and Culture. Honolulu: University of Hawaii Press.

Heisig, James W., and John C. Maraldo, eds. 1995. *Rude Awakenings: Zen, the Kyoto School, and the Question of Nationalism.* Honolulu: University of Hawaii Press.

Hervieu-Léger, Danièle. 1993. *La religion pour mémoire.* Paris: Cerf.

Hesse, Herman. 1922. *Siddhartha.* Berlin: S. Fischer.

Hickey, Shannon. 2010. "Two Buddhisms, Three Buddhisms, and Racism." *Journal of Global Buddhism* 11: 1–25.

Hirasawa, Caroline. 2008. "The Inflatable, Collapsible Kingdom of Retribution: A Primer on Japanese Hell Imagery and Imagination." *Monumenta Nipponica* 63 (1): 1–50.

Hobsbawm, Eric, and Terence Ranger, eds. 1983. *The Invention of Tradition*. Cambridge: Cambridge University Press.

Hong Kingston, Maxine. 1989 [1975]. *The Warrior Woman: Memoirs of a Girlhood among Ghosts*. New York: Vintage International Edition.

hooks, bell. 1994. "Waking Up to Racism." *Tricycle: The Buddhist Review* 4 (1): 42–45.

Hopkins, P. Jeffrey. 2001. "Tibetan Monastic Colleges: Rationality versus the Demands of Allegiance." In *Imagining Tibet: Perceptions, Projections, and Fantasies*, ed. Thierry Dodin and Heinz Räther, 257–268. Boston, MA: Wisdom Publications.

Hori, Victor Sogen. 1994. "Sweet-and-Sour Buddhism." *Tricycle: The Buddhist Review* 4 (1): 48–52.

Horinouchi, Isao. 1973. "American Buddhism: A Sociological Analysis of a Protestantized Japanese Religion." PhD diss., University of California, Davis.

Hubbard, Jamie. 1995. "Upping the Ante: budstud@millenium.end .edu." *Journal of the International Association of Buddhist Studies* 18 (2): 309–322.

Huber, Toni. 2008. *The Holy Land Reborn: Pilgrimage and the Tibetan Reinvention of Buddhist India*. Chicago: University of Chicago Press.

Hunter, Louise H. 1971. *Buddhism in Hawai'i: Its Impact on a Yankee Community*. Honolulu: University of Hawaii Press.

Imamura, Ryo. 1998. "Buddhist and Western Psychotherapies: An Asian American Perspective." In *The Faces of Buddhism in America*, ed. Charles S. Prebish and Kenneth K. Tanaka, 228–237. Berkeley: University of California Press.

Inda, Jonathan Xavier, and Renato Rosaldo. 2008. "Tracking Global Flows." In *The Anthropology of Globalization: A Reader*, ed. Jonathan Xavier Inda and Renato Rosaldo, 3–46. Rev. ed. Malden, MA: Blackwell.

Iwabuchi, Koichi. 2002. *Recentering Globalization: Popular Culture and Japanese Transnationalism*. Durham and London: Duke University Press.

Iwamura, Jane Naomi, and Paul Spickard, eds. 2003. *Revealing the Sacred in Asian and Pacific America*. New York and London: Routledge.

Jackson, Carl T. 1968. "The Meeting of East and West: The Case of Paul Carus." *Journal of the History of Ideas* 29: 73–92.

———. 1981. *The Oriental Religions and American Thought*. Westport, CT: Greenwood.

Jaffe, Richard. 2001. *Neither Monk nor Layman: Clerical Marriage in Modern Japanese Buddhism*. Princeton: Princeton University Press.

Jeung, Russell. 2005. *Faithful Generations: Race and New Asian American Churches*. New Brunswick, NJ: Rutgers University Press.

Johnson, Allan G. 2006. *Privilege, Power, and Difference*. 2nd ed. New York: McGraw-Hill.

Johnson, Charles. 1985. *Oxherding Tale: A Novel*. New York: Penguin Group.

———. 1990. *Middle Passage*. New York: Simon & Schuster.

———. 2004. "Foreword." *Nixon Under the Bodhi Tree and Other Works of Buddhist Fiction*, ed. Kate Wheeler, vii–x. Boston: Wisdom Publications.

Kachtick, Keith. 2003. *Hungry Ghost*. New York: HarperCollins.

———, ed. 2006. *You Are Not Here and Other Works of Buddhist Fiction*. Somerville, MA: Wisdom Publications.

Kamenetz, Rodger. 1994. *The Jew in the Lotus*. San Francisco: Harper.

Kapstein, Matthew. 2009. *Buddhism between Tibet and China*. Boston: Wisdom Publications.

Kashima, Tetsuden. 1977. *Buddhism in America: The Social Organization of an Ethnic Religious Organization*. Westport, CT: Greenwood.

Kaviraj, Sudipta. 2005. "An Outline of a Revisionist Theory of Modernity." *Archive of European Sociology* 46 (3): 497–526.

Kemper, Steven. 1984. "The Buddhist Monkhood, the Law, and the State in Colonial Sri Lanka." *Comparative Studies in Society and History* 26 (3): 401–427.

Ketelaar, James Edward. 1990. *Of Heretics and Martyrs in Meiji Japan: Buddhism and Its Persecution*. Princeton: Princeton University Press.

———. 1991. "Strategic Occidentalism: Meiji Buddhists at the World's Parliament of Religions." *Buddhist-Christian Studies* 11: 37–56.

Khema, Ayya. 1991. *When the Iron Eagle Flies: Buddhism for the West*. New York: Arkana.

———. 1997a. *Who Is My Self: A Guide to Buddhist Meditation*. Boston: Wisdom Publications.

———. 1997b. *I Give You My Life: The Autobiography of a Western Nun*, trans. Sherab Chodzin Kohn. Boston: Shambhala.

Kimbrough, R. Keller. 2006. "Tourists in Paradise: Writing the Pure Land in Medieval Japanese Fiction." *Japanese Journal of Religious Studies* 33 (2): 269–296.

Kippenberg, Hans G. 2002. *Discovering Religious History in the Modern Age*, trans. Barbara Harshaw. Princeton and Oxford: Princeton University Press.

Klein, Jennie. 2005. "Being Mindful: West Coast Reflection on Buddhism and Art." *Performance Arts Journal* 79: 82–90.

Kress, Gunther. 1987. "Genre in a Social Theory of Language: A Reply to John Dixon." In *The Place of Genre in Learning: Current Debates*, ed. Ian Reid, 35–45. Melbourne, Australia: Deakin University Center for Studies in Literary Education.

Lancaster, Lewis. 2012. "The Movement of Buddhist Texts from India to China and the Construction of the Chinese Buddhist Canon." In "Buddhism across Boundaries: The Interplay of Indian, Chinese, and Central Asian Source Materials," ed. John R. McRae and Jan Nattier. Special issue, *Sino-Platonic Papers* 222: 226–238.

Layman, Emma McCloy. 1976. *Buddhism in America*. Chicago: Nelson-Hall.

Lears, Jackson. 1981. *No Place of Grace: Antimodernism and the Transformation of American Culture, 1880–1920*. New York: Pantheon.

Lee, Tosi. 2004. "Fire Down Below and Watering, That's Life: A Buddhist Reader's Response to Marcel Duchamp." In *Buddha Mind in Contemporary Art*, ed. Jacquelyn Baas and Mary Jane Jacob, 124–138. Berkeley: University of California Press.

Levine, Sarah, and David Gellner. 2005. *Rebuilding Buddhism: The Theravada Movement in Twentieth-Century Nepal*. Cambridge: Harvard University Press.

Lewin, Bruno. 1994. "Activity of the Aya and Hata in the Domain of the Sacred," trans. Richard K. Payne, with Ellen Rozett. *Pacific World: Journal of the Institute of Buddhist Studies*, n.s. (10): 219–230.

Linzer, Judith. 1996. *Torah and Dharma: Jewish Seekers in Eastern Religions*. Northvale, NJ: J. Aronson.

Lippy, Charles H. 2009. *Introducing American Religion*. New York: Routledge.

Lopez, Donald S. 1998. *Prisoners of Shangri-La: Tibetan Buddhism and the West*. Chicago: University of Chicago Press.

———. 2002a. "Introduction." In *A Modern Buddhist Bible: Essential Readings from East and West*, ed. Donald S. Lopez, vii–xli. Boston: Beacon Press.

———. 2002b. "Introduction." In *Modern Buddhism: Readings for the Unenlightened*, vii–xli. London: Penguin.

———. 2006. *The Madman's Middle Way: Reflections on Reality of the Tibetan Monk Gendun Chopel.* Chicago: University of Chicago Press.

———, ed. 2008. *Buddhism and Science: A Guide for the Perplexed.* Chicago: University of Chicago Press.

Lutz, Antoine, John D. Dunne, and Richard J. Davidson. 2007. "Meditation and the Neuroscience of Consciousness: An Introduction." In *The Cambridge Handbook of Consciousness*, ed. Philip David Zelazo, Morris Moscovitch, and M. Evan Thompson, 499–554. Cambridge: Cambridge University Press.

Maffly-Kipp, Laurie. 1997. "Eastward Ho! American Religion from the Perspective of the Pacific Rim." In *Retelling U.S. Religious History*, ed. Thomas Tweed, 127–148. Berkeley: University of California Press.

Malalgoda, Kitsiri. 1976. *Buddhism in Sinhalese Society: 1750–1900.* Berkeley: University of California Press.

Malinowski, Bronislaw. 1948. *Magic, Science and Religion, and Other Essays.* Garden City, NY: Doubleday.

Malkki, Liisa. 1995. *Purity and Exile: Violence, Memory and National Cosmology among Hutu Refugees in Tanzania.* Chicago: University of Chicago Press.

Marquardt, Marie Friedmann. 2010. "An Anxious Traveler's Journal." Book Session on *Crossing and Dwelling: A Theory of Religion*, Annual Meeting of the American Academy of Religion, Atlanta, 20 October.

Mather, Cotton. 1702. *Magnalia Christi Americana, or, The Ecclesiastical History of New-England.* London: T. Parkhurst.

Matthews, Bruce. ed. 2005. *Buddhism in Canada.* London and New York: Routledge.

McDaniel, Justin. 2008. *Gathering Leaves and Lifting Words: Histories of Buddhist Monastic Education in Laos and Thailand.* Seattle: University of Washington Press.

McIntosh, Peggy. 2004. "White Privilege and Male Privilege." In *Oppression, Privilege, and Resistance: Theoretical Perspectives on Racism, Sexism, and Heterosexism*, ed. Lisa Heldke and Peg O'Connor, 317–327. New York: McGraw-Hill.

McLellan, Janet. 1999. *Many Petals of the Lotus: Asian Buddhist Communities in Toronto.* Toronto: Toronto University Press.

———. 2008. "Themes and Issues in the Study of North American Buddhists and Buddhism." In *Buddhists in North American Context*, ed. Paul Numrich, 19–50. Leiden and Boston: Brill.

———. 2008. *The Making of Buddhist Modernism*. New York: Oxford University Press.

Mitchell, Scott. 2006. "Sunday Morning Songs: English Language Gāthās in American Shinshū Temples." *The Pure Land* 22: 127–137.

———. 2008. "Taking Refuge in the Dharma: Post-Colonialism, Ritual Theory, and American Buddhist Studies." PhD diss., Graduate Theological Union.

———. 2010. "Locally Translocal American Shin Buddhism." *Pacific World: Journal of the Institute of Buddhist Studies*, 3rd ser. (12): 109–126.

Mitchell, Timothy. 2000a. "Introduction." In *Questions of Modernity*, ed. Timothy Mitchell, xi–xxvii. Minneapolis: University of Minnesota Press.

———. 2000b. "Preface." In *Questions of Modernity*, ed. Timothy Mitchell, vii–x. Minneapolis: University of Minnesota Press.

———. 2000c. "The Stage of Modernity." In *Questions of Modernity*, ed. Timothy Mitchell, 1–34. Minneapolis: University of Minnesota Press.

Miyazaki, Fumiko, and Duncan Williams. 2001. "The Intersection of the Local and the Translocal at a Sacred Site: The Case of Osorezan in Tokugawa Japan." *Japanese Journal of Religious Studies* 28 (3–4): 399–440.

Mochizuki, Shinko. Forthcoming. *A Doctrinal History of Pure Land Buddhism in China*, ed. Richard K. Payne and Natalie Quli, trans. Leo Pruden. Vol. 1. Berkeley: Institute of Buddhist Studies and BDK America.

Moran, Peter Kevin. 2004. *Buddhism Observed: Travellers, Exiles and Tibetan Dharma in Katmandu*. London: RoutledgeCurzon.

Moriya, Tomoe. 2000. *Yemyo Imamura: Pioneer American Buddhist*. Honolulu: Buddhist Study Center Press.

———. 2001. *America Bukkyō no tanjō*. Tokyo: Gendai shiryo shuppan.

Mullins, Mark R. 1988. "The Organizational Dilemmas of Ethnic Churches: A Case Study of Japanese Buddhism in Canada." *Sociological Analysis* 49 (3): 217–233.

Namgyal Rinpoche. 2004. *Body, Speech, and Mind: A Manual for Human Development*. Kinmount, ON: Bodhi Publishing.

Ñāṇamoli, Bhikkhu, trans. 1999. *The Visuddhimagga: The Path of Purification*. Seattle: BPS Pariyatti.

Nance, Richard F. 2012. *Speaking for Buddhas: Scriptural Commentary in Indian Buddhism*. New York: Columbia University Press.

Nattier, Jan. 1995. "Visible and Invisible: The Politics of Representation in Buddhist America." *Tricycle: The Buddhist Review* 5 (1): 42–49.

———. 1997. "Buddhism Comes to Main Street." *Wilson Quarterly* 21 (2): 72–80.

———. 1998. "Who Is a Buddhist? Charting the Landscape of Buddhist America." In *The Faces of Buddhism in America*, ed. Charles S. Prebish and Kenneth K. Tanaka, 183–195. Berkeley: University of California Press.

Nebesky-Wojkowitz, René de. 1998. *Oracles and Demons of Tibet: The Cult and Iconography of Tibetan Protective Deities*. 1st Indian ed. New Delhi: Paljor Publications.

Neumaier-Dargay, Eva K. 1995. "Is Buddhism Like a Tomato? Thoughts about the Transplantation of Buddhism to Germany: A Response to Martin Baumann." *Method and Theory in the Study of Religion* 7 (2): 185–194.

Niculescu, Mira. 2014. "'Juif-bouddhiste'? Conflictualités internes autour de l'adoption du bouddhisme par des juifs français." In *Quand le religieux fait conflit:* Désaccords, négociations ou arrangements, ed. Anne-Sophie Lamine, 137–148. Rennes: Presses Universitaires de Rennes.

Nongbri, Brent. 2008. "Dislodging 'Embedded' Religion: A Brief Note on a Scholarly Trope." *Numen* 55: 440–460.

———. 2013. *Before Religion: A History of a Modern Concept*. New Haven and London: Yale University Press.

Numrich, Paul David. 1996. *Old Wisdom in the New World: Americanization in Two Immigrant Theravada Buddhist Temples*. Knoxville: University of Tennessee Press.

———. 1998. "Theravāda Buddhism in America: Prospects for the Sangha." In *The Faces of Buddhism in America*, ed. Charles S. Prebish and Kenneth K. Tanaka, 147–161. Berkeley: University of California Press.

———. 2000. "How the Swans Came to Lake Michigan: The Social

Organization of Buddhist Chicago." *Journal for the Scientific Study of Religion* 39 (2): 189–203.

———. 2006. "Two Buddhisms Further Considered." In *Buddhist Studies from India to America: Essays in Honor of Charles S. Prebish*, ed. Damien Keown, 207–233. New York: Routledge.

Nyanaponika Thera. 1996 [1954]. *The Heart of Buddhist Meditation.* Kandy: Buddhist Meditation Society.

Obadia, Lionel. 2004. "Etre juif et bouddhiste." In *Des cultures et des Dieux: Repères pour une transmission du fait religieux*, ed. Jean-Christophe Attias and Esther Benbassa, 412–413. Paris: Fayard.

———. 2006. "Religions et modernité(s): Anciens débats, enjeux presents, nouvelle perspectives." *Socio-Anthropologie* 17–18. http://socio-anthropologie.revues.org/index448.html.

Oberoi, Harjot. 1994. *The Construction of Religious Boundaries: Culture, Identity, and Diversity in the Sikh Tradition.* Chicago and London: University of Chicago Press.

Omi, Michael, and Howard Winant. 2004. "Racial Formation." In *Oppression, Privilege, and Resistance: Theoretical Perspectives on Racism, Sexism, and Heterosexism*, ed. Lisa Heldke and Peg O'Connor, 115–142. New York: McGraw-Hill.

Ortiz, Fernando. 1995. *Cuban Counterpoint: Tobacco and Sugar*. Durham, NC: Duke University Press.

Pandita, U. 1993. *In This Very Life: The Liberation Teachings of the Buddha*, trans. Venerable U Aggacitta. Boston: Wisdom Publications.

Pattison, Eliot. 1999. *The Skull Mantra.* New York: St. Martin's Press.

Payne, Richard K. 2005. "Hiding in Plain Sight: The Invisibility of the Shingon Mission to the United States." In *Buddhist Missionaries in the Era of Globalization,* ed. Linda Learman, 101–122. Honolulu: University of Hawaii Press.

———. 2007. "Aparimitayus: 'Tantra' and 'Pure Land' in Medieval Indian Buddhism?" *Pacific World: Journal of the Institute of Buddhist Studies*, 3rd ser. (9): 273–308.

———. 2010. "From Kalimpong to Berkeley: Yogi Chen and Conflicting Practices of Sacred Auto/biography." Buddhism without Borders conference. Berkeley, CA.

———. 2011. "Why 'Buddhist Theology' Is Not a Good Idea." Keynote address for the Fifteenth Biennial Conference of the International Association of Shin Buddhist Studies, Kyoto. Forthcoming in *The Pure Land: Journal of the International Association of Shin Buddhist Studies.*

Pennington, Brian K. 2005. *Was Hinduism Invented? Britons, Indians, and the Colonial Construction of Religion.* Oxford: Oxford University Press.

Perreira, Todd LeRoy. 2004. "Sasana Sakon and the New Asian American: Intermarriage and Identity at a Thai Buddhist Temple in Silicon Valley." In *Asian American Religions: The Making and Remaking of Borders and Boundaries*, ed. Tony Carnes and Fengang Yang, 313–337. New York: New York University Press.

Pierce, Lori. 2000. "Constructing American Buddhisms: Discourse of Race and Religion in Territorial Hawaii." PhD diss., University of Hawaii.

———. 2006. "Asian Buddhist Communities from China and Japan." In *Encyclopedia of Women and Religion in North America*, ed. Rosemary S. Keller and Rosemary R. Ruether, 2:633–369. Bloomington: Indiana University Press.

Prebish, Charles S. 1978. "Reflections on the Transmission of Buddhism to America." In *Understanding the New Religions*, ed. Jacob Needleman and George Baker, 153–172: New York: Seabury.

———. 1979. *American Buddhism.* North Scituate, MA: Duxbury.

———. 1993. "Two Buddhisms Reconsidered." *Buddhist Studies Review* 10 (2): 187–206.

———. 1999. *Luminous Passage: The Practice and Study of Buddhism in America.* Berkeley: University of California Press.

———. 2002. "Studying the Spread and Histories of Buddhism in the West: The Emergence of Western Buddhism as a New Subdiscipline within Buddhism Studies." In *Westward Dharma: Buddhism beyond Asia*, ed. Charles S. Prebish and Martin Baumann, 66–84. Berkeley: University of California Press.

———. 2003. "Varying the Vinaya: Creative Responses to Vinaya." In *Buddhism in the Modern World: Adaptations of an Ancient Tradition*, ed. Steven Heine and Charles S. Prebish, 45–73. Oxford and New York: Oxford University Press.

Prebish, Charles S., and Kenneth K. Tanaka, eds. 1998. *The Faces of Buddhism in America.* Berkeley: University of California Press.

Preston, David. 1988. *The Social Organization of Zen Practice: Constructing Transcultural Reality.* Cambridge: Cambridge University Press.

Prothero, Stephen. 1996. *The White Buddhist: The Asian Odyssey of Henry Steel Olcott.* Bloomington: Indiana University Press.

Putnam, Hilary. 2002. *The Collapse of the Fact/Value Dichotomy and Other Essays.* Cambridge: Harvard University Press.

Pye, Michael. 1969. "The Transplantation of Religion." *Numen* 16: 234–239.

Queen, Christopher S. 1999. "Introduction." In *American Buddhism: Methods and Findings in Recent Scholarship*, ed. Duncan Ryūken Williams and Christopher S. Queen, xiv–xxxvii. Richmond, UK: Curzon Press.

———. 2000. *Engaged Buddhism in the West*. Boston: Wisdom Publications.

Quli, Natalie E. Fisk. 2008. "Multiple Buddhist Modernisms: Jhāna in Convert Theravāda." *Pacific World: Journal of the Institute of Buddhist Studies*, 3rd ser. (10): 225–249.

———. 2009. "Western Self, Asian Other: Modernity, Authenticity, and Nostalgia for 'Tradition' in Buddhist Studies." *Journal of Buddhist Ethics* 16: 1–39.

———. 2010. "Laicization in Four Sri Lankan Buddhist Temples in Northern California." PhD diss., Graduate Theological Union.

Raphaël, Liogier, and Bruno Étienne. 1997. *Etre bouddhiste en France aujourd'hui*. Paris: Hachette Littératures.

Rhys Davids, Caroline A. F. 1912. *Buddhism: A Study of the Buddhist Norm*. London: Williams & Norgate.

Rhys Davids, Thomas W. 1882. *Lectures on the Origin and Growth of Religion as Illustrated by Some Points in the History of Indian Buddhism*. Hibbert Lectures. New York: G. P. Putnam & Sons.

Robertson, Roland. 1992. *Globalization: Social Theory and Global Culture*. London: Sage Publications.

Robins, Kevin. 1991. "Tradition and Translation: National Culture in Its Global Context." In *Enterprise and Heritage: National Culture in Its Global Contexts*, ed. John Corner and Sylvia Harvey, 28–41. London: Routledge.

Rocha, Cristina. 2006. *Zen in Brazil: The Quest for Cosmopolitan Modernity*. Honolulu: University of Hawaii Press.

Roof, Wade Clark. 1993. *A Generation of Seekers: The Spiritual Journeys of the Baby Boom Generation*. San Francisco: Harper.

Rosaldo, Renato. 1989. *Culture and Truth: The Remaking of Social Analysis*. Boston: Beacon Press.

Rust, William Charles. 1951. "The Shin Sect of Buddhism in America." PhD diss., University of Southern California.

Salomon, Richard. 2012. "Aśvaghoṣa in Central Asia: Some Comments on the Recensional History of His Works in Light of Recent

Manuscript Discoveries." In "Buddhism across Boundaries: The Interplay of Indian, Chinese, and Central Asian Source Materials," ed. John R. McRae and Jan Nattier. Special issue, *Sino-Platonic Papers* 222: 86–105.

Salzman, Mark. 1991. *The Laughing Sutra: A Novel.* New York: Vintage Books.

Samuels, Jeffrey. 2007. "Buddhism and Caste in India and Sri Lanka." *Religion Compass* 1 (1): 120–130.

Sander, Lore. 2012. "Early Prakrit and Sanskrit Manuscripts from Xinjiang (Second to Fifth/Sixth Centuries C.E.): Paleography, Literary Evidence, and Their Relation to Buddhist Schools." In "Buddhism across Boundaries: The Interplay of Indian, Chinese, and Central Asian Source Materials," ed. John R. McRae and Jan Nattier. Special issue, *Sino-Platonic Papers* 222: 26–49.

Saricks, Joyce G. 2009. *The Reader's Advisory Guide to Genre Fiction.* 2nd ed. Chicago: American Library Association.

Sautter, Cia. 2002. "Chochmat: Rhymes with Spirit Rock." *Journal of Religion and Popular Culture* 1 (Spring), http://www.usask.ca/relst/jrpc/article-chocmat.html.

Schachter-Shalomi, Zalman. 1993. *Paradigmatic Shift.* North Vale, NJ: Jason Aaronson.

Seager, Richard Hughes. 1999. *Buddhism in America.* New York: Columbia University Press.

———. 2006. *Encountering the Dharma: Daisaku Ikeda, Soka Gakkai and the Globalization of Buddhist Humanism.* Berkeley, Los Angeles, and London: University of California Press.

Segal, Robert A. 2006. "All Generalizations Are Bad: Postmodernism on Theories." *Journal of the American Academy of Religion* 74 (1): 157–171.

Sen, Tansen. 2013. "Rediscovering and Reconstructing Buddhist Interactions between 'India' and 'China.'" Paper presented in the panel "Buddhism and Inter-Asian History," Association of Asian Studies conference, San Diego, CA.

Shankman, Richard. 2008. *The Experience of Samadhi.* Boston: Shambhala.

Sharf, Robert H. 1995a. "Buddhist Modernism and the Rhetoric of Meditative Experience." *Numen* 42 (3): 228–283.

———. 1995b. "Sanbōkyōdan: Zen and the Way of the New Religions." *Japanese Journal of Religious Studies* 22 (3–4): 417–457.

———. 1995c. "The Zen of Japanese Nationalism." In *Curators of the Buddha: The Study of Buddhism under Colonialism*, ed. Donald S. Lopez Jr., 107–160. Chicago: University of Chicago Press.

———. 1998. "Experience." In *Critical Terms in Religious Studies*, ed. Mark C. Taylor, 94–116. Chicago: University of Chicago Press.

Simmel, Georg. 2003 [1908]. *Le conflit*. Paris: Circé Poche.

Skaff, Jonathan Karam. 2012. *Sui-Tang China and Its Turko-Mongol Neighbors: Culture, Power, and Connections, 580–800*. Oxford and New York: Oxford University Press.

Skilling, Peter. 2009. "Theravāda in History." *Pacific World: Journal of the Institute of Buddhist Studies*, 3rd ser. (11): 61–93.

Slatter, Beryl. 1999. *Each Mind a Kingdom: American Women, Sexual Purity and the New Thought Movement, 1875–1920*. Berkeley and Los Angeles: University of California Press.

Smith, Jonathan Z. 2004. *Relating Religion: Essays in the Study of Religion*. Chicago: University of Chicago Press.

Smith, Sharon. 2003. "Widening the Circle: Communities of Color and Western Buddhist Convert Sanghas." In *Action Dharma: New Studies in Engaged Buddhism*, ed. Christopher Queen, Charles Prebish, and Damien Keown, 220–236. New York: Routledge.

Snodgrass, Judith. 2003. *Presenting Japanese Buddhism to the West: Orientalism, Occidentalism, and the Columbian Exposition*. Chapel Hill: University of North Carolina Press.

Snyder, Stephen, and Tina Rasmussen. 2009. *Practicing the Jhānas: Traditional Concentration Meditation as Presented by the Venerable Pa Auk Sayadaw*. Boston: Shambhala.

Sōen (Soyen), Shaku. 1993 [1913]. *Zen for Americans: Including the Sutra of Forty-Two Chapters*. New York: Barnes & Noble Books.

Spencer, Jonathan. 1990. "Tradition and Transformation: Recent Writing on the Anthropology of Buddhism in Sri Lanka." *Journal of the Anthropological Society of Oxford* 30 (2): 129–140.

Spiro, Melford. 1982. *Buddhism and Society: A Great Tradition and Its Burmese Vicissitudes*. Berkeley: University of California Press.

Spuler, Michelle. 1999. "The Adaptation of Buddhism to the West: Diamond Sangha Zen Buddhist Groups in Australia." PhD diss., University of Queensland.

Stalker, Nancy. 2006. "Suicide, Boycotts and Embracing Tagore: The Japanese Popular Response to the 1924 US Immigration Exclusion Law." *Japanese Studies* 26 (2): 150–170.

Stewart, Charles, and Rosalind Shaw. 1994. "Introduction." In *Syncretism/Anti-Syncretism: The Politics of Religious Synthesis*, ed. Charles Stewart and Rosalind Shaw, 1–26. New York: Routledge.

Strauss, C. T. 1922. *The Buddha and His Doctrine*. Port Washington, NY: Kennikat Press.

Suh, Sharon. 2004. *Being Buddhist in a Christian World: Gender and Community in a Korean American Temple*. Seattle and London: University of Washington Press.

Swearer, Donald K. 2003. "Aniconism versus Iconism in Thai Buddhism." In *Buddhism in the Modern World: Adaptations of the Ancient Tradition*, ed. Steven Heine and Charles S. Prebish, 9–26. New York: Oxford University Press.

Takaki, Ronald. 2008. *A Different Mirror: A History of Multicultural America*. 1st rev. ed. New York: Back Bay Books/Little, Brown & Co.

Tambiah, Stanley J. 1987. *Buddhism and the Spirit Cults in North-East Thailand*. Cambridge: Cambridge University Press.

———. 1990. *Magic, Science and Religion, and the Scope of Rationality*. Cambridge: Cambridge University Press.

Tan, Amy. 1989. *The Joy Luck Club*. New York: G.P. Putnam's Sons.

———. 1991. *The Kitchen God's Wife*. New York: G.P. Putnam's Sons.

———. 2005. "Grafting Identity: The Hawaiian Branches of the Bodhi Tree." In *Buddhist Missionaries in the Era of Globalization*, ed. Linda Learman, 77–100. Honolulu: University of Hawaii Press.

Tanaka, Kenneth K. 1999. "Issues of Ethnicity in the Buddhist Churches of America." In *American Buddhism: Methods and Findings in Recent Scholarship*, ed. Duncan Ryūken Williams and Christopher S. Queen, 3–19. Honolulu: Curzon Press.

Taylor, Charles. 2001. "Two Theories of Modernity." In *Alternative Modernities*, ed. Dilip Parameshwar Gaonkar, 172–196. Durham and London: Duke University Press.

Thurman, Robert, 1991. "Tibetan Psychology: Sophisticated Software for the Human Brain." In *Mindscience: An East-West Dialogue*, ed. Herbert Benson, Robert A. F. Thurman, Howard E. Gardner, Daniel Goleman, and the Harvard Mind Science Symposium, 51–74. Somerville, MA: Wisdom Publications.

———, trans. 1994. *The Tibetan Book of the Dead: The Great Book of Natural Liberation through Understanding in the In-Between*. New York: Bantam.

———. 2004. *Mahāyānasūtrālaṃkāra as the Universal Vehicle Discourse Literature.* New York: Columbia University Press.

Todorov, Tzvetan. 1990. *Genres in Discourse*, trans. Catherine Porter. Cambridge: Cambridge University Press.

Turner, Frederick Jackson. 1921. *The Frontier in American History.* New York: Holt.

Tweed, Thomas A. 1992. *The American Encounter with Buddhism 1844–1912: Victorian Culture and the Limits of Dissent.* Chapel Hill: University of North Carolina Press.

———. 1997a. "Asian Religions in America: Reflections on an Emerging Subfield." In *Religious Diversity and American Religious History: Studies in Traditions and Cultures*, ed. Walter H. Conser Jr. and Sumner B. Twiss, 189–217. Athens: University of Georgia Press.

———. 1997b. *Our Lady of the Exile: Diasporic Religion at a Cuban Catholic Shrine in Miami.* New York and Oxford: Oxford University Press.

———, ed. 1997c. *Retelling U.S. Religious History.* Berkeley: University of California Press.

———. 1999. "Night-Stand Buddhists and Other Creatures: Sympathizers, Adherents, and the Study of Religion." In *American Buddhism: Methods and Findings in Recent Scholarship*, ed. Duncan Ryūken Williams and Christopher S. Queen, 71–90. Surrey, UK: Curzon Press.

———. 2000. "Preface to the Paperback Edition." In *The American Encounter with Buddhism, 1844–1912: Victorian Culture and the Limits of Dissent*, xi–xxii. Chapel Hill and London: University of North Carolina Press.

———. 2002. "Who Is a Buddhist? Night-Stand Buddhists and Other Creatures." In *Westward Dharma: Buddhism beyond Asia*, ed. Charles S. Prebish and Martin Baumann, 17–33. Berkeley: University of California Press.

———. 2005. "American Occultism and Japanese Buddhism: Albert J. Edmunds, D. T. Suzuki, and Translocative History." *Japanese Journal of Religious Studies* 32 (2): 249–281.

———. 2006. *Crossing and Dwelling: A Theory of Religion.* Cambridge: Harvard University Press.

———. 2009. "Crabs, Crustaceans, Crabbiness, and Outrage: A Response." *Journal of the American Academy of Religion* 77 (2): 445–459.

———. 2011. "Theory and Method in the Study of Buddhism: Toward a 'Translocative' Analysis." *Journal of Global Buddhism* 12: 17–32.

Tweed, Thomas A., and Stephen Prothero, eds. 1999. *Asian Religions in America: A Documentary History*. New York and Oxford: Oxford University Press.

Tworkov, Helen. 1991. "Many Is More." *Tricycle: The Buddhist Review* 1 (2): 4.

Uchida, Kōyū. 1957. *Fushi no jinpō*. N.p.

Vallely, Anne. 2008. "Jewish Redemption by Way of the Buddha." In *New Age Judaism*, ed. Celia Rothenberg and Anne Vallely, 19–33. London: Vallentine Mitchell.

Van Esterik, Penny. 1992. *Taking Refuge: Lao Buddhists in North America*. Tempe: Program for Southeast Asian Studies, Arizona State University; Toronto: Centre for Refugee Studies, York University, York Lane Press.

Vásquez, Manuel A., and Marie Friedmann Marquardt. 2003. *Globalizing the Sacred: Religion across the Americas*. New Brunswick: Rutgers University Press.

Verchery, Lina. 2007. *The Trap: Fisherman and Buddhist Monks on Cape Breton: Two Worlds, One Idea*. DVD. 19 min. Montreal, PQ: National Film Board of Canada.

Vetter, Tilmann. 1988. *The Ideas and Meditative Practices of Early Buddhism*. Leiden: E. J. Brill.

Victoria, Brian Daizen. 1997. *Zen at War*. New York: Weatherhill.

Wallace, B. Alan. 2001. Interview by Brian Hodel. "Tibetan Buddhism in the West: Is it Working Here?" *Tricycle: The Buddhist Review* 10 (4).

———. 2003. "Introduction: Buddhism and Science—Breaking Down the Barriers." In *Buddhism and Science: Breaking New Ground*, ed. B. Alan Wallace, 1–30 New York: Columbia University Press.

Watson, James. 1988. "The Structure of Chinese Funerary Rights: Elementary Forms, Ritual Sequence, and the Primacy of Performance." In *Death Ritual in Late Imperial and Modern China*, ed. James L. Watson and Evelyn S. Rawski, 3–19. Berkeley: University of California Press.

Wenger, Tisa. 2009. *We Have a Religion: The 1920s Pueblo Indian Dance Controversy and American Religious Freedom*. Chapel Hill: University of North Carolina Press.

Whalen-Bridge, John, and Gary Storhoff, eds. 2009. *The Emergence of Buddhist American Literature*. Albany: State University of New York Press.

Wheeler, Kate, ed. 2004. *Nixon Under the Bodhi Tree and Other Works of Buddhist Fiction*. Somerville, MA: Wisdom Publications.

White, Marybeth. 2010. "That Luang: The Journey and Relocation of Lao Buddhism to Canada." In *Wild Geese: Buddhism in Canada*, ed. John S. Harding, Victor Sôgen Hori, and Alexander Soucy, 168–186. Montreal: McGill-Queen's University Press.

Williams, Duncan Ryūken, 2002. "Camp Dharma: Japanese-American Buddhist Identity and the Internment Experience of World War II." In *Westward Dharma: Buddhism beyond Asia*, ed. Charles Prebish and Martin Baumann, 191–200. Berkeley: University of California Press.

Williams, Duncan Ryūken, and Christopher S. Queen, eds. 1999. *American Buddhism: Methods and Findings in Recent Scholarship*. Surrey, UK: Curzon Press.

Williams, Duncan Ryūken, and Tomoe Moriya, eds. 2010. *Issei Buddhism in the Americas*. Urbana: University of Illinois Press.

Wilson, Jeff. 2009. *Mourning the Unborn Dead: A Buddhist Ritual Comes to America*. New York and Oxford: Oxford University Press.

———. 2012. *Dixie Dharma: Regionalism and Identity at a Buddhist Temple in the American South*. Chapel Hill: University of North Carolina Press.

Wilson, Mike. 1999. "Schisms, Murder, and Hungry Ghosts in Shangri-La." *Cross Currents* 49 (1): 25–38.

Wright, Brooks. 1957. *Interpreter of Buddhism to the West: Sir Edwin Arnold*. New York: Bookman Associates.

Wuthnow, Robert, and Wendy Cadge. 2004. "Buddhists and Buddhism in the United States: The Scope of Influence." *Journal for the Scientific Study of Religion* 43 (3): 363–380.

Yoshinaga, Shin'ichi. 2005. "Daisetsu to Swēdenborugu: sono rekishiteki haikei." 大拙とスウェーデンボルグ—その歴史的背景. *Shūkyō tetsugaku kenkyū* 22: 33–50.

Zagorin, Perez. 2003. *How the Idea of Religious Toleration Came to the West*. Princeton and Oxford: Princeton University Press.

Zürcher, Erik. 2012. "Buddhism across Boundaries: The Foreign Input." In "Buddhism across Boundaries: The Interplay of Indian, Chinese, and Central Asian Source Materials," ed. John R. McRae and Jan Nattier. Special issue, *Sino-Platonic Papers* 222: 1–25.

CONTRIBUTORS

MICHIHIRO AMA is Assistant Professor of Japanese at the University of Alaska, Anchorage.

HELEN J. BARONI is Associate Professor and Department Chair at the University of Hawai'i at Mānoa.

KIMBERLY BEEK is a researcher in the Religious Studies Department at McMaster University, Hamilton, Ontario.

ERIK BRAUN is Assistant Professor of Religious Studies at the University of Oklahoma.

JEANNINE CHANDLER is Visiting Professor of Asian History at the State University of New York, Albany.

WAKOH SHANNON HICKEY is Assistant Professor of Religious Studies at Notre Dame of Maryland University.

DAVID L. MCMAHAN is Charles A. Dana Professor of Religious Studies at Franklin and Marshall College.

SCOTT A. MITCHELL is Assistant Dean of Student Affairs at the Institute of Buddhist Studies at the Graduate Theological Union.

MIRA NICULESCU is a researcher at École des Hautes Études en Sciences Sociales, Paris.

RICHARD K. PAYNE is Dean and Yehan Numata Professor of Japanese Buddhist Studies at the Institute of Buddhist Studies.

NATALIE E. F. QULI is Adjunct Faculty at the Institute of Buddhist Studies and Assistant Editor of *Pacific World: Journal of the Institute of Buddhist Studies.*

RICHARD HUGHES SEAGER is Bates and Benjamin Professor of Religious Studies at Hamilton College, New York.

THOMAS A. TWEED holds the W. Harold and Martha Welch Endowed Chair in American Studies at the University of Notre Dame.

JEFF WILSON is Associate Professor of Religious Studies and East Asian Studies, Renison University College, University of Waterloo, Ontario.

INDEX